I0570326

SOUL ROAD

The Journey Home

A 1 Year Devotional

J.R. Canuel

ARPress
ILLUMINATING IDEAS,
EMPOWERING VOICES

ARPress
45 Dan Road Suite 5
Canton MA 02021

Hotline: 1(888) 821-0229
Fax: 1(508) 545-7580

Ordering Information:
Quantity sales. Special discounts are available on quantity purchases by corporations, associations, and others. For details, contact the publisher at the address above.

Printed in the United States of America.

ISBN-13:   Softcover 979-8-9899505-7-7
               eBook   979-8-9899505-8-4

Library of Congress Control Number: 2024904562

An Introduction and a Dedication

Soul Road *"The Journey Home"* was written as a way for all of us to share more quality time with God, and for us to draw closer to God as we travel along our own spiritual journey, our very own Soul Road. My hope is that through the Holy Spirit, my book becomes a bridge to God's Word. After reading each page a Bible verse has been placed at the bottom of the page. I pray that this verse moves your heart to open God's Holy Word, possibly even for the first time!

I know that there are quite a few devotionals out there to choose from, but **Soul Road *"The Journey Home"*** was written to be completely different. Every letter, every word, every sentence, and every page is a completely original! So, with all I am I truly believe that everything written in this book is a spiritual gift from our Lord. *I give all the glory to God!*

I dedicate **Soul Road *"The Journey Home"*** to it's one true author, God! The words I write are not my own. I am merely a messenger relaying to you the thoughts and inspirations from our Father.

To all my family and friends past and present, I could have never completed this book without your love, encouragement and most of all, your patience! Know each and every day that I pray for your salvation. Please know that God is always healing your heart, Jesus is always searching your soul and the Holy Spirit is always living in your life! *I thank you for your love! May God bless your journey home!*

A special thanks to my wife and best friend Kim & Meme You are my heart's inspiration and the love of my life! I Love you more than I could ever tell you!

Joe & Pepe

v

Foreword
By Gary Rosenberg

For as long as I have known Joe, it's been clear to me that in addition to his family, there are two primary passions that govern who he is: his faith and his music. In his first Soul Road compilation, it was a merging of these two passions. Here, in his second selection of writings (which are set to music at various times and places), the journey continues as he puts into words his thoughts, prayers and praises.

We live in a world where, much of the time, there is a tension between the work that pays the bills and the work of the heart. Or a rare few, these two are one and the same. For the rest of us, we dream of setting aside our "day jobs" and entering into a full-time reality of our labors meshing exactly with what we feel God made us to do. Joe and I talk about this quite often and I don't think he would mind me saying that he is still striving to bring that dream to fruition. Even if it doesn't pay the bills quite yet, though the work of his heart goes on. Continue the journey with him as you read through the pages that follow and as you walk your own Soul Road.

Blessings to you, Gary Rosenberg

A Special Note

The song "When I Think Of Heaven" **is dedicated to my friend and spiritual mentor Charlie Allen. Charlie has always filled my soul with the glory and the majesty of Heaven. Charlie is a main reason why I chose to write my second Soul Road book. Soon after my father's passing on September 13, 2015 I met with Charlie to talk and to pray. It was then that the idea of writing Soul Road "The Journey Home" was born! It was absolutely 100% his inspiration that gave me the start I really needed. It was also Charlie that gave this book its very name, "Soul Road, The Journey Home."**

So from the deepest corner of my soul, I thank you for every moment we've shared, from the bottom of my heart, I thank you for every hope we've hoped, and from the innermost parts of my soul, I thank you for every prayer we prayed! We've prayed a lot over the years! *I love you Yarlie!!!*

vi

A Prayer By Charlie Allen
Charlie's Prayer

ABBA Father, we come to Your gate of secrets, secrets of a man's heart towards you, towards Your Son, towards Your Spirit. You are all we have, You are all we need! We honor You, You are the One that was sufficient for the nation of Israel to escape Egypt. Joe and I escape the bondage of sin through Yeshua Hamashiach, through Jesus Christ. Often times Father, I think of how brutally Your Son was treated and then I see Him at the right hand of Your majesty. So many times, a tear comes to my eye because I realize, He is never, ever going to experience anything like that again! He's safe and we are forgiven! ***Thank You!***

Thank You Jesus for so great a Salvation. There are not words in our language that really shows our hearts. But You know them! In my brother Joe, You have caused and made an unusual brother. I pray that You would continue to flood Joe's heart and mind with a supernatural message, not entertainment but a supernatural message delivered by Your Holy Spirit that will set men, women and children free of their Egypt's! I love this man! ABBA, Father look at us, two brothers just sitting here with You, sitting here basking in Your love for us. As I hold hands with Joe, I am really holding hands with You Jesus, through Joe. Jesus work hope in Joe's heart, he works a message in every song!
And what a message!

Joe is the first one to admit, "I don't know what I'm going to write," but Lord You do, oh You do and that's good! Thank You Jesus, thank You ABBA and thank You Spirit of God! Holy! Holy! Amen and Amen!

May God bless this book and your journey home,
Charlie Allen

Revelation 2:10

Be faithful until death and I will give you the crown of life.
"Let the Holy Spirit Do, what the Holy Spirit Do!"

This Is My Prayer For You

I pray for your hands, your hands to be held
I pray for your soul, your soul to be saved
You ask me what I pray for
What I bring before the Lord

This is my prayer for you

I pray for your faith, your faith to be freed
I pray for your heart, your heart to be healed
You ask me what I pray for
What I lay down before the Lord

This is my prayer for you

I pray for the hope, when you have no hope
I pray for the strength, when you have no strength

I pray for salvation, the salvation of your soul
I pray for forgiveness, the forgiveness of your sin

You ask me what I pray for
What I offer to the Lord

I pray for your prayers, your prayers to find peace
I pray for your life, your life to know His love
You ask me what I pray for
What I lift up before the Lord

This is my prayer for you

January

COME HOLY SPIRIT

Come Holy Spirit

Come Holy Spirit now live within me
Open my heart to Your love, to Your love
Come Holy Spirit now work within me
Surround my life with Your love, with Your love

**And have my heart feel Your strength
And have my eyes see Your holy light
And have my soul know Your grace
And have my eyes see Your holy light**

Come Holy Spirit now move within me
Speak to my soul with Your love, with Your love
Come Holy Spirit now breathe within me
Renew my faith, with Your love, with Your love

***And have my words always speak Your truth
And have my prayers always know Your faith
And have my eyes always turn toward You
And have my sins always know Your grace
Always know Your grace, always know Your grace***

**And have my heart feel Your strength
And have my eyes see Your holy light
And have my soul know Your grace
And have my eyes see Your holy light**

Come Holy Spirit now live, within me
Open my heart to Your love, to Your love

Matthew 18:20

*For where two or three are gathered together
in My name, there am I in the midst of them.*

So I bid the Holy Spirit welcome!

Isn't It Time?

Isn't it time that you find your faith?
Isn't it time that you know His grace?
Isn't it time for your soul to believe?
Isn't it time for your eyes to see?

For you don't have forever
My child we can walk this road together
So cast away now all of your doubts
And find the faith that you cannot live without

Isn't it time for you to find your strength?
Isn't it time for you to call out His name?
Isn't it time for your heart to give in?
Isn't it time for your life to begin?

So lay down now all of your pain
For only the truth will remain
So lift up now all of your praise
For only the truth will remain

For you don't have forever
And we can walk this road together
So cast away now all of your doubts
And find the faith that you cannot live without

Matthew 7:7

Ask and it will be given to you, seek and you
will find, knock and it will be opened to you.

—3—

January 3ʳᵈ

Jesus Help Me To Stay

I've tried living my life on my own
And I've lied to everybody that I know
I've cried all the tears I can cry
And I've denied You without ever knowing why

I've heard this stirring deep in my soul
And I've learned there are things I can't control
I've spurned Your truth so many times
And I've yearned for Your truth to be mine

Jesus help me to understand
Jesus help me by taking my hand
Jesus help me to follow Your way
Jesus help me to pray
Jesus help me to stay

For You were always there, every time I fell down
To pick me up off of the ground

Every time I would fail, each time I'd give up
You have always been enough
For You are always enough

Jesus help me to understand
Jesus help me by taking my hand
Jesus help me to follow Your way
Jesus help me to pray
Jesus help me to stay

Psalm 119:1-2

Blessed are the undefiled in the way, who walk in the law of
the Lord! Blessed are those who keep His testimonies, who
seek Him with the whole heart!

—4—

Separated

Lord I know well all the sins of my heart
Lord I can tell when it keeps us apart

Lord I am here in my guilt and my shame
And Lord You are there bearing all of my blame

We're separated, separated once again

Lord here I fall once again upon my knees
Lord did You give all, so I could do just as I please

Lord am I so wrong now to question all my strength?
Lord help me to be strong, help me now to find my faith

We're separated, separated once again

*Lord You give me the gift of grace
So am I worthy to receive it?
Lord You offer me the love of Heaven
So am I ready to believe it?
Lord I'm ready to believe it!
Yes I'm ready to receive it!*

We're separated, separated never again

Lord I know well all the sins of my heart
Lord I can tell when it keeps us apart

Although at times we may feel separated from God

Isaiah 59:2

*But your iniquities have made a separation between you and
your God, and your sins have hidden His face from you, so
that He does not hear.*

Know God loves us more than we can ever imagine

John 3:16

*For God so loved the world, that He gave His only
Son, that whoever believes in Him should not*

I Don't Want To Sin Anymore

I don't want to sin anymore
I don't want to doubt anymore
I don't want to feel all of this shame
To feel this way again, I don't want to sin anymore

I don't want to cry anymore
I don't want to hurt anymore
I don't want to feel all of this pain
To feel this way again, I don't want to cry anymore

For I've never felt any more on my own
Any more on my own
For I've never felt so very much alone
So very much alone

I don't want to fail anymore
I don't want to fall anymore
I don't want to feel all of this blame
To feel this way again, I don't want to fail anymore

For I've never felt any more on my own
Any more on my own
For I've never felt so very much alone
So very much alone

I don't want to sin anymore
I don't want to feel all of this shame
To feel this way again, to feel this way again
I don't want to sin anymore

Romans 7:15

For what I am doing, I do not understand. For what I will
to do, that I do not practice, but what I hate, that I do.

When You Find Your Faith

There is healing, after your hurting
There is finding after your searching
When you find your faith

There is forgiving, after your sinning
There is hoping after your fearing
When you find your faith

**When you find your faith
Oh sweet faith you will know His great grace
When you find your faith
Oh sweet faith, you will know His strong strength
For your heart and for your soul
For your life and for your very own
When you find your faith**

There is believing, after your doubting
There is calming after your shouting
When you find your faith

*For fighting this battle all alone
Is no way to find your way home
And losing this fight all on your own
Is no way to find your Heavenly home
If you are fighting all alone
If you are fighting on your own*

There is healing, after your hurting
There is finding after your searching
When it is you find your faith

Romans 15:13

*Now may the God of love fill you with all joy and
peace as you trust in Him, so that you may overflow
with love by the power of the Holy Spirit.*

January 7TH

My Sinfulness

Lord all I see is my darkness
Lord I need Your light, Lord I need Your light

Lord all I feel is my weakness
Lord I need Your strength, Lord I need your strength

For only Your light will light up my darkness
For only Your strength will lift me from my weakness

Lord all I know is my blindness
Lord I need Your sight, Lord I need Your sight

Lord all I know is my sinfulness
Lord I need Your grace, Lord I need Your grace

For only Your sight will bring me out of my blindness
For only Your grace will forgive me of all my sinfulness

Lord it's for Your will, that I pray for
Lord it's for Your truth, that I hope for
For its only Your great will
That can ever heal this hurting heart
For it is only Your great truth
That can ever change each broken part
Each broken part, each broken part

For only Your light will light up my darkness
For only Your strength will lift me from my weakness
For only Your sight will bring me out of my blindness
For only Your grace will forgive me of all my sinfulness
My sinfulness

Psalm 51:1-2

Have mercy upon me, O' God according to Your lovingkindness
according to the multitude of Your tender mercies, blot out my
transgressions wash me thoroughly from my iniquity
and cleanse me from my sin.

New Life

I was dead in my sin and shame
I was dead then You called my name
I was dead now from the grave I'll rise
I was dead now by Your grace I'm alive

I was lost with no way home
I was lost wandering this world alone
I was lost then I reached out for Your hand
I was lost now with You my Lord I stand

For I was lost in the darkness, searching for Your light
I was hiding in the shadows, so far out of sight
Then I heard Your voice and I made my choice
For my Lord You saved me, You gave me new life
For my Lord You forgave me and gave me new life

I was scared when You took my hand
I was scared then I read Your plan
I was scared when You held me in Your arms
I was scared, now I'm safe from all harm

Never before, have I ever wanted more
Than to be forever free
To have my soul set free, my lost soul set free

For You saved me, my Lord You gave me a new life
For You found me, Lord You showed me my new life

I was dead in my sin and shame
I was dead then You called my name

Romans 6:4

Therefore we are buried with him by baptism into death,
that like as Christ was raised up from the dead by the glory
of the Father, even so we also should walk in newness of life.

January 9TH

Glorious

Lord I pray we have the eyes to see
And the ears to hear
And the heart to receive it

Lord I pray we have Your truth to speak
And Your love to share
And the faith to believe it

**And to shout to all the world
And to sing to all the earth
That You are glorious
Lord You are glorious!**

*Lord You are glorious
You are the light to all the earth
Lord You are glorious
You are the light to all the world
Lord You are glorious!*

**And to shout to all the world
And to sing to all the earth
That You are glorious
Lord You are glorious!**

Lord I pray we have the eyes to see
And the ears to hear
And the heart to receive it

Psalm 72:19

*Blessed be His glorious name forever glory!
Amen and amen!*

Lay It Down

My child come and see
My child come walk with Me
And I will show you everything

My child come and believe
My child come pray with Me
For you can tell me anything

**All that is now breaking your heart
All that is now tearing you apart, lay it down
Place it at the foot of My cross
All your of pain and all of your loss
Lay it down, lay it all down**

My child come and be free
My child come talk with Me
For you can share your everything

My child come and let it be
My child come and follow Me
For you can give to Me anything

*For I love you far more than you know
Even after all you've done
For I died for you, just for you
This battle was won!*

**All that is now breaking your heart
All that is now tearing you apart, lay it down
Place it at the foot of My cross
All your of pain and all of your loss
Lay it down, lay it all down**

Matthew 16:23

*But He turned and said to Peter, "Get behind Me, Satan!
You are an offense to Me, for you are not mindful of the
things of God, but the things of men.*

Lord You Love Me

Lord You love me, in spite of all of my sin
Lord You love me, in spite of all of my blame
All of my blame

Lord You love me, in spite of all of my lies
Lord You love me, in spite of all of my shame
All of my shame

**Even after my heart turns away
Even when my words remain the same
Even though my doubt returns again
Lord You love me, Lord You love me**

Lord You love me, in spite of all that I am
Lord You love me, in spite of all of my pain
All of my pain

*In all of my blame, Lord You love me
In all of my shame, Lord You love me
In all of my pain, Lord You love me
Lord You love me*

**Even after my heart turns away
Even when my words remain the same
Even though my doubt returns again
Lord You love me, Lord You love me
Lord You love me**

Romans 5:8

*But God demonstrates His own love toward us, in that
while we were still sinners, Christ died for us.*

Stand Strong

**Don't you give up, never give in
Stand strong against the wind
If the battle's long
And if the fight it goes wrong
Stand strong against the storm**

For your love is never lost
For your love is never gone
Know that love, it keeps on fighting on

For you are stronger than you know
And you are loved more than you think it shows
Just know the darkness
Always seems the darkest before the dawn
Stand strong

*For each and every step
Gets you a little closer towards home
For each and every prayer
Draws you a little nearer less alone*

**Don't you give up, never give in
Stand strong against the wind
If the battle's long
And if the fight it goes wrong
Stand strong against the storm**

Know the darkness
Always seems the darkest just before the dawn

Stand strong!

Ephesians 6:10

*Finally, my brethren, be strong in the
Lord and in the power of His might.*

Another Angel To Return With Jesus

So small, so perfect and so very wonderful
So strong, so little and so very defenseless

**You were gone too soon to have left us
Another angel to return with Jesus
You were gone too soon to have left us
Another angel to return, to return with Jesus**

So young, so fragile and so very beautiful
So loved, so alive and so much gentleness

*For you are a miracle
So fearfully and wonderfully made
For You are a promise
So fearfully and wonderfully made*

So adored, so precious and so very peaceful
So blessed, so gentle and so very blameless

**You were gone too soon to have left us
Another angel to return with Jesus
You were gone too soon to have left us
Another angel to return, to return with Jesus**

*On January 13, 1984, President Ronald Reagan issued a presidential
proclamation designating Sunday, January 22, 1984 as National
Sanctity of Human Life Day, noting that it was the 11th anniversary
of Roe v. Wade, in which the Supreme Court issued a ruling that
guaranteed women access to abortion. President Reagan was a
strong anti-abortion advocate who said that in Roe v. Wade
the Supreme Court "struck down our laws protecting
the lives of unborn children."*

Psalm 139:14

*I will praise You, for I am fearfully and wonderfully made,
marvelous are Your works and that my soul knows very well.*

Right On Up To The Sky

We are the beloved, we are the forgiven
We are the children of God
We are the believers, we are not forgotten
We are the nations of God

It's time we stand up and raise our hands up
Right on up to the sky
It's time we love more and look above more
And lift our eyes up on high
Right on up to the sky

Our Father He loves us, our Father He guides us
Right to where we all must go
Our Father He leads us, our Father He tells us
Just what we all need to know
His truth is all we need to know

We are the beloved, we are the forgiven
We are the children of God
We are the believers, we are not forgotten
We are the nations of God

It's time we stand up and raise our hands up
Right on up to the sky
It's time we love more and look above more
And lift our eyes up on high
Right on up to the sky

Romans 1:7

To all who are in Rome, beloved of God,
called to be saints, grace to you and peace
from God our Father and the Lord Jesus Christ.

Be My Deliverer

Lord I leave at Your cross, all I've gained, all I've lost
All I am, all I was and all I'll be
Lord I leave at Your throne, all I have, all I own
All I love, all I dream and all I've seen

**Blessed God be my Father
Jesus Christ be my Savior
Holy Spirit be my Comforter
Blessed God be my power
Jesus Christ be my Redeemer
Holy Spirit be my Deliverer**

**Lord I leave at Your feet, all I pray, all I seek
All I fear, all I doubt and all I believe
Lord I leave at Your side, all I show, all I hide
All my prayers, all my praise and all from my knees**

*And with an unfailing love, Lord You love me
And with an amazing grace, Lord You saved me
And by the power of Your cross
Lord You raised my soul
And with an unfailing love, Lord You love me*

**Blessed God be my Father
Jesus Christ be my Savior
Holy Spirit be my Comforter
Blessed God be my power
Jesus Christ be my Redeemer
Holy Spirit be my Deliverer**

Psalm 18:2

*The Lord is my Rock and my Fortress and my Deliverer,
my God, my Strength in whom I will trust, My shield
and the horn of my Salvation, my Stronghold.*

Everything Will Be Just Fine

Just beyond my doubt, is the faith that I need
Is the faith, that my soul now seeks
Just beyond my sin, is the grace that You give
Is the grace, that for me now forgives

**And all I have to do is lift my eyes to You
And everything will be just fine
And all I have to share is my all in prayer
And everything will be just fine, it will be just fine**

Just beyond my fear, is the love that is mine
Is Your love, for all my life
Just beyond my shame, is the love that Is real
Is the love, that my heart now feels

***Just beyond my hurt is Your healing for me
Just beyond my tears is Your trusting in me
Your trusting in me***

**And all I have to do is lift my eyes to You
And everything will be just fine
And all I have to share is my all in prayer
And everything will be just fine, it will be just fine
Everything will be just fine**

Psalm 123:1-4

*Unto You I lift up my eyes, O' You who dwell in the Heavens.
Behold, as the eyes of servants look to the hand of their
masters, as the eyes of a maid to the hand of her mistress,
so our eyes look to the Lord our God, Until He has mercy
on us. Have mercy on us, O' Lord, have mercy on us! For
we are exceedingly filled with contempt. Our soul is
exceedingly filled With the scorn of those who are
at ease, with the contempt of the proud.*

January 17TH

My Lord You Know

We show You our hate, You show us love
We show You our blindness, You show us sight
We show You our hurt, You show us peace
We show You our darkness, You show us Your light

For You know our heart
Just who we are and who we are not
For You know our soul
Just where we've been and where we will go
My Lord You know, my Lord You know

We show You our doubt, You show us faith
We show You our weakness, You show us strength
We show You our fear, You show us love
We show You our sinfulness, You show us grace

You know what lifts us up
You know what lets us down
You know what sets us straight
What spins our head around
You know what lifts us up
You know what lets us down
You know what sets us straight
What spins our head around

For You know our heart
Just who we are and who we are not
For You know our soul
Just where we've been and where we will go
My Lord You know, my Lord You know

We show You our heart, You show us Your cross
We show You our brokenness, You show us Your life

Psalm 139:1

O' Lord, You have searched me and known me.

I Am Here To Stay

Let me hold your trembling hands
Let me heal your troubled heart
Let me help your searching soul
Let me hear your beautiful song

**For I am always by your side
I'm never too far away and I am here to stay
For I am always by your side
I'm never too far away and I am here to stay**

*My child let Me in, please let Me forgive
Oh please let Me forgive
My child let Me stay, please let Me begin
Oh please let Me begin
To forgive your every sin*

**For I am always by your side
I'm never too far away and I am here to stay
For I am always by your side
I'm never too far away and I am here to stay**

Let Me hold your trembling hands
Let Me heal your troubled heart
Let Me help your searching soul
Let Me hear your beautiful song
Your beautiful song

John 4:13-15

*Jesus answered and said to her, "Whoever drinks of this water
will thirst again, but whoever drinks of the water that I shall
give him will never thirst. But the water that I shall give him
will become in him a fountain of water springing up into
everlasting life." The woman said to Him, "Sir, give me
this water, that I may not thirst, nor come here to draw.*

In Praise To The King

May the blind see again
May the dead rise to live again
In Your love, Lord in Your love

**May the deaf hear again
May the lame stand to walk again
In Your love, Lord in Your love**

**And may they dance, may they sing
May they gather together in praise to the King
In praise to the King**

May the dumb speak again
May the hurt be healed again
In Your love, Lord in Your love

And may who doubt believe again
May the lost be found again
In Your love, Lord in Your love

*May the weak find their strength
Lord in Your strength
And may all who seek find their truth
Lord in Your truth
May the sinner find their grace
Lord in Your grace*

*May all who doubt find their faith
Lord in Your faith
May all who doubt find their faith
Lord in Your faith*

And may they dance, may they sing
May they gather together in praise to the King
In praise to the King

Psalm 146:2

*While I live I will praise the Lord, I will sing
praises to my God while I have my being.*

Lord Jesus Come

In this world of love and fear
As we question why we're here
And in this world of hate and love
We look to Heaven so far above

**Lord Jesus come, now come to me
Lord Jesus find me on my knees
Lord we cry, we cry out Your name**

In this world of rich and poor
You guide us all now to Your door
And in this world of doubt and faith
You bless us all now with Your Grace

**Lord Jesus come, now come to me
Lord Jesus find me on my knees
Lord we cry, we cry out Your name**

*Lord I give to You my all, my everything
Lord I give to You my all, my everlasting*

In this world of free and bond
We search for strength from far beyond
And in this world of great and small
We look to You Father Lord of all

**Lord Jesus come, now come to me
Lord Jesus find me on my knees
Lord we cry, we cry out Your name
Lord Jesus come**

Revelation 22:20

He who testifies to these things says, "Surely I am coming quickly." Amen! Even so, come, Lord Jesus!

Your Mercy For Me

When in my hour of need
Lord I'll turn my eyes to Thee
When my strength it is lost
Lord I will turn to the cross

**And I will sing Lord You are worthy
And I will sing Lord of all Your glory
And I will sing Lord of Your mercy
Your mercy for me**

When my love it is gone
Lord I will turn to You alone
When my faith falls away
Lord I will turn to You and pray

**And I will sing Lord You are worthy
And I will sing Lord of all Your glory
And I will sing Lord of Your mercy
Your mercy for me**

*Lord I will shout, from the highest mountain
"Lord You are holy! Lord You are holy!"
Lord I will cry out, to the valley far below
"Lord You are holy! Lord You are holy!"*

**And I will sing Lord You are worthy
And I will sing Lord of all Your glory
And I will sing Lord of Your mercy
Your mercy for me**

Psalm 40:11

*Do not withhold Your tender mercies from me,
O' Lord, let Your lovingkindness and Your truth
continually preserve me.*

His Holy Word

There is truth, there is life
In His Holy Word
There is power, there is strength
In His Holy Word

**For there's a light, deep within the dark
For there is love, deep within your heart**

There is peace, there is joy
In His Holy Word
There is mercy, there is grace
In His Holy Word

**For there's a light, deep within the dark
For there is love, deep within your heart**

There is love, there is faith
In His Holy Word
There is worship, there is praise
In His Holy Word

***For there is healing, for the broken heart
For there are blessings, wherever you are
For there is healing, for the broken heart
For there are blessings, wherever you are***

There is truth, there is life
In His Holy Word

Proverbs 30:5

*Every word of God is pure, He is a shield
to those who put their trust in Him.*

Let Your Mercy Fall

My Lord Jesus, my Lord now bless us
Hold us secure now in Your arms
My Lord Jesus, my Lord now save us
Keep us all now safe from harm

**My Lord pour out Your love
Now from Heaven above
Lord now let Your mercy fall
My Lord fall fresh on me
Lord with all of Your glory
Lord now let Your mercy fall
Let Your mercy fall**

My Lord Jesus, my Lord now guide us
Wherever our lives they may go
My Lord Jesus, my Lord now heal us
Lord now heal our wounded souls

***Lord let it fall like the rain
That falls from the skies
Lord let it fall, like the tears
That fall from my eyes
Lord let it fall, Lord let it fall
Let Your mercy fall***

**My Lord pour out Your love
Now from Heaven above
Lord now let Your mercy fall
My Lord fall fresh on me
Lord with all of Your glory
Lord now let Your mercy fall
Let Your mercy fall**

Matthew 5:7

Blessed are the merciful, for they shall receive mercy.

Our Own Way Home

Each of us must find our own way home
Some of us are lost, some of us found

Each of us must find our own way home
Some of us are free, some of us bound

**For some of us pray, while some of us don't
Some of us are saved, while some of us won't
For each of us must find, our own way home
Our own way home**

Each of us must find our own way home
Some of us are hurt, some of us worn

Each of us must find our own way home
Some of us are healed, some of us torn

*We all need to turn our eyes up to the sky
We all need all of Heaven above
We all need to believe and be set free
We all need all of His love, all of His love
All of His love*

**For some of us pray, while some of us don't
Some of us are saved, while some of us won't
For each of us must find, our own way home
Our own way home**

Each of us must find, our own way home
Some of us are lost, some of us found

Ephesians 2:19

*Now, therefore, you are no longer strangers and foreigners,
but fellow citizens with the saints and members of the
household of God.*

Only If You Pray

God wants to help you now
God wants to lift you up
High above all of your hurt and all of your shame

God wants to guide your life
God wants to lead you home
Far away from all of your tears and all of your pain

**Well there is only one way and it's only if you pray
Yes there is only one way and it's only if you pray**

God wants to hold you close
God wants to draw you near
And to keep you safer, in His loving arms

God wants to show you more
God wants to free your faith
And to give you shelter, here in the storm

**Well there is only one way and it's only if you pray
Yes there is only one way and it's only if you pray**

***God wants to heal your heart
God wants to save your soul
God wants to love you more
More than you could ever know***

**Well there is only one way and it's only if you pray
Yes there is only one way and it's only if you pray**

Psalm 118:24

*This is the day the Lord has made,
we will rejoice and be glad in it.*

Lord I Surrender All

Lord I pray that Your love be my love
And that Your strength be my strength
Lord I pray that Your love be my love
And that Your faith be my faith
And that Your faith be my faith

**Lord I surrender all here at the foot of Your cross
All I am and ever hope to be
All I was and all You've seen in me
Lord I surrender all, Lord I surrender all**

Lord I pray that Your heart be my heart
And that Your life be my life
Lord I pray that Your truth be my truth
And that Your light be my light
And that Your light be my light

Lord I pray that Your will be my will
And that Your ways be my ways
Lord I pray that Your joy be my joy
And that Your days be my days
And that Your days be my days

**Lord I surrender all here at the foot of Your cross
All I am and ever hope to be
All I was and all You've seen in me
Lord I surrender all, Lord I surrender all**

Galatians 2:20

*I have been crucified with Christ, it is no longer I who live,
but Christ Who lives in me and the life which I now live in
the flesh I live by faith in the Son of God Who loved me
and gave Himself for me.*

All For The Glory Of The Lord

The sun greets the morning
As the stars welcome the night
The grass dances across the meadow
Just as the eagle now takes flight

The wind whispers Your name
As the ocean cries from the deep
The mountains stand in awe of You
Just as the rain it begins to weep
All for the glory of the Lord

Oh my Lord now hear my prayer
As I fall, as I kneel here
Oh my Lord now hear my song
That I will sing the whole day long
All for the glory of the Lord!

All creation sings Your praise
All creation declares Your beauty
All creation sings Your praise
All creation sings holy, holy, holy!
And all creation sings, all creation sings
All for the glory of the Lord

1 Corinthians 10:31

Whether you eat or drink, or whatever you
do, do all to the glory of God.

You Have Been Changed

What happens in your heart
Cannot stay within your heart
You'll have to sing it to all the world

What happens in your soul
Cannot stay within your soul
You'll have to shout it to all the earth

That you've gone from defeat to victory
From shame to grace
You've gone from bond to being free
From fear to faith, you have been changed

What happens in your life
Cannot stay within your life
You'll have to sing it to all the world

What happens in your faith
Cannot stay within your faith
You'll have to shout it to all the earth

From weakness to strength, from sorrow to joy
From darkness to light, from hurt to healed
You have been changed, you have been changed

That you've gone from defeat to victory
From shame to grace
You've gone from bond to being free
From fear to faith, you have been changed

What happens in your heart
Cannot stay within your heart
You'll have to sing it to all the world

Matthew 10:28

And do not fear those who kill the body
but cannot kill the soul. But rather fear Him
Who is able to destroy both soul and body in hell.

Let It Fall Down

There are clouds now darkening the sky
There are storms now surrounding your heart
And there are tears now falling like rain
But know there is love, know there is love
Wherever you are

**So let the rain fall down, let it fall all around
Let it wash away, all your hurt and your pain
So let the rain it fall, so let the rain it fall
Let it fall down**

*For there's healing to come, oh Lord let it be done
There's freedom and love, lift your eyes
Now look above*

*For there's blessings to flow, oh Lord now make it so
There's mercy and grace
Look to the skies, now cry out His name
Cry out His holy name*

Lord let the flood of Your love
Now wash me clean, Lord wash me clean
Lord let the flood of Your love
Now make me new, Lord make me new

**So let the rain fall down, let it fall all around
Let it wash away, all your hurt and your pain
So let the rain it fall, so let the rain it fall
Let it fall down**

Psalm 121:1-2

*I will lift up my eyes to the hills, from whence comes my help?
My help comes from the Lord, Who made Heaven and earth.*

You Lifted Me Up

I was drowning in my sin and shame
I was running from my hurt and pain
I was hiding from my pride and blame
It was then that You found me

I was searching for Your love and grace
I was needing all Your love and strength
I was falling far from Your truth and way
It was then that You raised me

High up off the ground
Far away from the crowd
You raised me up, You lifted me up

Your love is all I ever needed
Your strength is all I ever wanted
Your love is all that I was seeking
Your grace is all that I was praying for

Nothing more, nothing less
Only You and not myself
Nothing more, nothing less
Only You and not myself

High up off the ground
Far away from the crowd
You raised me up, You lifted me up

Psalm 36:7

How precious is Your loving kindness, O' God!
Therefore the children of men put their trust
under the shadow of Your wings.

I Need Jesus

I need Jesus, yeah I need His love
I need Jesus and all of Heaven above
I need Jesus, yeah I need His strength
I need Jesus and the gift of His grace
I need Jesus and the gift of His grace

I need Jesus, yeah I need His love
I need Jesus, now to save my soul
I need Jesus, yeah I need His truth
I need Jesus, now to see me through
I need Jesus, now to see me through

I need Jesus, yeah I need His cross
I need Jesus, when all seems lost
I need Jesus, yeah I need His scars
I need Jesus, for He will heal my heart

I need Jesus, yeah I need His love
I need Jesus, now to save my soul
I need Jesus, yeah I need His truth
I need Jesus, now to see me through
I need Jesus, now to see me through

I need Jesus, yeah I need His cross
I need Jesus, when all seems lost
I need Jesus, yeah I need His scars
I need Jesus, for He will heal my heart

I need Jesus, yeah I need His love
I need Jesus, now to save my soul
I need Jesus, yeah I need His truth
I need Jesus, now to see me through
I need Jesus, now to see me through

Philippians 4:19

And my God shall supply all your need according
to His riches in glory by Christ Jesus.

February

A Little Closer To Thee

A Little Closer To Thee

Lord I pray for Your mercy
Your forgiveness and Your grace
Lord I pray for Your glory
Your kindness and Your strength

**For only through my prayers
Will You ever draw, nearer to me
For only through my prayers
Will I ever draw a little closer to Thee
A little closer to Thee**

For me to be nearer, Lord is what I pray
For me to be closer, closer than yesterday
Closer than yesterday

*Lord find me here kneeling
Find me here praying, I'm praying to You
Lord find me here hoping
Lord find me here waiting, I'm waiting for You
To be a little closer to Thee*

**For only through my prayers
Will You ever draw, nearer to me
For only through my prayers
Will I ever draw a little closer to Thee
A little closer to Thee**

Romans 12:1

*I beseech you therefore, brethren, by the mercies
of God, that ye present your bodies a living sacrifice,
Holy, acceptable unto God, which is your
reasonable service.*

Right Now, Today

Have you been changed by His love?
Have you been saved by His grace?

Have you been healed by His love?
Have you been lifted up by His strength?

For only His love can ever change your heart
For only His grace can ever save your soul
For only His love can ever heal your hurt
For only His strength can ever lift you up

So have you been washed by His blood?
Have you been moved by His truth?

Have you been held within His arms?
Have you been freed by His holy word?

For only His blood can ever wash your sin
For only His truth can help you find what you seek
For only His arms can ever keep you safe
For only His holy word can ever set you free

Have you ever been so alone and so afraid?
Have you ever been so alarmed and so ashamed?
Let Him make you clean, right now today

Have you been changed by His love?
Have you been saved by His grace?

I John 4:1-3

Beloved, do not believe every spirit, but test the spirits, whether they are of God, because many false prophets have gone out into the world. By this you know the Spirit of God, every spirit that confesses that Jesus Christ has come in the flesh is of God and every spirit that does not confess that Jesus Christ has come in the flesh is not of God. And this is the spirit of the Antichrist, which you have heard was coming, and is now already in the world.

How Many Tears Have You Dried?

There's an old church standing, at the top of the hill
There's a dirt road winding, leading past the lumber mill
There's a cross still hanging, above an old weathered door
There's a sign still reading, **"Salvation Can Be Yours!"**

**Lord I wonder just how many prayers
Have been prayed 'round these old walls
How many hopes here were lifted high?
Lord I wonder just how many tears
Have been cried before this cross
Just how many tears, oh Lord have You dried?**

I imagine the children playing, down by the river in the sun
Near the cool water running, just as the Pastor had begun
There are souls here wading, gently placed under the blue sky
With the Holy Spirit's blessing, all to be raised up to new life

*There's an old cemetery resting
Down below there in the field
There are names that are now fading
Now as time it takes its yield
As I walk among the flowers blooming
Now growing all around
It's the silence of their whispering
That is now the only sound*

**Lord I wonder just how many prayers
Have been prayed 'round these old walls
How many hopes here were lifted high?
Lord I wonder just how many tears
Have been cried before this cross
Just how many tears, oh Lord have You dried?**

Revelation 7:17

*For the Lamb which is in the midst of the throne shall feed them,
and shall lead them unto living fountains of waters, and God
shall wipe away all ears from their eyes.*

All I Am Is Yours

Lord I come to You this morning
With all of my guilt and my shame

Lord I share with You this morning
All of my sin and my blame
All I am is Yours, all I am is Yours

**With all of my soul, every day of my life
All I am is Yours, all I am is Yours
With all of my hope, every prayer in my heart
All I am is Yours, all I am is Yours**

Lord I bring to You this morning
All of my joy and my praise

Lord I sing to You this morning
All of my words and my songs
All I am is Yours, all I am is Yours

***Lord all I am is Yours, all I was ever meant to be
Lord all I am is Yours, all that You now see in me
All that You now see in me***

**With all of my soul, every day of my life
All I am is Yours, all I am is Yours
With all of my hope, every prayer in my heart
All I am is Yours, all I am is Yours**

Lord I pray with You this morning
With all of my faith and my soul
All I am is Yours, all I am is Yours

Isaiah 6:8

*Also I heard the voice of the Lord, saying "Whom shall I send,
and who will go for Us?" Then I said, "Here am I! Send me."*

We Are All So Beautiful

We are all so beautiful, in the eyes of the Lord
We are all so beautiful, in the eyes of the Lord
All so perfect in every way, all so wonderfully made

**With each heart, with each soul, with each life
And with each and every love
With each thought, with each tear, with each breath
And with each and every prayer
We are all so beautiful**

We are all so beautiful, in the eyes of the Lord
We are all so beautiful, in the eyes of the Lord
All so perfectly planned, all so wonderfully grand

**With each heart, with each soul, with each life
And with each and every love
With each thought, with each tear, with each breath
And with each and every prayer
We are all so beautiful**

*God must just laugh, God must just cry
God must shake His head, look around and just wonder why
Why we are the way we are
Why we do the things we do*

*God must just laugh, God must just cry
For God knows our heart far better than we do
God knows our thoughts long before we even move
For God knows our intents, all the choices that we choose
All the moments that we lose
God knows our heart, for we are so beautiful
In the eyes of The Lord*

Song of Solomon 4:7

You are all fair my love and there is no spot in you.

If We All Loved Jesus

If we all loved Jesus, there'd be no more hurting
There would be only life
If we all loved Jesus, there'd be no more darkness
There would be only light, so let it shine
So let it shine

If we all loved Jesus, there'd be no more searching
There would be only love
If we all loved Jesus, there'd be no more sadness

There would be only love, so let it shine
So let it shine

There would be no more crying, only joy to behold
There would be no more lying, only truth to be told
There'd be only praying and His blessings to unfold
There'd be only praying and His blessings to unfold

If we all loved Jesus, there'd be no more doubting
There would be only faith
If we all loved Jesus, there'd be no more weakness
There would be only strength, so let it shine
So let it shine

There would be no more crying, only joy to behold
There would be no more lying, only truth to be told
There'd be only praying and His blessings to unfold
There'd be only praying and His blessings to unfold

If we all loved Jesus, there'd be no more sadness
There would be only His love, only His love

Psalm 143:8

Cause me to hear Your lovingkindness in the morning,
for in You do I trust, cause me to know the way in
which I should walk, for I lift up my soul to You.

That's What I Pray For

To know Your will, for my life
To hear Your truth, through the lies
That's what I pray for, that's what I pray for

To feel Your love, heal my heart
To seek Your grace, to save my soul
That's what I pray for, that's what I pray for

**When I am down, upon my knees
And my prayers, are lifted to Your throne
You hear my prayer, You know that I'm here
That's what I pray for, that's what I pray for**

*No not one breath is ever in vain
For the angels make known
To You my love
No not one doubt will ever remain
For the angels make known
To You my love, my love*

**When I am down, upon my knees
And my prayers, are lifted to Your throne
You hear my prayer, You know that I'm here
That's what I pray for, that's what I pray for**

*No not one breath is ever in vain
For the angels make known to You my love
No not one doubt will ever remain
For the angels make known to You my love, my love*

To know Your will, for my life
To hear Your truth, through the lies
That's what I pray for, that's what I pray for

Luke 11:1

Now it came to pass, as He was praying in a certain place,
when He ceased, that one of His disciples said to Him, "Lord,
teach us to pray, as John also taught his disciples."

Know God Is Faithful

In the midst of the storm, when you think you're alone
Know God is faithful, know God is faithful, right to the end
In the midst of the fight, when you've lost all your might
Know God is faithful, know God is faithful
Right to the end, to the end

When the winds seem too strong
When battles seem to take too long
Know that God is by your side, He's along for the ride
And when the winds they beat you down
When battles take you to the ground
Know God is at your side, He's along for the ride
For He's more than faithful, know that God is faithful

In the midst of the night, when dark seems to defeat the light
Know God is faithful, know God is faithful
Right to the end, to the end

When the winds seem too strong
When battles seem to take too long
Know that God is by your side, He's along for the ride
And when the winds they beat you down
When battles take you to the ground
Know God is at your side, He's along for the ride
For He's more than faithful, know that God is faithful

In the midst of the rain, when you've been shaken again
Know God is faithful, know God is faithful
Right to the end, to the end

1 Corinthians 10:13

No temptation has overtaken you except such as is common to man, but God is faithful, who will not allow you to be tempted beyond what you are able, but with the temptation will also make the way of escape, that you may be able to bear it.

February 9TH

Come And Follow Me

Come and follow me
Come and set your lost soul free
Come and follow me
Come and have your blind eyes see

**Come for the first time
Come for the very first time
Come as never before
Come find forgiveness
Come find forgiveness and grace
Come just open this door
Just come, just come**

Come and follow me
Come and see just what your life can be
Come and follow me
Come and find peace eternally

***And lay down your sin, let your life begin
Lay down all that you are, lay down your shame
Just cry out my name, lay down all of your heart
Just come, just come***

**Come for the first time
Come for the very first time
Come as never before
Come find forgiveness
Come find forgiveness and grace
Come just open this door
Just come, just come**

Matthew 4:19-20

Then He said to them, "Follow Me and I will make you fishers of men." They immediately left their nets and followed Him.

Just As It Should Be

Lord I leave my sins at Your cross
All of my shame, all I have lost
And all will be found, within the sound
Lord of Your voice, Lord of Your voice

When all will be, just as it should be
When we all see, all You want us to see
When we are free, yes when we are free
Then all will be, just as it should be
Just as it should be

With no more crying, no more death
With no more weeping, only joy in every breath
With no more fears, with no more tears
When all will be, just as it should be
Just as it should be

So Lord I leave, my sins at Your cross
All of my shame, all I have lost
All will be found, within the sound
Lord of Your voice, Lord of Your voice

When all will be, just as it should be
When we all see, all You want us to see
When we are free, yes when we are free
Then all will be, just as it should be
Just as it should be

Hebrews 7:27

Who does not need daily, as those high priests, to offer up
sacrifices, first for His own sins and then for the people's,
for this He did once for all when He offered up Himself.

Oh Father Please

Oh Father please, help me to change
Oh Lord help me, to never remain the same
Oh Father please, help me to learn
Oh Lord help me, to no longer doubt Your word

And to always step out in my faith
And to always trust now in Your strength
And to always shout, out all of my praise
And to always cry, out Your holy name

Oh Father please, help me to stand
Oh Lord help me, to become a better man
Oh Father please, help me to pray
Oh Lord help me, to be on my knees to stay

And to always step out in my faith
And to always trust now in Your strength
And to always shout, out all of my praise
And to always cry, out Your holy name

So high above the mountains, so high above the seas
So high above the valleys, You are whispering to me
So high above the clouds, so high above the crowds
Lord You are calling out to me
Lord You are calling out to me

Oh Father please, help me to change
Oh Lord help me, to never remain the same

Ezekiel 11:19

Then I will give them one heart, and I will put a new spirit
within them, and take the stony heart out of their flesh
and give them a heart of flesh.

In The Arms Of The Lord

In the arms of the Lord
Where forever I will find my rest
In the arms of the Lord
Where forever my soul will be blessed

**Where along the glassy sea
My Lord will walk there with me
And I will praise Him for eternity
And I will praise Him eternally**

In the arms of the Lord
Where forever my heart it will sing
In the arms of the Lord
Where forever I am finally free

***Where together we will fall
All as one before His throne
Where together we will come
And all gather at His throne, as His own***

**Where along the glassy sea
My Lord will walk there with me
And I will praise Him for eternity
And I will praise Him eternally**

In the arms of the Lord
Where forever I will find my rest

Deuteronomy 33:27

The Eternal God is your Refuge and underneath are the everlasting arms. He will thrust out the enemy from before you, And will say, 'Destroy!'

Come Glory

We all hurt, we'll all hurt no more
We all fail, we'll all fail no more

Come glory, we'll all shine

We all sin, we'll all sin no more
We all fall, we'll all fall no more

Come glory, we'll all shine

**We will all dance in glory
We will sing "Glory to the Lord!"
We will all dance in glory
We will sing "Holy is the Lord!"
Holy is the Lord**

We all doubt, we'll all doubt no more
We all cry, we'll all cry no more

Come glory, we'll all shine

**We will all dance in glory
We will sing "Glory to the Lord!"
We will all dance in glory
We will sing "Holy is the Lord!"
Holy is the Lord**

**Come glory, every knee shall bow
Come glory, every voice will shout
Come glory, every heart will sing
Come glory, we will give You everything!**

We all hurt, we'll all hurt no more
We all fail, we'll all fail no more

Hebrews 9:28

*So Christ was offered once to bear the sins of many.
To those who eagerly wait for Him He will appear a
second time, apart from sin, for salvation.*

A Special Kind Of Love

May His love now carry you, may His light now shine through
May His love now always find you where you are
May His grace surround you
May His strength now breakthrough
May His love now always find you where you are

For there's a love, a special kind of love
One that reaches deep into your heart
For there's a love, a lasting kind of love
One that will forever set your life apart

There is a God above so full of grace and love
Who now awaits to forgive you of your sin
And there is a God on high Who loves both you and I
Who now awaits for your life to begin

For there is power in His name
And there is love for all the lost
For there's forgiveness in His grace
And there's Salvation at His cross

May your faith grow every day
May your life know amazing grace
May each and every prayer
Always come straight from your heart

May His love now carry you, may His light now shine through
May His love now always find you where you are

For there's a love, a special kind of love
One that reaches deep into your heart
For there's a love, a lasting kind of love
One that will forever set your life apart

Proverbs 3:5-6

Trust in the Lord with all your heart and lean not on your
own understanding In all your ways acknowledge Him
and He shall direct your paths.

A Little Something To Pray For

Lord I need a little bit of Your love
I need a little bit of Your faith
Lord I need a little bit of Your love
I need a little bit of Your grace

Lord I need a little bit of Your life
I need a little bit of Your strength
Lord I need a little bit of Your light
I need a little bit of Your prayer

**Lord I need a little something to believe in
A little something to mean just a little more
Lord I need a little something
A little something to pray for**

Lord I need a little bit of Your truth
I need a little bit of Your peace
Lord I need a little bit of Your heart
I need a little bit of Your sweet release

**Lord I need a little something to believe in
A little something to mean just a little more
Lord I need a little something
A little something to pray for**

Philippians 4:6

*Be anxious for nothing, but in everything by prayer and
supplication, with thanksgiving, let your requests
be made known to God.*

Oh Child Of God

Oh child of God, oh child of the King
Now lift up your eyes and take in everything

Oh child of God, oh child of the King
Now lift up your hands and let your praises sing

**He's whispering your name, He's calling you home
Just follow your faith, be still and know
For He's waiting here with His arms open wide
He's drawing you near, inviting you inside**

Oh child of God, oh child of the King
Now lift up your eyes and take in everything

Oh child of God, oh child of the King
Now lift up your hands and let your praises sing

**He's whispering your name, He's calling you home
Just follow your faith, be still and know
For He's waiting here with His arms open wide
He's drawing you near, inviting you inside**

Oh child of God, oh child of the King
Now lift up your eyes and take in everything

Oh child of God, oh child of the King
Now lift up your hands and let your praises sing
Oh child of God, oh child of the King
Now lift up your eyes and take in everything

Galatians 3:26

For you are all sons of God through faith in Christ Jesus.

So Are You Born Again?

Are you born again? Is your soul now saved?
Are you washed in His blood?
Are you forgiven by grace? Is your heart now healed?
Have you been cleansed in the flood?

For you were dead in your sin
So lost and far from home
So separated and set apart
And so very much alone
So very much alone

Are you held in His arms? Is your life now alive?
Are you strong in His strength?
So are your hands raised up high? Is your faith now on fire?
Are you calling out His name?

Are you ready now to begin
To fall down upon your knees?
He is so ready now to forgive
So just ask of the Lord
"My Lord please!"

To save me, to hold me, to never let me go
To love me, to keep me, to never let me go

For I was dead in my sin
So lost and far from home
So separated and set apart
And so very much alone
So very much alone

So does nothing remain? Is your life changed?
So are you born again?

John 3:3

Jesus answered and said to him, "Most assuredly, I say to you,
unless one is born again, he cannot see the Kingdom of God.

You Walked That Road For Me

Lord You laid down Your very life for me
It was for my soul, it was for my soul

Lord You cried all Your tears for me
It was for my soul, it was for my soul

**In every day that You lived
In every step that You walked
Oh Jesus You shed Your blood for me
With every heart that You loved
In every drop of blood
Oh Jesus You walked that road for me**

Lord You prayed Your every prayer for me
It was for my soul, it was for my soul

Lord You gave all Your grace for me
It was for my soul, it was for my soul

**In every day that You lived
In every step that You walked
Oh Jesus You walked that road for me
With every heart that You loved
In every drop of blood
Oh Jesus You shed Your blood for me**

Lord You shared all of Your love for me
It was for my soul, it was for my soul

Matthew 27:33-37

*And when they had come to a place called Golgotha, that is to say,
Place of a Skull, they gave Him sour wine mingled with gall to drink.
But when He had tasted it, He would not drink. Then they crucified
Him, and divided His garments, casting lots, that it might be
fulfilled which was spoken by the prophet: "They divided My
garments among them, And for My clothing they cast lots."
Sitting down, they kept watch over Him there. And they put
up over His head the accusation written against Him:*

THIS IS JESUS THE KING OF THE JEWS

Lord How Long Until We Gather?

Lord how long until we gather all together at Your throne?
Lord how long until we gather and we worship You alone?
All together at Your throne

Lord how long until we gather all to shout Your victory?
Lord how long until we gather and with all the angels sing?
All to shout Your victory

Lord is today the day when we see You in the clouds?
Lord is today the day when we all hear the trumpet sound?
Lord is today the day when in glory You appear?
Lord is today the day when we will all draw near?
Lord is today the day?

Lord how long until we gather and we bow down at Your feet?
Lord how long until we gather and we rejoice in death's defeat?
And we bow down at Your feet

Lord how long until we gather and we all shout out Your name?
Lord how long until we gather and as one we lift all our praise?
And we all shout out Your name

Lord is today the day when we see You in the clouds?
Lord is today the day when we all hear the trumpet sound?
Lord is today the day when in glory You appear?
Lord is today the day when we will all draw near?
Lord is today the day?

Lord how long until we gather all together at Your throne?

Revelation 3:10

*Because you have kept My command to persevere, I also
will keep you from the hour of trial which shall come upon
the whole world, to test those who dwell on the earth.*

All The Way To The Cross

May this song sung from our hearts
Lift high now to Heaven

May this prayer prayed from our souls
Reach all the way to the cross

And may we all bow down
To Your glory, may we all bow down

Lord may we all know Your grace
Know Your grace
Lord may we all know Your mercy
Know Your mercy
Lord may we all know Your strength
Know Your strength
May we all bow down

May this song sung from our hearts
Lift high now to Heaven

May this prayer prayed from our souls
Reach all the way to the cross

And may we all bow down
To Your glory, may we all bow down
All the way to the cross

Hebrews 12:2

Looking unto Jesus the author and finisher of our faith,
Who for the joy that was set before Him endured the cross,
despising the shame and has set down at the right
hand of the throne of God.

Here At The Saviors Feet

There's a love and there's a forgiveness
In your soul's time of need
There's a love and there's a promise
In that your soul can believe

**You can be made new
Yes you can now be born again
You can be made whole
And be set free of your every sin
Just lay your burdens down
Here at the Savior's feet
Just cast down your crowns
Here at the Savior's feet**

And Lord I cry out in all my praise
For You have heard my voice
And Lord I'll cry out for all my days
For You have heard my voice

*My Holy Father, my Host of Heaven
Lord I'll lift Your name
My Holy Father, my God of glory
Lord I'll praise Your name
I will praise Your name, Your holy name*

**You can be made new
Yes you can now be born again
You can be made whole
And be set free of your every sin
Just lay your burdens down
Here at the Savior's feet
Just cast down your crowns
Here at the Savior's feet**

Matthew 15:30

*Then great multitudes came to Him, having with them the
lame, blind, mute, maimed and many others and they
laid them down at Jesus' feet and He healed them.*

You Are Never Alone

When there is love in your every word
Know Jesus that He hears you
When there is loss in your every hurt
Know Jesus that He is near you

**For He is always there, right by your side
For He is always there, there to guide you home
For you are never alone**

When there is pain in your every tear
Know Jesus that He will hold you
When there is love in your every prayer
Know Jesus that He has told you

*Jesus has told you, Jesus has shown you
All of the truth you will ever need
Jesus has given you, He has forgiven you
Of every sin from which you now bleed*

*So when there's joy in your every praise
Know Jesus that He sings with you
And when there's strength in your every fear
Know Jesus that He stands with you*

**For He is always there, right by your side
For He is always there, there to guide you home
For you are never alone**

When there is love in your every word
Know Jesus that He hears you

Romans 8:35

*Who shall separate us from the love of Christ? Shall
tribulation, or distress, or persecution, or famine, or
nakedness, or peril, or sword?*

February 23RD

His Only Hope And Prayer

When you're down and you're low
And you feel like there's nowhere to go
And your heart has been broken in two

So close your eyes and please pray
Because right now, right here today
There is a Savior, Who is waiting to comfort you

For it is His only hope and prayer
To find you kneeling upon your knees right there
Praying for His mercy and His grace

To hear you calling out His name
To hear you praying with all your faith
To hear you crying out His name with all of your praise

That when you feel like there's nowhere to go
When your heart has been broken in two
Just close your eyes and please pray
Because right now, right here today
There is a Savior Who is waiting to comfort you

For it is His only hope and prayer
To find you kneeling upon your knees right there
Praying for His mercy and His grace

To hear you calling out His name
To hear you praying with all your faith
To hear you crying out His name with all of your praise

For it is His only hope and prayer

Jeremiah 29:11-13

For I know the thoughts that I think toward you, says the Lord,
thoughts of peace and not of evil, to give you a future and a
love. Then you will call upon Me and go and pray to Me and
I will listen to you. And you will seek Me and find Me, when
you search for Me with all your heart.

—56—

Only By Your Love

Only by Your sacrifice do I live, do I breathe
Only by Your surrender have I the faith to believe

Lord only by Your love that first loved me
Lord only by Your love that has set me free

Only by Your suffering do I know Your grace, Your love
Only by Your salvation have I love of Heaven above

Lord Your love bore my blame
Took my pain carried all of my shame
Lord Your love bore my blame
Took my pain carried all of my shame

Lord only by Your love that saved my soul
Lord only by Your love that has made me whole

Lord only by Your love that first loved me
Lord only by Your love that has set me free

Lord only by Your love that saved my soul
Lord only by Your love that has made me whole

Only by Your forgiveness
Only by Your forgiveness and Your grace

Mark 12:29-31

Jesus answered him, "The first of all the commandments is
'Hear, O' Israel, the Lord our God, the Lord is one. And you shall love
the Lord your God with all your heart, with all your soul, with all your
mind and with all your strength.' This is the first commandment.
And the second, like it, is this, You shall love your neighbor as
yourself. There is no other commandment greater than these."

Lord This Is My Prayer

Lord give me the eyes to see
Give me the ears to hear
And a heart that feels
Lord give me the gifts to give
Give me the time to share
And a faith that is real

Oh my Lord this is my prayer
As I'm kneeling here
Oh my Lord this is my prayer
As I draw now near
Lord this is my prayer

Lord give me the love to dream

Give me a soul that sings
And a heart that loves
Lord give me this life to live
Give me the truth to speak
And the chance to rise above

Lord I pray not for the riches of this world
But for Your glory to come
Lord I pray not for the rule over this earth
But for Your will to be done

Oh my Lord this is my prayer
As I'm kneeling here
Oh my Lord this is my prayer
As I draw now near
Lord this is my prayer

Psalm 102:1

Hear my prayer, O' Lord and let my cry come to You.

Sinner Come Home

If you are weary, so weary and worn
Jesus is calling, He's calling you home

If you are broken, so broken and down
Jesus is calling, He's calling you now

**So come home sinner, sinner come home
No longer will you ever be, ever be alone
So come home sinner, sinner come home
No longer will you ever be, will you ever be alone**

If you are troubled, so troubled and torn
Jesus is calling, He's calling you home

If you are wounded, so wounded and hurt
Jesus is calling, He's calling you now

*So come now touch the scars that for you He bore
So come now touch the crown that for you He wore
Touch every wound, every scar
Know that with every drop of blood
You are washed clean, you are washed clean*

**So come home sinner, sinner come home
No longer will you ever be, ever be alone
So come home sinner, sinner come home
No longer will you ever be, will you ever be alone**

So come home sinner, sinner come home

Luke 15:10

*Likewise, I say to you, there is joy in the presence
of the angels of God over one sinner who repents.*

Will I Ever Learn?

There's so much to pray for, so many people are hurting
There's so much to pray for, so many people are searching
And I just can't seem to find the time
I can't seem to be bothered, why?

There's so much to pray for, so many people are falling
There's so much to pray for, so many people are calling
And I just can't seem to find the time
I can't seem to be bothered, why?

**You hold our prayers, there within Your hands
The angels bring You our every word
Just when I could be, down on my knees
I turn the other way, Lord will I ever learn?
Will I ever learn?**

There's so much to pray for, so many people are crying
There's so much to pray for, so many people are trying
And I just can't seem to find the time
I can't seem to be bothered, why?

*Lessons are expensive when they are never learned
Expecting the Lord to bless you, when in return
You can't find the time, you can't be bothered, why?*

**For You hold our prayers, there within Your hands
The angels bring You our every word
Just when I could be, down on my knees
I turn the other way, Lord will I ever learn?
Will I ever learn?**

Proverbs 1:7

*The fear of the Lord is the beginning of knowledge,
but fools despise wisdom and instruction.*

Prayer Will Always Win

When I am weaker and I need to be stronger
When I am further and I need to be closer

**When I give in, when it is I sin
My heart it needs to know
That prayer will always win**

When I am searching and I need to be finding
When I am hurting and I need to be healing

***Forgiveness is the victory, over the darkness
Compassion is the victory, over your weakness***

So when I am drowning and I need to be breathing
And when I am sinning and I need to be praying

**When I give in, when it is I sin
My heart it needs to know
That prayer will always win
When I begin, when again I sin
My soul it needs to know
That prayer will always win
Prayer will always win**

When I am weaker and I need to be stronger
When I am further and I need to be closer
Prayer will always win

John 16:33

*These things I have spoken to you, that in Me you may
have peace. In the world you will have tribulation, but
be of good cheer, I have overcome the world.*

Here Praying For Your Will

Tonight I'm searching, for a little love within a heart
Tonight I'm looking, for a little love where you are
Tonight I'm pleading, for a little peace upon the earth
Tonight I'm hoping, for a little faith around the world

And I know that sometimes, that it gets just a little hard
And I know that sometimes that it takes just a little time
Lord find me still, here praying for Your will

Tonight I'm reaching, for a little hand to hold
Tonight I'm watching, for a little sign from above
Tonight I'm praying, for a little prayer to be heard
Tonight I'm hoping, for a little faith around the world

And I know that sometimes, that it gets just a little hard
And I know that sometimes that it takes just a little time
Lord find me still, here praying for Your will

From deep in my heart, 'O' Lord hear me cry out
From deep in my soul, 'O' Lord hear me shout out loud
Right out loud!

Tonight I'm searching, for a little love within a heart
Tonight I'm looking, for a little love where you are

1 Corinthians 15:58

Therefore, my beloved brethren, be steadfast, immovable,
always abounding in the work of the Lord, knowing that
your labor is not in vain in the Lord.

March

Our Hope and Stay

Our Hope And Stay

Jesus our Salvation, Jesus our Forgiveness
Jesus our Everything, our Lord and our King
Jesus our Perfection, Jesus our Holiness
Jesus our Everlasting, our Lord and our King

From age to age, from heart to heart
From prayer to prayer, from our worlds apart
He in glory born, He in glory came
Now in glory Lord, You are our hope and stay

Jesus our Restoration, Jesus our Righteousness
Jesus our Beginning, our Lord and our King
Jesus our Foundation, Jesus our Faithfulness
Jesus our Thanksgiving, our Lord and our King

From age to age, from heart to heart
From prayer to prayer, from our worlds apart
He in glory born, He in glory came
Now in glory Lord, You are our hope and stay

Jesus our Salvation, Jesus our Forgiveness
Jesus our Everything, our Lord and our King

Psalm 119:114

You are my hiding place and my shield,
I hope in Your word.

His Beautiful Light

Know that after the clouds and rain
Know that the sun will shine again
Know that after your hurt and pain
Know that your heart it will heal again

**So don't you lose faith, don't you lose hope
So don't you give in, don't you give up
For the Lord He is working in every moment of your life
So don't you lose faith, don't you lose hope
So don't you give in, don't you give up
For the Lord He's always shining
His beautiful light, His beautiful light**

*It's so easy to think that nothing will work out right
It's so easy to think that nothings ever going to change
When You believe, when you hold on
When you have faith, you need to be strong*

**For the Lord He is always shining
For the Lord He is always shining
For the Lord He is always shining, His beautiful light
For the Lord He is always shining, His beautiful light**

2 Corinthians 4:6

*For it is the God Who commanded light to shine out of
darkness, Who has shone in our hearts to give the light of
the knowledge of the glory of God in the face of Jesus Christ.*

I Am Free!

I am free from the chains that bound me
Free from the sins that surrounded me
I am free, I am free!

I am free, from the world that has lied to me
Free from the hurt that's haunted me
I am free, I am free!

I am free from all my blame, from all my shame
I am free because my Savior set me free
I am free from all my tears, from all my fears
I am free because my Savior died for me
Because my Savior set me free, I am free!

It took His pain, every drop of His blood
It took His strength, every step that He walked
It took all He had to give, so that I would be free and live
It took all of His life, so that I would survive

I am free, from the life that I lived for me
Free by Your grace that You gave to me
I am free, I am free!

I am free from all my blame, from all my shame
I am free because my Savior set me free
I am free from all my tears, from all my fears
I am free because my Savior died for me
Because my Savior set me free, I am free!

I am free because my Savior died for me
I am free!

Psalm 51:10-11

Create in me a clean heart, O' God and renew a steadfast
spirit within me. Do not cast me away from Your presence
and do not take Your Holy Spirit from me.

For All Of Forever

Lord I give to You my all, I pray that I never fall
Lord I give to You my heart, I pray that we never part

**And that we always stay together
For all of forever
And that we always love one another
For all of forever**

Lord I give to You my soul, I pray for Your control
Lord I give to You my life, I pray for Your Heavenly light

*And that nothing ever separates us
That nothing ever tears us apart
And that nothing ever weakens us
Or ever changes the way we are now
The way that we are now*

Lord I give to You my faith, I pray for Your great strength
Lord I give to You my sins, I pray each one You forgive

**And that we always stay together
For all of forever
And that we always love one another
For all of forever**

Now walking together
Now praying together
Now being together
Now staying together
For all of forever

1 Chronicles 16:34

*Oh, give thanks to the Lord, for He is good!
For His mercy endures forever.*

It Has Changed My Heart

I want to tell you all about, the saving grace of Jesus
Tell you all about His hope and His everlasting love

I want to share this all with you, the forgiving grace of Jesus
Share with you His holy word and His amazing love

**That for your life He died, for your hurt He cried
He poured out every drop of blood
To wash your sins just like a flood
All to make you clean, all to make you clean**

I want to sing this song for you, to sing of what His grace can do
For it can change your heart, it can change your heart

I'll sing of what it's done for me, I'll sing of how it's set me free
For it has changed my heart, it has changed my heart

**That for my life He died, for my hurt He cried
He poured out every drop of blood
To wash my sins just like a flood
All to make me clean, all to make me clean**

I want to tell you all about, the saving grace of Jesus
Tell you all about His hope and His everlasting love

I'll sing of what it's done for me, I'll sing of how it's set me free
For it has changed my heart, it has changed my heart

2 Corinthians 5:17

*Therefore, if anyone is in Christ, he is a new creation,
old things have passed away, behold, all things have
become new.*

Inside My Heart Is Where You Reside

You've always been enough, never given up on me
You've always shown me love, never turned away from me

You have always heard my prayers, never didn't listen to me
You've always held me when I was scared
You've never walked away from me

You have always been here by my side
You have always been here along for the ride
You have always been here since my first cry
Here deep inside my heart, is where You reside
Is where You reside

We have never been too far apart
I know always just where You are
We have never been separated
For You have always been here deep inside my heart
You have always been here deep inside my heart

You have always been here by my side
You have always been here along for the ride
You have always been here since my first cry
Here deep inside my heart, is where You reside
Is where You reside

You've always been enough, never given up on me

Ezekiel 36:26

I will give you a new heart and put a new spirit within you,
I will take the heart of stone out of your flesh and give
you a heart of flesh.

March 7TH

Lord You Know

Lord You know my every prayer
Long before I ever fall to my knees and pray

Lord You know my every word
Long before I ever open my mouth to say

What I need, what I feel
What is wrong, just what I am seeking
Lord You know, Lord You know, Lord You know

Lord You know my every thought
Long before my mind it starts racing
Lord You know my every fear
Long before I realize just what I am facing

Lord You know when I'm crying
Just what makes me cry
Lord You know when I'm trying
Just what makes me try
Or just give in, or just give up
All the moments when I've had too much
Or not enough
Lord You know, Lord You know

Lord You know my every heartbeat
Long before I ever take a breath to breathe

Lord You know my every memory
Long before I ever open up my eyes to see

All the glory of, all the beauty of
All the mercy of, just all the majesty of Your majesty
Lord You know, Lord You know, Lord You know

Psalm 7:9

Oh, let the wickedness of the wicked come to an end,
but establish the just, for the righteous God tests
the hearts and minds.

To Our Glorious One

We lift up, our eyes now to Heaven
We lift up, our hands now in praise
All to our Lord, all to our Lord

Let's lift our prayers now to His throne
Let's lift our souls now in freedom
All to our God, all to our God

All to our Glorious One, our Glorious One

**Lord may Your church now arise
And have our praise fill all the skies
All over the world, all over the world**

**Lord may Your church now bow down
And have our songs now resound
All over the earth, all over the earth**

We lift up, our hopes to Your cross
We lift up, our love with all our heart
All to our King, all to our King

All to our Glorious One, our Glorious One

Holy Father we will sing, all our praise to Your name
Holy Father we will pray, all our prayers in Your name
Lord in Your name

**Lord may Your church now arise
And have our praise fill all the skies
All over the world, all over the world**

**Lord may Your church now bow down
And have our songs now resound
All over the earth, all over the earth**

All to our Glorious One!

James 5:13

*Is anyone among you suffering? Let him pray.
Is anyone cheerful? Let him sing psalms.*

March 9TH

I'll Pray For You

I'll pray for you
In all that you're going through
I'll pray for you
That's just what I'm gonna do

**Because sometimes it's His hope
That you have to find
And sometimes it's His hope
That's just on time
So I will pray for you
That's what I'm gonna do**

I'll pray for you
For everything breaking your heart
I'll pray for you
For that's a great place to start

*On my knees, is where you'll find me
On my knees, is where I'm gonna be
I'll pray for you, that's what I'm gonna do*

I'll pray for you
For that's just what you mean to me
I'll pray for you
His grace is what I want You to see

**Because sometimes it's His hope
That you have to find
And sometimes it's His hope that's just on time
So I will pray for you
That's what I'm gonna do**

I'll pray for you, in all that you're going through

Colossians 1:3

*We give thanks to God, the Father of our
Lord Jesus Christ, praying always for you.*

—72—

He Will Welcome You Home

Are you so weary and worn?
So tired and torn? So lonely and lost?
Are you so broken and bare?
So silent and scared? So afraid and alone?
So come back home
So come back home

With His arms now open wide
He will welcome you inside
With His song singing to your soul
He will welcome you home
He'll welcome you home

Is your brokenness, all that you know?
Is your loneliness, all that you show?
Is your emptiness, all that you feel?
Is His forgiveness, all that you need?
All that you need

Are you so weary and worn
So tired and torn? So lonely and lost?
Are you so broken and bare?
So silent and scared? So afraid and alone?

So come back home
So come back home

Matthew 19:24

Again I say to you, "It is easier for a camel to go through
the eye of a needle, than for a rich man
to enter the Kingdom of God."

All Of Creation

Everything in the Heavens
And everything on the earth
My Lord it is Yours, my Lord it is Yours

Everything in Your kingdom
And everything that has breath
My Lord it is Yours, my Lord it is Yours

And all of creation cries out Your name
And of the nation's now sing of Your praise
They sing of Your praise

Everything in the valley
And everything in the mountains high
My Lord it is Yours, my Lord it is Yours

Everything in the oceans
And everything across the sky
My Lord it is Yours, my Lord it is Yours

And all of creation cries out Your name
And of the nation's now sing of Your praise
They sing of Your praise

Everything everlasting
And everything that's wonderful
It declares the glory of Your name
Everything glorious, everything that is beautiful
It declares the glory of Your praise!

Hebrews 11:3

By faith we understand that the worlds were framed
by the word of God, so that things which are seen
were not made of things visible.

Hallelujah Praise The Lord!

My doubt may cross my mind
Your faith fills my soul
My hurt may bruise this life
Your love heals this heart

Hallelujah, praise the Lord!

My tears may fill my eyes
Your faith dries each one
My pain may bring me down
Your love lifts me up

Hallelujah, praise the Lord!

It's when I think that I've given up
It's then I know that You are enough
It's when I think that I have given in
It's then I know that I am now forgiven

It's when I love that I will make it through
It's then I know that all my hope is in You
It's when I lay my everything down
It's then I know that You are surrounding me
You are all around me

My sin may darken my soul
Your grace it lights the way
My fear may hold me back
Your strength it drives me on

Hallelujah, praise the Lord!

Psalm 95:1

Oh come, let us sing unto the Lord, let us make
a joyful noise to the Rock of our salvation.

Mercy

Oh what a debt I owe
My Lord have mercy on my soul
And oh it's such a long road home
My Lord have mercy on my soul

For the way that I have been
For the depths Lord of all my sin
Oh what a debt I owe
My Lord have mercy on my soul
Oh my Lord have mercy on my soul

Holy Father our Host of Heaven
Lord we lift Your name on high
Holy Father our God of Glory
Lord we praise Your name we cry

Oh my Lord You're my Morning Star
Shining brighter than the sun
Oh my Lord You're the Hope of my Heart
Holy Father, Spirit, Son, the Holy One

My dear Lord this is my prayer to You
Lord to bless me in all that I do
In every trial that I go through
My dear Lord I will give my thanks to You

Oh what a debt I owe
My Lord have mercy on my soul
Oh my Lord have mercy on my soul
Holy Father, our Host of Heaven
Lord we lift Your name on high
Holy Father, our God of Glory

Luke 6:36

Therefore be merciful, just as your Father also is merciful.

Lord Because Of You

Lord I have changed all that I can change
Lord I am not the same
Lord I have prayed all that I can pray
Lord no I am not the same
Lord nothing now remains

For You have changed every part of me
For everything that You see has changed
All of my heart, all of my soul
All of my life has been made whole
It's all because of You!

For Lord Your light is all I want to see
Lord I am not the same
Lord Your grace is Your gift of love to me
Lord no I am not the same
Lord nothing now remains

Lord Your life it is my reason to believe
For Lord Your faith is now my everything
Lord Your name is the very air I breathe
Lord Your love it is my reason to sing

Lord of Your love and of Your grace
Lord of Your cross that took my place
Lord of Your hope and forgiveness
That has set me free
Lord it was Your great love for me

For You have changed every part of me
For everything that You see has changed
All of my heart, all of my soul
All of my life has been made whole
It's all because of You!

2 Corinthians 5:21

For He made Him who knew no sin to be sin for us,
that we might become the righteousness of God in Him.

That's What Hope Is For

When you're at the end of the line
When you have run out of time
When your heart can't take any more
That's what hope is for

When there are no more words left to say
When you've prayed all you can pray
When there is nothing in your life that's sure
That's what hope is for

Just when you've given up, just when you give in
Know His forgiveness is there to forgive, is there to forgive
Just when you've let go, just when you can't hold on
Know that His strength it's always strong, it is always strong

So just hold on, just be strong
It won't be long, just be strong

For there's a miracle, ready to do the impossible
For there's a miracle, ready to do the improbable

So just hold on, just be strong
It won't be long, just be strong

Just when you've given up, just when you give in
Know His forgiveness is there to forgive, is there to forgive
Just when you've let go, just when you can't hold on
Know that His strength it's always strong, it is always strong

So just hold on, just be strong
It won't be long, just be strong
That is what hope is for

Proverbs 18:10

The name of the Lord is a strong tower,
the righteous run to it and are safe.

Lord You Know My Everything

Lord You know my heart
All I am, all I'm not
Lord You know my soul
All my hurt, all my hope

Lord You know my life
All my dark, all my light
Lord You know my faith
All my doubt, all my strength

**Lord You know everything
There is to know about me
Everything I try to hide
Lord You know everything
There is to know inside me
Everything I try to deny
Lord You know my everything**

*My every thought, my every sin
All that is deep within
My every hope, my every dream
All my every word
And all that they really mean*

Lord You know my heart
All I am, all I'm not
Lord You know my soul
All my hurt, all my hope

Psalm 139:7-10

*Where can I go from Your Spirit? Or where can I flee from
Your presence? If I ascend into Heaven, You are there, If I
make my bed in hell, behold, You are there. If I take the
wings of the morning and dwell in the uttermost parts
of the sea, even there Your hand shall lead me and
Your right hand shall hold me.*

That Is Love

Lord You know the depths of my shame
This is the very reason that You came

Lord You know the weight of my sin
You are to suffer and to die
And You'd do it all over again

That is love, that is love

Lord You know the darkness of my heart
Still You prayed for my soul, with all You are
Lord You know the burdens of my blame
This is the very reason
The reason that You came

That is love, that is love

You see the cross and You know what is to come
You feel the loss between a Father and His Son

And that is love, that is love
That is love

Matthew 6:5-13

And when you pray, you shall not be like the hypocrites. For they love to pray standing in the synagogues and on the corners of the streets, that they may be seen by men. Assuredly, I say to you, they have their reward. But you when you pray, go into your room and when you have shut your door, pray to your Father Who is in the secret place and your Father Who sees in secret will reward you openly. And when you pray, do not use vain repetitions as the heathen do. For they think that they will be heard for their many words. "Therefore do not be like them. For your Father knows the things you have need of before you ask Him. In this manner, therefore pray,

Our Father in Heaven, hallowed be Your name. Your Kingdom come. Your will be done on earth as it is in Heaven. Give us this day our daily bread. And forgive us our debts as we forgive our debtors. And do not lead us into temptation, but deliver us from the evil one. For Yours is the Kingdom and the power and the glory forever. Amen!"

Only God

Only God can take a sinner
And make in him a saint
Only God can move the mountain
With just a mustard seed of faith

Only God can calm the waters
With just a breath of His holy word
Only God can bring you to your knees
So that we will someday learn

**Only God can heal your heart
Although you feel unworthy
Only God can save your soul
And give you sweet victory**

Only God can lift your life
And raise you high above
Only God can take your tears
And dry them all with His love
And dry them all with His love

**Only God can heal your heart
Although you feel unworthy
Only God can save your soul
And give you sweet victory
Only God!**

Acts 4:12

Nor is there is salvation in no one else, for there is no other name under Heaven given among men by which we must be saved.

When Heaven Comes

When Heaven comes, we will have every answer
To all the questions we now ask
When Heaven comes, we will know every reason
To every problem we now have

**Like why do they have to die so young?
When they have everything to live for?
Like why for them does eternity come?
When every moment seems like forever**

When Heaven comes, we'll have every solution
To all the issues we now face
When Heaven comes, we'll know every explanation
For every truth we now replace

**Like why do we always separate?
When there's every reason to come together?
Like why we lose love and we always find hate?
When every moment gives us the answer**

*I want to be the one with my arms held high
I want to be the one who Your name cries
I want to be the one with my soul open wide
I want to be the one, who never says goodbye*

When Heaven comes, we will have every answer
To all the questions we now ask

2 Peter 3:13

*Nevertheless we according to His promise look for new
Heavens and a new earth in which righteousness dwells.*

My Lord Come Down

My Holy Father, my Lord in Heaven
Hear my prayer, Lord hear my prayers
My Glorious Father, my Lord in Heaven
Hear my cry, Lord hear my cries

My Lord come down and fill my heart
For Lord Your love it has set me apart
My Lord come down and fill my soul
For Lord Your love it has made me whole
Lord Your love it has made me whole

My loving Father, my Lord in Heaven
Hear my praise, Lord hear my praises
My merciful Father, my Lord in Heaven
Hear my song, Lord hear my songs

Lord I am not worthy to kneel before You
I am not worthy to kneel before You now
Lord I am not worthy to draw near You
I am not worthy to draw near to Your throne

My Lord come down and fill my heart
For Lord Your love it has set me apart
My Lord come down and fill my soul
For Lord Your love it has made me whole
Lord Your love it has made me whole

Isaiah 64:1-3

Oh, that You would rend the Heavens! That You would come down! That the mountains might shake at Your presence as fire burns brushwood, as fire causes water to boil to make Your name known to Your adversaries, that the nations may tremble at Your presence! When You did awesome things for which we did not look, You came down, the mountains shook at Your presence.

A Little Hope And Faith

You can heal a heart, with just one word of hope
Heal a heart with just one word of hope
With just one word of hope

You can save a soul, with just one prayer of faith
Save a soul, with just one prayer of faith
With just one prayer of faith

**So with just a little hope
Yeah with just a little faith
You can move a mountain of stone
So with just a little hope
Yeah with just a little faith
You can lead the lost one's home
You can lead them home**

You can give a gift, with just one act of love
Give a gift, with just one act of love
With just one act of love

You can lift a life, with just one song of praise
Lift a life, with just one song of praise
With just one song of praise

**So with just a little hope
Yeah with just a little faith
You can move a mountain of stone
So with just a little hope
Yeah with just a little faith
You can lead the lost one's home
You can lead them home**

Hebrews 11:1

*Now faith is the substance of things hoped
for, the evidence of things not seen.*

The Flicker Of A Flame

There is more to a prayer than being upon your knees
Be careful what you pray for, it's what you may receive

There is more to a faith than for you just to believe
Know it's the blind man, he too dreams of what he sees

But we're no more than the flicker of a flame
So self-important to the end we remain
Wasting time gathering greed, we can never tame
And if you haven't learned
Nothings left behind, but just a stone, just a name

There is more to a life than to hurry up, stand in line
When it's early to work, your best clothes on, now be on time There is
more to a love than a phone call and a dime
Each must search their own heart for the reason and the rhyme

So seek the courage that awaits within your fears
Pursue the strength that rests beyond your tears
Break the bondage that keeps you a prisoner here
Believe in the faith that has now become so clear

But we're no more than the flicker of a flame
So self-important to the end we remain
Wasting time gathering greed, that we can never tame
And if you haven't learned
Nothings left behind, but just a stone, just a name

There is more to a prayer than being upon your knees
Be careful what you pray for
It's what you may receive

James 4:14

Whereas you do not know what will happen tomorrow.
For what is your life? It is even a vapor that appears for
a little time and then vanishes away.

My Mighty Savior

Savior, may Your will be done here
May Your kingdom come here to this place
Oh my Savior, may Your truth be heard here
May I speak Your words here in this place

Oh my Savior, my mighty Savior
May I feel Your power, at this very hour
Oh my Savior, my mighty Savior
May I feel Your love, from Heaven above

Savior, may Your love abound here
May Your grace be found here and surround this place
Oh my Savior, may Your hope be known here
May Your strength be shown here all around this place

Oh my Savior, my mighty Savior
May I feel Your power, at this very hour
Oh my Savior, my mighty Savior
May I feel Your love, may I feel Your love
May I feel Your love, from Heaven above

Savior, may Your will be done here
May Your kingdom come here to this place

Luke 1:69

And has raised up a Horn of Salvation for
us in the house of His servant David.

I Won't Look Back

Lord I will follow to where You lead
Lord all of my tomorrows are held in Your keep

Lord I will follow to where You are
Lord all of my sorrows You hold in Your heart

And Lord I will go, where You ask me to go
And Lord I will stay, where You want me to stay
Lord I won't look back, no I won't look back
Lord I won't look back

For Lord You are my Guiding Light, always showing me
Always showing me the way home
You are my Morning Star, always leading me
Always leading me home, leading me home

And Lord I will go, where You ask me to go
And Lord I will stay, where You want me to stay
Lord I won't look back, no I won't look back
Lord I won't look back

Lord I will follow to where You lead
Lord all of my tomorrows are held in Your keep

Luke 9:62

But Jesus said to him, "No one, having put his hand to the
plow and looking back, is fit for the Kingdom of God."

The Savior Of The World

The Savior of the world cared enough for my soul
That He walked the road to Calvary

The Savior of the world cared enough for my soul
That He died to set my soul free

**All to forgive, all that I have done
All to forget, all that I once was
The Savior of the world
Cared enough for my soul
That He walked the road to Calvary**

The Savior of the world cared enough for my soul
That He suffered upon that tree

The Savior of the world cared enough for my soul
That He gave all, so my blind eyes may see

**All to forgive, all that I have done
All to forget, all that I once was
The Savior of the world
Cared enough for my soul
That He suffered upon that tree**

*He could have just passed me by
And never heard, never heard my cry
He might have never called my name
And left me here drowning in my shame
Yet He drew me near, He drew me near*

The Savior of the world cared enough for my soul
That He walked the road to Calvary
The Savior of the world cared enough for my soul
That He died to set my soul free

John 4:14

*But whoever drinks of the water that I shall give him will never
thirst. But the water that I shall give him will become in him
a fountain of water springing up into everlasting life.*

Share With Me Your Hope

Lord now break these chains, that are holding me down
Lord now break these chains
That are now keeping me bound

Lord now break this heart, that is now nothing but stone
Lord now break this heart
That is now keeping me here alone

**Bring me to my knees
Open up my eyes, touch my very soul
Bring me to Your cross
Show to me Your cost, share with me Your hope
Share with me Your hope**

*Lord now break these chains, that are holding me down
Lord now break these chains
That are keeping me bound, keeping me bound
Lord now break this heart, that is nothing but stone
Lord now break this heart
That is keeping me alone, keeping me alone*

Lord now save my soul, that is now keeping us apart
Lord now save my soul
That's now keeping us apart

**Bring me to my knees
Open up my eyes, touch my very soul
Bring me to Your cross
Show to me Your cost, share with me Your hope
Share with me Your hope**

Colossians 1:27

*To them God has chosen to make known among the
gentiles the glorious riches of this mystery, which is
Christ in you the hope of glory.*

Glory Bound

I do not know the last breath I'll breathe
For I do not know the last sight my eyes will see
I do not know the last prayer I'll pray
For I do not know the last word my words will say

So here and now I want You to know
Just how much You mean to my soul
With every hope I lift up
With every hope I lay down
Lord it's all in the hope that I will be, glory bound

I'm just trying to live, within every moment
For whom that I love
I'm just trying live, within every minute
For You that I love
Not to look too far ahead, not to look too far behind
Lord to thank You for this day
And to make my yesterday's a little harder to find

I do not know the last breath I'll breathe
For I do not know the last sight my eyes will see
I do not know the last prayer I'll pray
For I do not know the last word my words will say

So here and now I want You to know
Just how much You mean to my soul
With every hope I lift up
With every hope I lay down
Lord it's all in the hope that I will be, glory bound

Psalm 79:9

Help us, O' God of our salvation, for the glory of Your name,
and deliver us and provide atonement for our sins,
for Your name's sake!

That's Where I Want To Be

Wherever You are, my love is
Wherever You are, my hope is

Wherever You are, my joy is
Wherever You are, my grace is

**With all of my heart
I want to be just where You are
And with all of my soul
I want to go just where You go
Ever closer to Your side
Nearer all of the time
That's where I want to be**

Wherever You are, my faith is
Wherever You are, my life is

Wherever You are, my truth is
Wherever You are, my peace is

**With all of my heart
I want to be just where You are
And with all of my soul
I want to go just where You go
Ever closer to Your side
Nearer all of the time
That's where I want to be**

Deuteronomy 4:29

*But from there you will seek the Lord your God and
you will find Him if you seek Him with all your heart
and with all your soul.*

Right Beside Of Me

Lord You are my Guiding Light
Now that shines upon the darkest night
Always leading me home, leading me home

Lord You are my Morning Star
Now that shines in my darkest hour
Always leading me home, leading me home

**For no matter where it is that I am
No matter where it is that I will be
For You are always, Lord You are always
Right beside of me
No matter where it is that I will go
No matter where it is Lord, I will follow
No matter where it is Lord, I will follow
For You are always, Lord You are always
Right beside of me
Right beside of me, right beside of me**

Lord You are my Guiding Light
Always leading me home, leading me home

Psalm 16:8

*I have set the Lord always before me, because
He is at my right hand I shall not be moved.*

Nearer To You

I know You want the best for me
Everything to work out fine, everything to work out fine

I know You're looking out for me
Everything to be ok, everything to be ok

**So why do I walk away from You
Just when You're drawing me closer, closer to You
Why do I run so far from You
Just when You're bringing me nearer, nearer to You**

I know You want the most from me
Everything that I can give, everything that I can give
I know You're asking a lot of me
Everything that's in my soul, everything that's in my soul

*For it's in the grace that You gave
In the life You lost
For it's in the price that You ppaaiid
That covered all my cost
For it's in the hope that You had
That would save my soul
For it's in the song that You sang
Now it's my heart You hold
For You gave Your all to me*

**So why do I walk away from You
Just when You're drawing me closer, closer to You
Why do I run so far from You
Just when You're bringing me nearer, nearer to You
Nearer to You**

I know You want the best for me
Everything to work out fine, everything to work out fine

Hebrews 10:22

*Let us draw near with a true heart in full assurance of faith,
having our hearts sprinkled from an evil conscience and
our bodies washed with pure water.*

Lord Lead Me

It is in my moments of weakness
Lord that I need Your strength
It is in my moments of hopelessness
Lord that I need Your faith

**My Lord lead me, right to where You are
My Lord draw me, closer to Your heart**

It is in my times of darkness
Lord that I need Your light
It is in my times of blindness
Lord that I need Your sight

**My Lord lead me, right to where You are
My Lord draw me, closer to Your heart**

No matter how far away that I go
No matter how much I think that I know
You are leading me, You are leading me home

***I pray for Your will when I have no will
I pray for Your strength when I have no strength
For only Your strength will have me do
All that I need to
I pray for Your faith when I have no faith
I pray for Your hope when I have no hope
For only Your hope will see me through
To be all that's true***

**My Lord lead me, right to where You are
My Lord draw me, closer to Your heart**

Lord lead me

Psalm 5:8

*Lead me, O' Lord in Your righteousness because of my
enemies, make Your way straight before my face.*

April

Rise Again

April 1ST

Rise Again

I know what lies ahead, all that is to come
I know of all the suffering, just what now must be done

I know that they'll greet Me and throw palms at My feet
They'll think they've defeated Me, you just watch what will be!

**For I will rise, rise again, for I've overcome, the battle's done
And the victory has been won, for I will rise, rise again
For I've conquered the grave, your soul to save
All by the power of My holy name!
For I will rise again**

They will drive nails deep into my feet and hands
They will say and do things that they don't understand
The crowd will cry **"Pilot, crucify Him!"**
And I will pray **"Lord they know not what they do today!"
Father. please forgive them!"**

*By the power of this cross, all their tears will be washed away
By the blood that I shed, all their sin will be swept away
Father make it so, please make it so*

**For I will rise, rise again, for I've overcome, the battle's done
And the victory has been won, for I will rise, rise again
For I've conquered the grave, your soul to save
All by the power of My holy name!
For I will rise again**

Luke 24:46

*Then He said to them, thus it is written and thus it was
necessary for the Christ to suffer and to rise from the
dead the third day.*

I Will Hold Onto Your Cross

I will hold, I will hold onto Your cross
I will hold, I will hold onto Your cross

With all I am, with all my faith
With all I have, with all my strength
I will hold, I will hold onto Your cross

Though this world will try to separate us
Keep us far apart
I will hold onto You my Lord Jesus
With all of my heart

I will hold, I will hold onto Your cross
I will hold, I will hold onto Your cross

With all I am, with all my faith
With all I have, with all my strength
I will hold, I will hold onto Your cross

I won't let go, I will hold on, with all my might
I won't let go, I will hold on, with all my life

I will hold, I will hold onto Your cross
I will hold, I will hold onto Your cross

With all I am, with all my faith
With all I have, with all my strength
I will hold, I will hold onto Your cross
I will hold, I will hold onto Your cross

Luke 23:32-33

There were also two others, criminals, led with Him to be put to death. And when they had come to the place called Calvary, there they crucified Him and the criminals, one on the right hand and the other on the left.

April 3RD

At The Foot Of Jesus's Cross

At the foot of Jesus's cross
I will lay all my burdens down
I will fall upon holy ground, here at the foot of Jesus's cross

At the foot of Jesus's cross
It is where my soul will be found
Where His grace is all around, here at the foot of Jesus's cross

**Where all that I have done, all that I have been
It means everything to Him
Where just who that I am, where all that I believe
All my sin He now forgives
All of it right here, at the foot of Jesus's cross**

*And I want to show Him
Just how much I've changed
How much my life has changed
And I want to give Him
All of the love that remains
And so much now remains*

**Where all that I have done, all that I have been
It means everything to Him
Where just who that I am, where all that I believe
All my sin He now forgives
All of it right here, at the foot of Jesus's cross
And all of it right here, all of it right here
At the foot of Jesus's cross**

At the foot of Jesus's cross
It is where I hear the angel's song
It is here just where I belong, here at the foot
Here at the foot, of Jesus's cross

Matthew 26:28

*For this is My blood of the new testament, which
is shed for many for the remission of sins.*

—98—

The Passion

With every drop of blood
That You shed for me
With every tear You cried
Each one that set me free

With every bead of sweat
That fell upon dirty ground
With every eye that Your eyes met
As You searched the crowd

**With every insult thrown
Screamed out in Your name
With every vacant stare, oh my Lord
You bore that blame**

**With every lash that Your back felt
Never once in pain did You cry out
With every step that Your feet walked
Such hate heard, heard in every shout**

With every breath of dust
Life into this life You breathe
With every hit of the hammer hard
That Your gentle hands received

With every sigh Your mother sighed
Falling down, there at Your feet
With every prayer Your Father prayed
For it is now, that Your eyes meet

**With every drop of blood
That You shed for me
With every tear You cried
Each one that set me free**

John 19:17-18

*And He, bearing His cross, went out to a place called the
Place of a Skull, which is called in Hebrew, Golgotha, where
they crucified Him and two others with Him, one on
either side and Jesus in the center.*

April 5TH

Christ The Lord Has Risen Today

Christ the Lord has risen today
For He has rolled the stone away
Christ the Lord has made a way
For He gave all upon this day
And He is alive, He is alive!

Christ the Lord has risen today
For He has washed our sins away
Christ the Lord our debt He paid
For He poured out His heart this day
And He is alive, He is alive!

For Christ the Lord has overcome
The work of the Father has now been done
With every drop of blood He shed
For my sins my Savior suffered and bled
And He is alive, He is alive!

O' death, where is thy sting?
For the victory it has been won
O' death, where is thy sting?
For the victory it has been won

Christ the Lord has risen today
For He has rolled the stone away
Christ the Lord has made a way
For He gave all upon this day
And He is alive, He is alive!

Mark 16:6

He said to them, "Do not be alarmed, You seek Jesus of Nazareth, Who was crucified. He is risen! He is not here. See the place where they laid Him."

Come To The Cross

You will find the truth
That your words have been waiting for
All in the truth of the Lord
You will find the love
That your heart has been hoping for
All in the love of the Lord

**So just come now to the cross
And just fall down on your knees
And there's where you'll find, all you have lost
Just come now to the cross**

You will find the strength
That your life has been longing for
All in the strength of the Lord

You will find the hope
That your soul has been searching for
All in the hope of the Lord

**So just come now to the cross
And just fall down on your knees
And there's where you'll find, all you have lost
Just come now to the cross**

1 Corinthians 1:17

For Christ did not send me to baptize, but to preach the gospel, not with wisdom of words, lest the cross of Christ should be made of no effect.

In The Garden Of Gethsemane

In the Garden of Gethsemane
You are deep in prayer and alone
You take a moment as Your own

In the Garden of Gethsemane
Upon your knees You now fall
For You hear Your Fathers' call

**In the Garden of Gethsemane
You are deep in prayer and alone**

In the Garden of Gethsemane
Through tears of blood You pray
By a kiss You will be betrayed

In the Garden of Gethsemane
You watch over the apostles sleep
Your promise made is one You keep

**In the Garden of Gethsemane
Through tears of blood You pray**

*In the Garden of Gethsemane
It is for my very sins that You cry
It is for my sins that You will die
Bound in chains You are led away*

*In the Garden of Gethsemane
Our very sin has brought You here
Your moment of truth is near
You'll forgive what they do today*

In the Garden of Gethsemane
You are deep in prayer and alone

Matthew 26:36-39

*Then Jesus came with them to a place called Gethsemane and
said to the disciples, "Sit here while I go and pray over there."
He went a little farther and fell on His face and prayed, saying,
"O' My Father, if it is possible, let this cup pass from
Me, nevertheless, not as I will, but as You will."*

My Savior King

On a cross You died for us
Lord You gave up Your life
And on that hill Your blood was spilled
As a perfect sacrifice

**Hallelujah my Lord Jesus
Hallelujah my Savior King
Hallelujah my Lord Jesus
Hallelujah my Savior King**

And in our place our debt was paid
With every beat of Your heart
And on that tree Your suffered for me
With every tear, wound and scar

**Hallelujah my Lord Jesus
Hallelujah my Savior King
Hallelujah my Lord Jesus
Hallelujah my Savior King**

***And on that day a way was made
To share in Your victory
And on that day You broke the chains
All to set our lost souls free
All to set our lost souls free***

**Hallelujah my Lord Jesus
Hallelujah my Savior King**

Philippians 3:20

*For our citizenship is in Heaven, from which we also
eagerly wait for the Savior, the Lord Jesus Christ.*

You Will Find Your Forgiveness

Come all the broken, come all the lost
Come all the wounded, come to the cross
Come all the weary, for here you'll find rest
Come every sinner, for here you'll be blessed

**You will find, your forgiveness
For your sin, for your sin
You will find, His faithfulness
To forgive, to forgive**

Come all the burdened, come now draw near
Come any hour, come dry your tears
Come all the weakened, for here you'll find strength
Come every sinner, for here you'll find grace

*No matter how lonely you are
You are never alone
No matter how far away you are
You are never far from home*

Come all the broken, come all the lost
Come all the wounded, come to the cross
Come all the weary, for here you'll find rest
Come every sinner, for here you'll be blessed

**You will find, your forgiveness
For your sin, for your sin
You will find, His faithfulness
To forgive, to forgive**

Psalm 103:12

*As far as the east is from the west, so far has
He removed our transgressions from us.*

Nothing But The Blood

Nothing but the blood, the blood of Jesus
Can ever save my soul, can ever save my soul
Nothing but the blood, the blood of Jesus
Will ever make me whole, will ever make me whole

Nothing but the blood, the blood of Jesus
Can ever heal my heart, can ever heal my heart
Nothing but the blood, the blood of Jesus
Will ever set me apart, will ever set me apart

**Nothing but the blood that did flow down
That fell upon dirty ground
The blood that was shed for me
Nothing but the blood that did pour out
That my life can't live without
The blood that has now set me free**

Nothing but the blood, the blood of Jesus
Can ever bear my blame, can ever bear my blame
Nothing but the blood, the blood of Jesus
Will ever wash away my shame
Will ever wash away my shame

**Nothing but the blood that did flow down
That fell upon dirty ground
The blood that was shed for me
Nothing but the blood that did pour out
That my life can't live without
The blood that has now set me free**

Nothing but the blood, the blood of Jesus
Can ever save my soul, can ever save my soul

Romans 5:9

*Much more then, being now justified by His blood,
we shall be saved from wrath through Him.*

On The Third Day

On the third day at early dawn
They gathered together in their room
And on the third day they prayed alone
They lifted prayers up to the Lord

And they prayed halleluiah, halleluiah
Halleluiah He is the Lord our God
And they prayed halleluiah, halleluiah
Halleluiah He is the Lord
The Lord our God

On the third day with gifts in hand
They walked the road towards the tomb
And on the third day as they drew near
They found the stone had been removed

And they sang, halleluiah, halleluiah
Halleluiah, He's rolled away the stone
And they sang, halleluiah, halleluiah
Halleluiah, He's rolled away the stone

On the third day they entered in
And He had risen just as He had said
And on the third day the angel spoke
"Why do you seek the living among the dead?"

So sing halleluiah, halleluiah
Halleluiah, praise the Lord for He arose
So sing halleluiah, halleluiah
Halleluiah He is the Lord our God
So sing sang halleluiah, halleluiah
Halleluiah He's rolled away the stone
On the third day

1 Corinthians 15:4

And that He was buried and that He rose again
the third day according to the Scriptures.

Who Will Come To The Cross?

Who will come, come to the cross?
All who seek the Saviors love
Who will come, come to the cross?
All who need the Healers touch

**All of the broken and all of the hurting
All of the wounded and all of the lost
All of the searching and all of the forgiven
All of the faithful who have paid the cost
So who will come, come to the cross?**

Who will come, come to the cross?
All who seek the Saviors grace
Who will come, come to the cross?
All who need the Healers strength

***All who've made it through
Through the driving rain
All who've made it through
Through the suffering and the pain***

**Are you one of the broken, one of the hurting?
One of the wounded, one of the lost
Are you one of the searching, one of the forgiven?
One of the faithful who has paid the cost**

So will you come to where the Savior died?
So will you come to where for you He cried?
So will you come to where love has no end?
So will you come to where for you He rose again?

Who will come, come to the cross?
All who seek the Saviors love

Matthew 16:24

*Then Jesus said to His disciples, "If anyone desires to
come after Me, let him deny himself and take
up his cross and follow Me.*

What More Can I Do?

So what have I left to do? What have I left to prove?
Aren't My prayers enough to believe?
The very price I paid to set you free

So what is there left to say? What is there left to pray?
Aren't My words enough for you to hear?
The very truth that will set you free

**What more can I do? What more can I do?
To prove My love, to prove My love for you
My love for you**

So what have I left to give? What have I left to forgive?
Are not My wounds enough for you to see?
With every drop of blood that has set you free

*What more can I show you now?
Is there a way I can reach you somehow?
Is there something I might have missed?
Or is your heart so broken, that it cannot be fixed?
What more can I do?*

So what have I left to do? What have I left to prove?
My love for you, all My love for you

1 Peter 2:21

*For to this you were called, because Christ also suffered
for us, leaving us an example, that you should follow His steps.*

There's Forgiveness At The Cross

At the cross there is hope
At the cross there is grace
At the cross there is love, sweet love

At the cross there is peace
At the cross there is strength
At the cross there is love, sweet love

And for your broken heart there is healing
And for your wounded soul
There's forgiveness at the cross

At the cross there is joy
At the cross there is praise
At the cross there is love, sweet love

At the cross there is truth
At the cross there is faith
At the cross there is love, sweet love

And for your broken heart there is healing
And for your wounded soul
There's forgiveness at the cross

For there is hope there is grace
There is peace and there is strength
For there is joy there is praise
There is truth and there is faith, oh there is faith

At the cross there is life
At the cross there is prayer
At the cross there is love, sweet love, oh there is love

Philippians 2:8

And being found in fashion as a Man, He humbled Himself
and became obedient unto death, even the death of the cross.

It Was His Sacrifice

Lay down your burdens, lay down all your sins
Lay down your sorrows, here where grace it begins
Lay down your worries, lay down all your fears
Lay down your failures, now come close and draw near
Just lay down your every doubt

**For this is where your Savior He bled
For this is where all of His love it ran red
For this is where your Savior He died
For this is where He gave His very life
It was His sacrifice**

Lay down your bruises, lay down all your heart
Lay down your weakness here, for He knows just who you are
Lay down your blessings, lay down your hopes
Lay down your praises here, at the foot of His cross
Just lay down your every doubt

*For this is where He gave, for this is where He gave
For this is where He gave His very life*

**For this is where your Savior He bled
For this is where all of His love it ran red
For this is where your Savior He died
For this is where He gave His very life
It was His sacrifice**
Just lay down your every doubt

1 John 2:2

*And He is the propitiation for our sins and not for
ours only, but also for the sins of the whole world.*

The Love Of The Cross

Lord how I can find salvation?
How can I find redemption?
After all that I've done, after all that I've done

Lord how I can know Your mercy?
How can I know Your glory?
After all that I've done, after all that I've done

Lord I know, that my debt is paid
Paid by the love of the cross
Lord I know, that my chains are broken
Broken by the love of the cross

Lord how will I see Your beauty?
How will I see Your majesty?
After all that I've done, after all that I've done

And to see, all You want for me
And to know, all You want me to be

Lord I know, that my debt is paid
Paid by the love of the cross
Lord I know, that my chains are broken
Broken by the love of the cross

John 15:13

Greater love hath no man than this,
if someone lay down his life for his friends.

All The Glory Of His Love

It took a sacrifice, it took a surrender
It took a life lost, it took an old rugged cross
It took a nailed scarred hand, it took a crown of thorns
It took blood to be shed, it took His blood to run red

All to save my soul, so that I may know
All the glory of His love, the glory of His love

It took an innocent man, it took the sins of sinners
It took a battle won, it took God's only Son
It took Calvary, it took Gethsemane
It took an empty grave, it took a stone rolled away

All to save my soul, so that I may know
All the glory of His love, the glory of His love

It took an angry crowd, it took a dusty road
It took every ounce of strength, it took all His faith
It took a Mothers tears, it took a Fathers love
It took everything, it took a risen King

It took an amazing love, an amazing grace
An amazing strength, an amazing faith
All to change my heart, all just to forgive
Just for me, all to live, forever, together

All to save my soul, so that I may know
All the glory of His love, the glory of His love

Isaiah 60:1

Arise, shine, for your light has come! And
the glory of the Lord is risen upon you.

In Heaven's Keep

Go to be with Jesus, now fly into His arms
He will be there to greet you
He will keep you safe from all harm

Go to be in Heaven, where you will know His love
Your loved ones will be waiting
At Your home in Heaven above

**Where no more tears will you weep
Where no more death will you feel
On angel's wings you will soar
In Heaven's keep forevermore**

Go to be in glory, where every fear is gone
Join the choirs of hallelujah
For you are just where You belong

So go to be with Jesus, just fly into His arms
He is there to greet you
He will keep you safe from all harm

**Where no more tears will you weep
Where no more death will you feel
On angel's wings you will soar
In Heaven's keep forevermore**

Revelation 21:1-3

*Now I saw a new Heaven and a new earth, for the first Heaven
and the first earth had passed away. Also there was no more
sea. Then I, John, saw the Holy City, New Jerusalem, coming
down out of Heaven from God, prepared as a bride adorned
for her husband. And I heard a loud voice from Heaven
saying, "Behold, the tabernacle of God is with men and
He will dwell with them and they shall be His people.
God Himself will be with them and be their God."*

April 19TH

I Know Of A Savior

You tell me that you're searching now
For someone to dry your tears
You tell me that you're hoping for
For someone to calm your fears

**Well I know of a Savior, a Shelter in the storm
I know of a Savior, for all that you've done wrong
I know of a Savior**

You tell me that you're reaching out
For someone to know just where you are
You tell me that you're praying for
For someone to heal your heart

**Well I know of a Savior, a Shelter in the storm
I know of a Savior, for all that you've done wrong
I know of a Savior**

You tell me that you're hoping for
Someone to know that you're there
You tell me that you're searching for
For someone that will care

*Someone to help you stand when it is that you fall
Someone to take your hand when the mountain seems too tall
Well I know of a Savior, I know of a Savior*

**Well I know of a Savior, a Shelter in the storm
I know of a Savior, for all that you've done wrong
I know of a Savior**

Luke 19:10

*For the Son of man has come to seek and
to save that which was lost.*

— 114 —

Lord Wash Me Clean

Search me oh God and know all my heart
Search me oh Lord and know every part
Search me oh God and know all my sin
Search me oh Lord and know where I begin

**So here fall down, down at Your cross
With all of my gain and all of my loss
So here fall down, down at Your throne
Lord wash me clean, make me Your own**

Search me oh God and know all my soul
Search me oh Lord and know all I know
Search me oh God and know all my life
Search me oh Lord and show to me Your light

*For too long, I have closed my eyes
I have been a fool, here in disguise
I've let show my weakness and not Your great strength
I've let show all my doubt and not Your great faith
Until today, until today!*

**So here fall down, down at Your cross
With all of my gain and all of my loss
So here fall down, down at Your throne
Lord wash me clean, make me Your own**

Search me oh God and know all my heart

1 John 1:7

*But if we walk in the light, as He is the light we have
fellowship with one another in the blood of Jesus
His Son cleanses us from all sin.*

April 21ST

To The Cross

When my soul is aching
When my heart is breaking
I lift my eyes to the cross

And when my hopes are fading
When my strength is straining
I lift my eyes to the cross, to the cross

And when I am lonely
When I am on my own
When I am lonely
When I'm so very far from home
Yes when I am lonely
When I am so very much alone
I lift my eyes, yes I lift my eyes
To the cross

When my tears are flowing
When my fears are showing
I lift my eyes to the cross

And when my faith is failing
When my doubt is gaining
I lift my eyes to the cross, to the cross

And when I am lonely
When I am on my own
When I am lonely
When I'm so very far from home
Yes when I am lonely
When I am so very much alone
I lift my eyes, yes I lift my eyes
To the cross

1 Corinthians 1:18

For the word of the cross is folly to those who are perishing,
but to us who are being saved it is the power of God.

Just Lay Them All Down

Nothing is more beautiful than the face of Christ
Nothing is more wonderful than the hope of the Lord
Nothing is more merciful than the grace of Christ
Nothing is more bountiful than the love of the Lord

**So come to Me, come to My cross
Lay all your burdens down, just lay them all down
So come to Me, come to My cross
Lay all your sins around, just lay them all down
Just lay them all down**

*For you're so tired and so torn, so weary and so worn
Just lay them all down, just lay them all down
For you're so lonely and so lost, so tattered and so tossed
Just lay them all down, just lay them all down*

For nothing is more beautiful than the face of Christ
Nothing is more wonderful than the hope of the Lord
Nothing is more merciful than the grace of Christ
Nothing is more bountiful than the love of the Lord

**So come to Me, come to My cross
Lay all your burdens down, just lay them all down
So come to Me, come to My cross
Lay all your sins around, just lay them all down
Just lay them all down**

Matthew 11:28-30

Come to Me, all you who labor and are heavy laden and I will give you rest. Take My yoke upon you and learn from Me, for I am gentle and lowly in heart and you will find rest for your souls. For My yoke is easy and My burden is light.

Your Cross Is What I Need To Find

Your eyes are all I want to see, Your side is where I long to be
Your name is all I want to call, Your feet are where I long to fall

Your voice is all I want to hear, Your love is what I long to share
Your hope is all I want to know, Your home is where I long to go

Your cross is what I need to find
Your throne's where I leave my all behind
Your arms are all I need to hold
Your truth is of all the truth, I need to be told

Your faith is all I want to believe, Your heart is all I long to feel
Your hands are all I want to hold, Your face is all I long to behold

I need to, I want to, be with You every day
I need You, I want You, now in every way
For Your words are all I want to speak
Your truth is all I long to seek
Your light is all I want to shine
Your grace is all I long to find
Your words are all I want to speak
Your truth is all I long to seek
Your light is all I want to shine
Your grace is all I long, I long to find

Your cross is what I need to find
Your throne's where I leave my all behind
Your arms are all I need to hold
Your truth is of all the truth, I need to be told

Your eyes are all I want to see, Your side is where I long to be

Galatians 6:14

*But God forbid that I should boast except in the cross of our
Lord Jesus Christ, by whom the world has been crucified to
me and I to the world.*

Can't You Hear Me Calling Out Your Name?

You tell me that your heart's been broken
By such cruel words that have been spoken
So more than anything, I want to heal your heart

You tell me that your soul's been shaken
By so many lies that your trust's been taken
So more than anything, I want to save your soul

**Can't you hear Me calling, calling out your name?
Here in the darkness know, that I will be your light
Can't you hear Me calling, calling out your name?
Here in your weakness know, that I will be your strength
Can't you hear Me calling out your name?**

You tell me that your life's been losing
By the choices you have been choosing
So more than anything, I want to lead your life

**Can't you hear Me calling, calling out your name?
Here in the darkness know, that I will be your light
Can't you hear Me calling, calling out your name?
Here in your weakness know, that I will be your strength
Can't you hear Me calling out your name?**

Acts 22:16

*And now why are you waiting? Arise and be baptized and
wash away your sins, calling on the name of the Lord.*

Here At The Foot Of His Cross

There is hope and there is strength
There is mercy and there is grace
And there is a love, all about this place
Here at the foot of His cross

There is truth and there is faith
There is worship and there is praise
And there's a love, all around His face
Here at the foot of His cross

**And you can lay down, your every sin now
And you can lift up, your empty cup
And you can lay down, your every sin now
And you can lift up, your empty cup
At the foot of His cross, at the foot of His cross**

There is prayer and there is light
There is forgiveness and there is life
And there's a love, that burns so bright
At the foot of His cross

**And you can lay down, your every sin now
And you can lift up, your empty cup
And you can lay down, your every sin now
And you can lift up, your empty cup
At the foot of His cross, at the foot of His cross**

There is hope, there is strength
At the foot of His cross

John 19:25-27

Now there stood by the cross of Jesus His mother and His mother's sister, Mary the wife of Clopas and Mary Magdalene. When Jesus therefore saw His mother and the disciple whom He loved standing by, He said to His mother, "Woman, behold your son!" Then He said to the disciple, "Behold your mother!" And from that hour that disciple took her to his own home.

The Bread Of Life

There's a Savior Who is ready
To show you all His grace, all of His strength
There's a Savior Who is ready
To give you all His love, all of Heaven above

So will your heart now believe?
Are your eyes ready to see?
Love's Pure Light, the Bread of Life

There's a Savior Who is ready
To share with you all of His hope, all to save your soul
There's a Savior Who is ready
To help you to find your rest, for you to be so blessed

Know that He suffered, for your every sin
So let forgiveness begin, let forgiveness begin
And know that He died, for your every lie
So let's give salvation a try, give salvation a try
What do you now have to lose?
It is your choice to choose, your choice to choose

There's a Savior Who is ready
To show you all His grace, all of His strength
There's a Savior Who is ready
To give you all His love, all of Heaven above

So does your heart now believe?
Are your eyes ready to see?
Love's Pure Light, the Bread of Life

John 6:35

And Jesus said to them, "I am the bread of life. He who comes to Me shall never hunger and he who believes in Me shall never thirst."

Take Them All Away

In times that are the saddest
In times that are the hardest
Lord I lift my eyes to Thee
In times that I'm the weakest
In times that are the darkest
Lord I lift my eyes to Thee
I lift my eyes to Thee

**And through, all my tears that I cry
Lord may You wash them all away
And through, all my questions why
Lord may You take them all away, all away**

*Oh Lord, take them, far from me
Oh Lord, make them, too hard to see
Oh Lord, with my eyes, as blind as they've been
Oh Lord, take them all away again, all again*

**And through, all my tears that I cry
Lord may You wash them all away
And through, all my questions why
Lord may You take them all away, all away**

In times that are the saddest
In times that are the hardest
Lord I lift my eyes to Thee
In times that I'm the weakest
In times that are the darkest
Lord I lift my eyes to Thee
I lift my eyes to Thee

Mark 10:27

*But Jesus looked at them and said, "With men it is impossible,
but not with God, for with God all things are possible."*

At This Cross

At this cross I kneel, well here my hurt is healed
Oh what love I feel, for me

At this cross I cry, well here my tears are dried
Oh what joy I find, for me, oh for me

**Well no other place can there be
Where Your pain and suffering
Where each drop of blood
Has set me free, than at this cross, at this cross**

At this cross I pray, well here my soul is saved
Oh what a price You paid for me

At this cross I fall, well here my heart it calls
Oh what grace gave all, for me, oh for me

*It was Your death, that brought me new life
It was Your surrender, Your perfect sacrifice
It was my sin, that was laid at Your feet
Lord it was every failure, that You made Your victory!*

So at this cross I kneel, well here my hurt is healed
Oh what love I feel, for me, oh for me

**Well no other place can there be
Where Your pain and suffering
Where each drop of blood
Has set me free, than at this cross
Than at this cross**

Mark 15:39

*So when the centurion, who stood opposite Him, saw that
He cried out like this and breathed His last, he said,
"Truly this Man was the Son of God!"*

It's A Glorious Day

For I can hear the trumpet sound
May it throughout all the earth resound
For I can hear my name be called
For He has now opened the scroll!

**It's a glorious day
For He has rolled the stone away
For His death has made a way
It's a glorious day
For it's the only reason why He came
For His life has shown us the way
It's a glorious day**

*Praising, praying, walking Heaven with You
Singing, dancing, talking forever with You*

We'll all rise to join Him in the sky
As we rise we'll see Him eye to eye
Our broken bodies will be made new
And we'll spend all of eternity with You

**It's a glorious day
For He has rolled the stone away
For His death has made a way
It's a glorious day
For it's the only reason why He came
For His life has shown us the way
It's a glorious day**

Titus 2:13

*Looking for the blessed hope and the glorious appearing
of our great God and Savior Jesus Christ.*

He Is Alive!

I can hear the angels sing
I can hear the bells of Heaven ring
And they're all ringing
All over the earth, tonight
He is alive, alive! He is alive!

I can hear, the nations say
I can hear the voice of the faithful pray
And they're all praying
All across the earth, tonight
He is alive, alive! He is alive!

To every soul, all over the earth
Lift up your hands, lift up your praise
To every heart, all over the world
Lift up your hands, cry out His name
Lift up your hands, cry out His holy name

Alive, for He has conquered the grave
Alive, for He died, it was for my soul to save

I can hear the angels sing
I can hear the bells of Heaven ring
And they're all ringing
All over the earth, tonight

He is alive, alive! He is alive!

Revelation 1:18

I am He Who lives and was dead and behold, I am
alive forevermore. Amen! And I have the keys
of hades and of death.

May

Behold

Behold

All for my broken heart
He was wounded, He was scarred
And the light of His love it will shine
The light of His love it will shine

All for the weak and the poor
He has opened Heaven's door
And the sound of His name it will rise
And the sound of His name it will rise

**Oh behold, behold the Lord
Now in all of His glory, high and lifted up
Now in all of His beauty, high and lifted up
Oh behold, oh behold**

All for the lost and the lame
He's made a path, He's made a way
And the truth of His word it will stand
And the truth of His word it will stand

**Oh behold, behold the Lord
Now in all of His glory, high and lifted up
Now in all of His beauty, high and lifted up
Oh behold, oh behold**

*Oh behold the wonder
All the glory of the Lord
Oh behold the splendor
All the glory of the Lord*

All for the weak and the poor
He has opened Heaven's door

John 1:29

*The next day John saw Jesus coming toward him and said,
"Behold! the Lamb of God Who takes away the sin of the world!"*

All For The Love Of Your Love

I'm praying for Your will, Lord Your perfect will
Lord there is no other prayer
I'm praying for Your truth, Lord Your perfect truth
Lord there is no other prayer

I'm raising my arms in surrender
All for the love of Your love
I'm lifting my eyes up in wonder
All for the love of Your love
All for the love of Your love

I'm praying for Your hope, Lord Your perfect hope
Lord there is no other prayer
I'm praying for Your grace, Lord Your perfect grace
Lord there is no other prayer

All for Your love to comfort my soul
All for Your love to lead me home

So I'm raising my arms in surrender
All for the love of Your love
I'm lifting my eyes up in wonder
All for the love of Your love
All for the love of Your love
All for the love of Your love

I'm praying for Your will, Lord Your perfect will
Lord there is no other prayer

Matthew 19:26

But Jesus looked at them and said to them, "With men this is impossible, but with God all things are possible."

Your Love Is

Lord Your love it is my hope
Lord Your love it is my everything
Lord Your love it is my strength
Lord Your love it is so amazing
Your love is

Lord Your love it is my joy
Lord Your love it is never ending
Lord Your love it is my peace
Lord Your love it is so unfailing
Your love is

Lord Your love it is my grace
Lord Your love it is my everlasting
Lord Your love it is my praise
Lord Your love it is my thanksgiving
Lord Your love is

Lord Your love is my faith
Lord Your love it is my beginning
Lord Your love is my life
Lord Your love it is so forgiving
Your love is

Lord Your love it is my grace
Lord Your love it is my everlasting
Lord Your love it is my praise
Lord Your love it is my thanksgiving
Lord Your love is

Lord Your love is my truth
Lord Your love it is so unchanging

Isaiah 30:18

*Therefore the Lord will wait, that He may be gracious to You
and therefore He will be exalted, that He may have mercy
on you. For the Lord is a God of justice, blessed are all
those who wait for Him.*

Great Is Your Grace

Lord we are Your sons, Lord we are Your daughters
Oh our Holy Father, Lord we love You like no other

For we are Your nations, Lord we are Your children
And we cry out, Lord with all of creation

**So great is Your glory, so great is Your love
So great is the power, of all of Heaven above
So great is Your mercy, so great is Your strength
So great is Your forgiveness, Your everlasting grace**

*Our God of glory, just how great Thou art
Lord we stand in awe of all that You are
Our Host of Heaven, our Prince of Peace
Lord our hearts we lift up, Lord all to Thee*

Lord at Your cross, we lay down our lives
Lord at Your cross, our hands are lifted high
Lord where You are, is where we want to be
Lord by Your side, You beside of me

**So great is Your glory, so great is Your love
So great is the power, of all of Heaven above
So great is Your mercy, so great is Your strength
So great is Your forgiveness, Your everlasting grace**

Acts 4:33

*And with great power the apostles gave witness to
the resurrection of the Lord Jesus. And great grace
was upon them all.*

We Are All Here Together

With a heart of thanksgiving
Lord we come before Your throne
With the hope of forgiveness
Lord we come as Your own

We're to love one another
Like the Father, Spirit, Son
We're to stand here together
To always stand together as one

So Lord we come, as a child to the Father
Lord we come, as one heart to another
Lord we come, as one church in praise forever
Lord we come, we are all here together

Lord we come now as Your children
Lord we come as one of Your lost
Lord we come now as one nation
Lord we all come to Your cross

Lord we come now as Your faithful
Lord we come as Your loved
Lord we come now as hopeful
So that we may see Heaven above

For there's a song Lord now in our souls
May we sing it now, may we sing it out loud
For there's a hope Lord in our hearts
For we were without, we once had our doubts

So Lord we come, as a child to the Father
Lord we come, as one heart to another
Lord we come, as one church in praise forever
Lord we come, we are all here together

With a heart of thanksgiving, Lord we come before Your throne

Hebrews 4:16

Let us therefore come boldly to the throne of grace, that we
may obtain mercy and find grace to help in time of need.

His Forgiveness For My Soul

When I walk, when I walk, walk into Heaven
I want to hold, I want to hold His nail scarred hands
When I walk, when I walk, walk into Heaven
I want to stare, into the eyes of the Great I Am

I want to feel His loving embrace
To hear Him say "My son you're home"
I want to know of His sweet grace
For Him to share with me
His forgiveness for my soul
His forgiveness for my soul

When I walk, when I walk, walk into Heaven
I want to bow, I want to bow down at His feet
When I walk, when I walk, walk into Heaven
I want to shout, I want to shout His victory!

And for all eternity
I will thank Him for the grace He's shown
And for all eternity
I will thank Him for the love I've known
For the love I've known

When I walk, when I walk, walk into Heaven
I want to join, I want to join the angel's song
When I walk, when I walk, walk into Heaven
I want to sing of all my love in my Heavenly home
Yes I want to sing of all my love
Yes I want to sing of all my love
I want to sing of all my love in my Heavenly home
In my Heavenly home

Acts 5:31

*Him, God has exalted to His right hand to be Prince and
Savior, to give repentance to Israel and forgiveness of sins.*

I'm Sending You All My Prayers

I'm sending you all my prayers
In the hope that this finds you there
And to surround you now
In the comfort of the Lord

I'm sending you all my prayers
In the hope that He draws you near
And to be all around you now
In the arms of our God

*In all that you are going through
I pray for His peace and love
In all that you have to do
I pray now to Heaven above
That He finds you, He holds you
He keeps you safe from all harm
That He meets you, He draws you
Into His loving arms*

*That He finds you, that He holds you
That He keeps you safe from all harm
That He meets you, that He draws you
Into His loving arms*

So I'm sending you all my prayers
In the hope that this finds you there
And to surround you now
And to be all around you now
In the comfort of the Lord
In the arms of our God

Romans 15:30

*Now I beg you, brethren, through the Lord Jesus Christ
and through the love of the Spirit, that you strive
together with me in prayers to God for me.*

All My Worship And All My Praise

I was dead, but now I live
I was bond, but now I'm free
I was lame, but now I walk
I was blind, but now I see

**For Lord You've shown me
Your love and mercy
Your forgiveness and Your grace
All I can give to You, is my life lived for You
And all of my worship and all my praise**

I was broken, but now I'm healed
I was lost, but now I'm found
I had fallen, but now here I stand
I was gone, but now I'm home
I was gone, yes I was gone

**For Lord You've shown me
Your love and mercy
Your forgiveness and Your grace
All I can give to You, is my life lived for You
And all of my worship and all my praise**

I was dead, but now I live
I was bond, but now I'm free
I was lame, but now I walk
I was blind, but now I see
Lord now I see
Oh now I see!

1 Thessalonians 5:11

*Therefore comfort each other and edify
one another, just as you also are doing.*

For You Have Set This Captive Free

I am alive, all because of Your faithfulness
I will survive, all because of Your forgiveness
All because of the tears You wept
All because of the promises You kept to me, all for me

I am Your own, all because of Your loving kindness
I bow at Your throne, all because of Your blessedness
All because of the tears You wept
All because of the promises You kept to me, all for me

**For You have set this captive free
For this is what You have done for me
For You've won the battle for my soul
For in Your victory I've been made whole
In Your name, Lord in Your name**

*Lord in Your name, I am Yours, yes I am Yours
Lord in Your name, You are mine, yes You are mine*

**For You have set this captive free
For this is what You have done for me
For You've won the battle for my soul
For in Your victory I've been made whole
In Your name, Lord in Your name**

*Lord in Your name, I am Yours, yes I am Yours
Lord in Your name, You are mine*
Yes You are mine!

Luke 4:18

*The Spirit of the Lord is upon me, because He has anointed me
to preach the gospel to the poor, He has sent me to heal the
brokenhearted, to proclaim liberty to the captives and recovery
of sight to the blind, to set at liberty those who are oppressed.*

Worship And Believe

Give to the Lord, with all of your heart
-Give to the Lord, with all that you are

All glory to His name, all honor and all praise

Lift to the Lord, with all of your hope
Lift to the Lord, with all of your soul
All glory to His name, all honor and all praise

**Lord I will follow to where You guide me
Lord I will worship, I will worship and believe
Lord I'll be faithful to where You lead me
Lord I will worship, I will worship and believe**

Trust in the Lord, now all that you love
Trust in the Lord, now in all of Heaven above!
All glory to His name, all honor and all praise

Share with the Lord, now all of your prayers
Share with the Lord, now all of your cares
All glory to His name, all honor and all praise

**Lord I will follow to where You guide me
Lord I will worship, I will worship and believe
Lord I'll be faithful to where You lead me
Lord I will worship, I will worship and believe**

*Lord I will hold on, to Your cross
With all of my strength
Lord I will hold on, to Your cross
With all of my life, with all of my life*

Give to the Lord, with all of your heart
Give to the Lord, with all that you are
All glory to His name, all honor and all praise

Deuteronomy 6:4-5

*Hear, O' Israel, the Lord our God, the Lord Is one!
You shall love the Lord your God with all your heart,
with all your soul and with all your strength.*

For My Life

Lord Your truth, Lord Your perfect truth
Lord Your will, Lord Your perfect will
It's what I pray for, it's what I pray for
Lord for my life, Lord for my life, for my life

Lord Your love, Lord Your perfect love
Lord Your hope, Lord Your perfect hope
It's what I pray for, it's what I pray for
Lord for my life, Lord for my life, for my life

**For You, are the very breath I breathe
For You, are the beauty my eyes see
For You, are the very beat of my heart
And the mercy I seek, for my life**

Lord Your peace, Lord Your perfect peace
Lord Your grace, Lord Your perfect grace
It's what I pray for, it's what I pray for
Lord for my life, Lord for my life, for my life

*You've shown to me my freedom
Broken every chain I wore, every chain I bore
You've given to me this promise
To set my soul free and be so much more
Be so much more, in my life*

Lord Your truth, Lord Your perfect truth
Lord Your will, Lord Your perfect will
It's what I pray for, it's what I pray for
Lord for my life, Lord for my life, for my life
It's what I pray for, it's what I pray for
Lord for my life, Lord for my life, for my life

Romans 12:2

*And do not be conformed to this world, but be transformed
by the renewing of your mind, that you may prove what is
that good and acceptable and perfect will of God.*

Only With Jesus

You'll never find your healing
In this lost and broken world
You'll never know true salvation
Anywhere here upon this earth

Only now with your eyes now lifted
Only now upon your fallen knees
Will you ever know the saving grace of
A Savior such as this, only with Jesus

You'll never end your searching
Without ever opening your eyes
You'll never know His forgiveness
Anywhere or at anytime

For only in the moment
When all your gain is loss
For only when you bow down
At the foot of His cross
For only when you can't go on
And you still have so very far to go
For only with Jesus will you ever know

For Jesus You are my Lord, I will now follow You J
esus You are my King in all that I go through
For Jesus You are my Lord, I will follow You
Jesus You are my King in all that I go through

Only now with your eyes now lifted
Only now upon your fallen knees
Will you ever know the saving grace of
A Savior such as this, only with Jesus

1 John 5:6

This is He Who came by water and blood, Jesus Christ,
not only by water, but by water and blood. And it is the
Spirit Who bears witness, because the Spirit is truth.

Your Endless Grace

In this communion, Lord I lift up my sins
All to Your throne, all to You alone
In this communion, Lord I lay down my life
All to Your love, all to Heaven above

For I'm alive, all because You died for me
For I survive, all because You set my soul free
All by Your blood, all by the price that You paid
All by Your endless grace, Your endless grace

In this communion, Lord I share with You my soul
All to Your heart, all to Who You are
In this communion, Lord I cry out my prayers
All to Your name, all to You in praise

For I'm alive, all because You died for me
For I survive, all because You set my soul free
All by Your blood, all by the price that You paid
All by Your endless grace, Your endless grace

For Your body is the bread, Your blood the wine
It was Your sacrifice, You gave Your life for mine
For in every drop of blood, for in every tear You cried
It was Your surrender, that saved my life

In this communion, Lord I lift up my sins
All to Your throne, all to You alone
In this communion, Lord I lay down my life
All to Your love, all to Heaven above

Ephesians 2:8

For by grace you have been saved through faith,
and that not of yourselves, it is the gift of God.

This Is Who I Am

For this is who I am, I'm lifting up my heart
Praising all You are, this is who I am

For this is who I am, I'm leaning on Your love
Praising Heaven above, this is who I am

**All for You my Lord, this song of love I sing
All for You my God, this gift of love I bring**

For this is who I am, I'm believing in all You've done
Praising every battle won, this is who I am

For this is who I am, I'm laying down all my life
Praising Your sacrifice, this is who I am

**All for You my Lord, this song of love I sing
All for You my God, this gift of love I bring**

For this is who I am, I'm searching all of my soul
Praising my All in All, this is who I am

For this is who I am, I'm lifting up my heart
Praising all You are, this is who I am

**All for You my Lord, this song of love I sing
All for You my God, this gift of love I bring**

Psalm 63:4

*Thus will I bless Thee while I live, I will
lift up my hands in Your name.*

Call Out For Jesus

When your heart it is breaking
When your soul it is searching
When your life it is losing
When your faith it is doubting
Call out, for Jesus

**Call out, call out for Jesus
When your hope is gone, when all seems lost
Call out, call out for Jesus
Just when you need Him the most
Call out for Jesus**

When your hands they are shaking
When your tears they are falling
And when your fear it is growing
And when your strength it is failing
Call out, for Jesus

***And here, in the midst of the storm
His strength, His strength will make you strong
And here, in the times you can't go on
His strength, His strength will make you strong***

**Call out, call out for Jesus
When your hope is gone, when all seems lost
Call out, call out for Jesus
Just when you need Him the most
Call out, call out for Jesus**

Call out, call out
Call out, call out for Jesus

Romans 10:13

For whoever calls on the name of the Lord shall be saved.

The Power In Your Prayers

I pray for the hurting of your heart
The comfort of His cross
To know that God's not very far away

I pray for the promise of His peace
The searching of your soul
To know that God is in control

For you to find the healing in His hands
The life within His love, the life within His love
For you to find the worship in His words
And the power in your prayers
The power in your prayers

To know that the finding of your faith
Will bring you closer to the One Who loves you
To know that the stirring of your strength
Will draw you nearer to the One Who cares
The most for you

I pray for the hoping of your hope
The truth of His tears
To know that God is lifting up your life

For you to find the healing in His hands
The life within His love, the life within His love
For you to find the worship in His words
And the power in your prayers
The power in your prayers

Mark 11:24

Therefore I say to you, whatever things you ask
when you pray, believe that you receive them
and you will have them.

It's All Been Just For You

You've got tears that keep on falling
You've got cries that keeps on calling
Calling out for Me

You've got a heart that keeps on hurting
You've got a soul that keeps on searching
Searching here for Me

Well I am right here, waiting for you
With arms open wide, to welcome you inside
And it's all true, that everything that I do
It's all been just for you

Well you've got doubt that keeps on doubting
Still you've got faith that keeps on believing
Believing in Me

You've got sin that needs forgiving
You've got arms that keep on reaching
Reaching out for Me

Well I am right here, waiting for you
With arms open wide, to welcome you inside
And it's all true, that everything that I do
It's all been just for you

You've got faith that keeps on believing
Believing in Me

2 Corinthians 1:3-4

Blessed be the God and Father of our Lord Jesus Christ, the
Father of mercies and God of all comfort, Who comforts us in
all our tribulation, that we may be able to comfort those who
are in any trouble, with the comfort with which we ourselves
are comforted by God.

I'm Always Right Here

I'll never leave you, never forsake you
I'll never leave your side
I'll always love you, always care for you
I'll always be there My child

**Although it's now that
You feel that I'm so very far away
Although right now that
You feel now that I just won't stay
Well I'm always right here, I'm always right here**

*I am always here to hold your trembling hand
I am always doing everything I can
I am always here to heal your breaking heart
I am always doing anything I can
For this is just Who I am*

I'll never stop showing, how much I love you
I'll never let you go
I'll never stop giving, all I have to you
I'll always let you know

**Although it's now that
You feel that I'm so very far away
Although right now that
You feel now that I just won't stay
Well I'm always right here, I'm always right here**

Romans 8:37-39

*Yet in all these things we are more than conquerors through
Him Who loved us. For I am persuaded that neither death nor
life, nor angels nor principalities nor powers, nor things present
nor things to come, nor height nor depth, nor any other created
thing, shall be able to separate us from the love of
God which is in Christ Jesus our Lord.*

This I Need To Know

If I fix my eyes upon You and never look away
If I always stay true and follow every word You say

**Will You bless my life? Will You change my heart?
Will You chase away all of my doubt?
Will You hold me close? Will You never let me go?
Will You always love me? Lord, this I need to know**

So if I lay down my soul and surrender all my faith
If turn over control and look to You for my strength

*For so many things, in my life I've lied about
But Your truth came crashing in with a shout
For so many times, in my life I've given up
But Your love it lifted me, but Your love it lifted me
So high above all my hurt*

So if I fall down on my knees and raise up all of my hope
If my promises I keep and pray all my faith to show

**Will You bless my life? Will You change my heart?
Will You chase away all of my doubt?
Will You hold me close? Will You never let me go?
Will You always love me? Lord, this I need to know
Will You bless my life? Lord, this I need to know**

Psalm 24:5

*He shall receive blessing from the Lord and
righteousness from the God of his salvation.*

For The One I Love

For the one I love, I'll do anything
Yes I'll give My everything
For the one I love, I'll lay down My life
Yes I will sacrifice

**Just for you, just for you My love
Just for you, just for you My child**

For the one I love, I will carry this cross
Yes I will pay this cost
For the one I love, I will surrender
Yes I will surrender My all

**Just for you, just for you My love
Just for you, just for you My child**

***No one will love you more than I
No one has shown you more than I
And I would do it all again***

***I'll dry every tear that you cry
I'll forever be right by your side
And I would do it all again***

**Just for you, just for you My love
Just for you, just for you My child
For the one I love**

For the one I love, I'll do anything

Hebrews 9:23

Therefore it was necessary that the copies of the things in the Heavens should be purified with these, but the Heavenly things themselves with better sacrifices than these.

His Strength Will Make You Strong

You need to pray to the Lord
To be found upon your knees, upon your knees
You need to lift up to the Lord
All your soul's deepest needs, your soul's deepest needs

For only then find your peace, in the midst of the storm
For only then find your strength, when you cannot go on
For His strength, will make you strong

You need to turn to the Lord
Like never before, like never before
You need to share with the Lord
Your everything and more and so much more

For only then find your peace, in the midst of the storm
For only then find your strength, when you cannot go on
For His strength, will make you strong

So in your sadness, His joy will be your joy
And in your sinfulness, His grace will be your grace
Here in your darkness, His light will be your light
And in your weakness, His strength will be your strength

You need to pray to the Lord
To be found upon your knees, upon your knees
You need to lift up to the Lord
All your soul's deepest needs, your soul's deepest needs

Psalm 18:2

The Lord is my Rock and my Fortress and my Deliverer.
My God, my Strength, in Whom I will trust, my Shield
and the Horn of my Salvation, my Stronghold.

Only Your Song

Lord show me my lies, show me Your truth
Lord look deep inside to where I cannot hide

Lord show me my sin, show me Your grace
Lord open my eyes, please awaken my faith

For only Your song can ever sing to my soul
Show me where I am to stay
Show me where I am to go
For only Your song can ever sing to my soul

And it brings me to tears, just how You love me
All that You've done, that it was all just for me
And it brings so much joy now to my heart
All that You've done that it was all just for me

For only Your song can ever sing to my soul
Show me where I am to stay
Show me where I am to go
For only Your song can ever sing to my soul

Lord show me my lies, show me Your truth
Lord look deep inside to where I cannot hide

Revelation 5:9

And they sang a new song, saying, "You are worthy
to take the scroll, and to open its seals, for You were
slain and have redeemed us to God by Your blood out
of every tribe and tongue and people and nation.

My Holy One

Like the sunrise, in the morning
Lord Your love is so beautiful

And like the sunset, in the evening
Lord Your love is so beautiful

**And Lord I stand, in awe of You
For all You are, for all You do
And Lord I owe, my all to You
For all You've done, my Holy One**

*Lord Your love, won't let me go
Lord Your love, it always holds on
Lord Your love, will stay by my side
Forever faithful, forever mine*

Like the sunrise, in the morning
Lord Your love is so beautiful

And like the sunset, in the evening
Lord Your love is so beautiful

**And Lord I stand, in awe of You
For all You are, for all You do
And Lord I owe, my all to You
For all You've done, my Holy One**

1 Peter 4:7-11

*But the end of all things is at hand, therefore be serious and
watchful in your prayers. And above all things have fervent
love for one another, for "love will cover a multitude of sins."
Be hospitable to one another without grumbling. As each one
has received a gift, minister it to one another, as good stewards
of the manifold grace of God. If anyone speaks, let him speak as
the oracles of God. If anyone ministers, let him do it as with
the ability which God supplies, that in all things God may be
glorified through Jesus Christ, to whom belong the glory
and the dominion forever and ever. Amen.*

Oh What A Moment It Will Be

Oh what a moment it will be
When Jesus comes for me
Oh what a moment it will be
When Jesus' face I see

When glory comes right through the clouds
He calls my name and the trumpet sounds
His glory sings and I hear His song
I'll know forever's come and it is time
For Him to bring me home

Oh what a moment it will be
When Jesus sets me free
Oh what a moment it will be
When Jesus' arms I reach

When glory comes right through the clouds
He calls my name and the trumpet sounds
His glory sings and I hear His song
I'll know forever's come and it is time
For Him to bring me home

Oh what a moment it will be
When Jesus comes for me

1 Thessalonians 4:13-15

But I do not want you to be ignorant, brethren, concerning
those who have fallen asleep, lest you sorrow as others who
have no hope. For if we believe that Jesus died and rose again,
even so God will bring with Him those who sleep in Jesus. For
this we say to you by the word of the Lord, that we who are
alive and remain until the coming of the Lord will by no
means precede those who are asleep.

For All Eternity Forever

You've prepared a place for me
Where I will run and my soul is free
And I will cry out Your holy name, forever
You've prepared a place for me
Where my blind eyes will finally see
And I will now praise Your holy name, forever

**And we will walk by the glassy sea
And we will talk when it's just You and me
And I will thank You for all eternity, forever**

You've prepared a place for me
Where it's Your song that my soul will sing
And I will shout out Your holy name, forever

**And we will walk by the glassy sea
And we will talk when it's just You and me
And I will thank You for all eternity, forever**

You've prepared a place for me
Where my heart's as safe as it can be
And I will worship your holy Name
And I will worship your holy Name
And I will worship Your holy name, forever

**And we will walk by the glassy sea
And we will talk when it's just You and me
And I will thank You for all eternity, forever**

You've prepared a place for me
Where I will run and my soul is free
And I will cry out Your holy name forever

John 10:28-30

*And I give them eternal life and they shall never perish,
neither shall anyone snatch them out of My hand. My
Father Who has given them to Me, is greater than all
and no one is able to snatch them out of My Father's
hand. I and My Father are One.*

May 26TH

I Will Meet You With All The Angels

I will meet you at the gates
Yes I will meet you at the gates
And on the day of glory, we will all celebrate
Yes I will meet you at the gates

I will meet you at His throne
Yes I will meet at His throne
And on the day of glory, we will join as one
Yes I will meet You at His throne

I will meet you in the clouds
Yes I will meet you in the clouds
And on the day of glory, we will hear the trumpet sound
Yes I will meet you in the clouds

I will meet you at His side
Yes I will meet you at His side
And on the day of glory, when we all arrive
Yes I will meet you at His side

I will meet you at His feast
Yes I will meet you at His feast
And on the day of glory, we will all know His peace
Yes I will meet you at His feast

I will meet you with all the angels
Yes I will meet you with all the angels
And on the day of glory, when we hear Heaven's bells
I will meet you
Yes I will meet you with all the angels

1 Thessalonians 4:16-17

For the Lord Himself will descend from Heaven with a shout,
with the voice of an archangel, and with the trumpet of God. And
the dead in Christ will rise first. Then we who are live and remain shall
be caught up together with them in the clouds to meet the Lord
in the air. And thus we shall always be with the Lord.

Come On Down To The River

For there's a river that is flowing
From Heaven's shore down to your soul
And that river's never-ending
It will change your life forevermore
It will change your life forevermore

So come on down to the river
Come on down have your life begin
Come on down to the river
Come on down and wash away your sin

And that river's ever running
From Heaven's throne straight to your heart
And that rivers ever healing
Your every wound, your every scar
Your every wound, your every scar

For it is glory wide and mercy deep
Forever faithful, forever free
And it is waiting for both you and me
Forever faithful, forever free

So come on down to the river
Come on down have your life begin
Come on down to the river
Come on down and wash away your sin

Matthew 3:13-17

Then Jesus came from Galilee to John at the Jordan to be baptized by him. And John tried to prevent Him, saying, "I need to be baptized by You and are You coming to me?" But Jesus answered and said to him, "Permit it to be so now, for thus it is fitting for us to fulfill all righteousness." Then He allowed him.

When He had been baptized, Jesus came up immediately from the water and behold, the Heavens were opened to Him and He saw the Spirit of God descending like a dove and alighting upon Him. And suddenly a voice came from Heaven, saying, "This is My beloved Son, in whom I am well pleased."

Tell Me Whom Shall I Fear?

Come to the cross and lay your burdens down
For at His feet your forgiveness is found

Lift up your eyes and behold all His glory
For at His feet your salvation is His story

Whom shall I fear when my Lord is right here?
Whom shall I fear when my God is so close?
When my enemies draw near
Tell me whom shall I fear?

Only by His grace, are my sins they are forgiven
For at His feet, is where His grace it is given
I need not be afraid, for His love is all I need
For at His feet my Savior died, He did bleed

For it's in the love of God
In the gift of His mercy
For it's in the hope of Heaveenn
In the sight of His beauty
That His salvation it is shown
That His redemption it is known

Whom shall I fear when my Lord is right here?
Whom shall I fear when my God is so close?
When my enemies draw near
Tell me whom shall I fear?

Come to the cross and lay your burdens down
For at His feet your forgiveness is found

Psalm 27:1

The Lord is my light and my salvation, Whom shall I fear?
The Lord is the strength of my life, of whom shall I be afraid?

Forgive Me Father

Forgive me Father, for so often I sin
Help me find my grace in You
Forgive me Father, for so often I doubt
Help me find my faith in You

Change my heart, change my life
Have my words speak Your truth
Hear my prayers, hear my cries
Have my hope come alive in You

Forgive me Father, for so often I fail
Help me find my trust in You
Forgive me Father, for so often I fall
Help me find my strength in You

For I've been rescued, been set free
I've been restored by Your love for me
I've been redeemed, been made new
I've been reborn, by Your words of truth

Lord may I thank You, for all the days of my life
Lord may I thank You, for all the days of my life

Forgive me Father, for so often I sin
Help me find my grace in You

Matthew 6:14-15

*For if you forgive men their trespasses, your Heavenly
Father will also forgive you. But if you do not forgive
men their trespasses, neither will your Father
forgive your trespasses.*

Here At The Table Of The Lord

There is a hope here for your heart
Here at the table of the Lord
There is a song here for your soul
Here at the table of the Lord

**May the saint and the sinner, may they all come home
And may the lost and the found, never again be alone**

There is a place here for your prayers
Here at the table of the Lord
There is a light here for your life
Here at the table of the Lord

**For here you'll find grace for all of your sin
Here you'll find faith, just where your faith it begins**

*For at this table the Lord He is here
Closer than a friend, so very near
For at this table the Lord He is here
Closer than He has ever been, so very near
The Lord He is here*

There is a hope here for your heart
Here at the table of the Lord
There is a song here for your soul
Here at the table of the Lord

**May the saint and the sinner, may they all come home
And may the lost and the found, never again be alone
Never again be alone**

1 Corinthians 10:21

*You cannot drink the cup of the Lord and the cup of
demons, you cannot partake of the Lord's table and
of the table of demons.*

There Will Be A Victory

There will be a victory
Over your sin, over worry and pain
There will be a victory
Over your hurt, over guilt and shame

Never again will you cry one tear
For there will be no more tears
Never again will you feel one fear
For there will be no more fears

There will be a victory
Over your doubt, your sorrow and blame
There will be a victory
Over your grief, over your loss and over your chains
For there will be a victory

Never again will you cry one tear
For there will be no more tears
Never again will you feel one fear
For there will be no more fears
For there will be no more tears
For there will be no more fears

For there will be a victory!

1 Corinthians 15:50-52

Now this I say, brethren, that flesh and blood cannot inherit the Kingdom of God, nor does corruption inherit incorruption. Behold, I tell you a mystery, we shall not all sleep, but we shall all be changed in a moment, in the twinkling of an eye, at the last trumpet. For the trumpet will sound, and the dead will be raised incorruptible and we shall be changed.

June

By The Grace Of God

By The Grace Of God

I am saved by the grace of God
Yes I am saved by the grace of God
Nothing I have done, nor any battle won
Yes I am saved by the grace of God

I am healed by the grace of God
Yes I am healed by the grace of God
Nothing on my own, not by works shall I boast
Yes I am healed by the grace of God

**It's only grace, to save my soul
It's only grace, to make me whole
It's only grace, that will save my soul
It's only grace, only grace, it's only grace, only grace**

I am changed by the grace of God
Yes I am changed by the grace of God
You have drawn me here
Yes You have drawn me near
Yes I am changed by the grace of God

**It's only grace, to save my soul
It's only grace, to make me whole
It's only grace, that will save my soul
It's only grace, only grace, it's only grace, only grace**

I am saved, by the grace of God

Romans 3:23-24

*For all have sinned and fall short of the glory of God,
being justified freely by His grace through the
redemption that is in Christ Jesus.*

June 2ND

It's What You Are All About

Are we just so very afraid?
Are our hearts so broken and in pain?
We need to let You in, we need to let You in

Are we just so very ashamed?
Are our eyes always looking away?
We need to let You begin, we need to let You begin

**To bring us back to life
To change our very lives
To move within our faith
To renew our weakened strength
To heal us from the inside out
To take us far away from our doubt
It is what You are all about**

Are we just so very alone?
Are our hearts only made of stone?
We need to let You win, we need to let You win

**To bring us back to life
To change our very lives
To move within our faith
To renew our weakened strength
To heal us from the inside out
To take us far away from our doubt
It is what You are all about**

So are we so very much more than alive?
Or are our souls just trying to survive?
We need to let You forgive, we need to let You forgive

Psalm 27:14

*Wait on the Lord, be of good courage and He shall
strengthen your heart, wait I say on the Lord!*

All Things

God gives to you mountains, to teach you how to climb
God gives to you wounds, so one day you will be healed

God gives to you valleys, so you will learn to lift your eyes
God gives to you tears, so that one day they will be dried

**Know all things work together
For those that love the Lord
According to His purpose
According to His will, so be still**

God gives to you words, so you can choose what not to say
God gives to you fear, so you can find your courage to stay

God gives to you doubts, for you to find your faith
God gives to you an empty heart, so that it may be filled

*Oh Lord how long? We're waiting so patiently
Oh Lord how long?
We're anticipating our sweet release*

**Know all things work together
For those that love the Lord
According to His purpose
According to His will, so be still**

Romans 8:28

*And we know that all things work together for good
to them that love God, to them who are the called
according to His purpose.*

For This Is Not My Home

For this is not my home
I'm just a soul who's passing through
For there is nothing here I own
All I have my Lord, belongs to You

For this is not my home
I'm just a soul who's waiting 'round
So across this world I will roam
All I have my Lord, belongs to You

For all I am and all I'll ever be
All I was, all that You set free
It is Yours, it is Yours

For this is not my home
I'm just a soul who's spending some time
For I will be traveling on
All I have my Lord, belongs to You

For all I am and all I'll ever be
All I was, all that You set free
It is Yours, it is Yours

For this is not my home
I'm just a soul who's passing through
All I have my Lord, belongs to You

Hebrews 13:14

For here we have no continuing city
but we seek the one to come.

So Turn To Jesus

He will always love you, always stand there beside you
He will always hold you safe within His arms

He will always lead you, always be there to guide you
He will always keep you safe from all harm

So turn to Jesus when your heart it is hurting
So turn to Jesus when your soul it is searching
So turn to Jesus when your faith it is failing
He will never leave you here alone
He will lead you all the way back home
He will lead you home

He will always heal you, always be so strong for you
He will always lift you high above your hurt

He will always be near you, always surround you
He will always bless you in whatever lesson you need to learn

So keep your eyes open wide, have them lifted to the sky
So keep your soul so very still, always be praying for His will
And hear His voice, high above the noise, and turn to Jesus

So turn to Jesus when your heart it is hurting
So turn to Jesus when your soul it is searching
So turn to Jesus when your faith it is failing
He will never leave you here alone
He will lead you all the way back home
He will lead you home

He will always love you, always stand there beside you
He will always hold you safe within His arms

Acts 3:19-21

*Repent therefore and be converted, that your sins may be blotted
out, so that times of refreshing may come from the presence of
the Lord and that He may send Jesus Christ, Who was preached
to you before, whom Heaven must receive until the times of
restoration of all things, which God has spoken by the
mouth of all His Holy prophets since the world began.*

Through The Eyes Of Our Faith

May our praise always be the praise
That lifts Your name on high
And may Your name always be the name
Always be the name that we cry

And may our prayers always be the prayers
That pray for Your mercy and Your grace
And may we always see, may we always see

Through the eyes of our faith

May our song always be the song
That sings of Your great love
And may Your light always be the light
That always shines from Heaven above

And may our hearts always be the hearts
That long for Your mercy and Your grace
And may we always see, may we allwwaays see

Through the eyes of our faith

May we always be, may we always be
Strong within Your strength
May we always speak, may we always speak
Through the words of our praise

And may our hearts always be the hearts
That long for Your mercy and Your grace
And may we always see, may we always see

Through the eyes of our faith

Ephesians 1:16-18

*Do not cease to give thanks for you, making mention of
you in my prayers, that the God of our Lord Jesus Christ,
the Father of glory, may give to you the Spirit of wisdom
and revelation in the knowledge of Him, the eyes of your
understanding being enlightened, that you may know
what is the hope of His calling, what are the riches
of the glory of His inheritance in the saints.*

I'm In Need Of Your Love

My heart it is hurting
So tired of all the crying
My soul it is searching
I'm so tired of all the running
And I'm in need of, I'm in need of Your love

My life it is losing
So tired of all the quitting
My faith it is failing
I'm so tired of all the doubting
And I'm in need of, I'm in need of Your love

I need Your hands, to lift me from where I am
I need to be held within Your arms
I need Your hope, to lead my lost soul home
I need all Your love to keep safe
From all harm, from all harm

I am in need of, I am in need of Your love
I am in need of, I am in need of Your love

I need Your hands, to lift me from where I am
I need to be held within Your arms
I need Your hope, to lead my lost soul home
I need all Your love to keep safe
From all harm, from all harm

I'm in need of Your love

Isaiah 41:11-13

"Behold, all those who were incensed against you shall
be ashamed and disgraced, they shall be as nothing and
those who strive with you shall perish. You shall seek them
and not find them, those who contended with you. Those
who war against you shall be as nothing, as a nonexistent
thing. For I, the Lord your God, will hold your right hand,
saying to you, 'Fear not, I will help you.'

Only God's Love

Only God's love can ever save your soul
Only God's love will ever heal your heart
For only God's love will bring you home
Make your life His very own
Only God's love can ever save your soul

Only God's love can ever change your mind
Only God's love will ever lead your life
For only God's love will light the way
Bring you nearer to Him today
Only Gods love can ever lead your life

You won't see unless you have the eyes to see
You won't hear until you have the ears to hear
You won't know unless you open up your heart
And give in, give up and let in, His love

Only Gods love can ever find your faith
Only Gods love will ever seal your sin
For only God's love will bid you to come
Keep you at His side so close
Only God's love can ever find your faith

You won't see, unless you have the eyes to see
You won't hear, until you have the ears to hear
You won't know, unless you open up your heart
And give in, give up and let in, His love

Only Gods love can ever free your fears
Only Gods love will ever tell the truth
For only Gods love will forever show
That He loves you more than you know
Only Gods love will ever free your fears

Only God's love can ever save your soul

1 John 4:7-8

Beloved let us love one another, for love is of God and everyone who loves is born of God and knows God. He who does not love does not know God, for God is love.

With All That I Am

Lord I will stand there before You
And I will speak Your name
Lord I will fall down before You
And I will sing all my praise

With all of my heart, with all of my soul
With all that I am, with all that I know
With all of my heart, with all of my soul
With all that I am, with all that I know
Lord I will stand there before You
And I will speak Your name

Lord I will kneel there before You
And I will lift up my eyes
Lord I will cry out before You
And I will lay down my life

With all of my heart, with all of my soul
With all that I am, with all that I know
With all of my heart, with all of my soul
With all that I am, with all that I know
Lord I will kneel there before You
And I will lift up my eyes

Lord I will stand there before You
And I will speak Your name

Psalm 96:9

Oh worship the Lord in the beauty of holiness!
Tremble before Him, all the earth.

His Love Will Set You Free

Throughout all the ups and downs
Throughout all the in-betweens
His love is a light, a light within the dark
His love is there wherever, wherever you are

Throughout all the broken roads
Throughout all your hopes and dreams
His love is a prayer, a prayer within your heart
His love is there wherever, wherever you are

**For His love will set you free, it will break every chain
That you just cannot see, for His love will set you free**

Throughout all the tears and pain
Throughout all the times of doubt
His love is a song, a song within your soul
His love is there wherever, wherever you go

*Breaking every bond, holding you down
Bringing you safe into His arms
Lifting you higher, drawing you closer
Keeping you safe from all harm*

**For His love will set you free, it will break every chain
That you just cannot see, for His love will set you free**

Throughout all the ups and downs
Throughout all the in-betweens
His love is a light, a light within the dark
His love is there wherever, wherever you are

John 8:31-32

*Then Jesus said to those Jews who believed Him, "If you abide
in My word, you are My disciples indeed and you shall know
the truth and the truth shall make you free."*

Where Would I Be?

Where would I be Lord without Your strength?
Without Your cross, or Your never-ending grace
Where would I be Lord without Your hope?
Without Your truth or Your everlasting love

**Without Your forgiveness
Lord without Your salvation
Without Your faithfulness
Lord without Your restoration
Where would I be?**

Where would I be Lord without Your faith?
Without Your peace, or Your beautiful name
Where would I be Lord without Your glory?
Without Your victory or Your never-ending mercy

*In the darkness I may go
But I'm never without hope
In the light forever You'll reign
Where forever I will praise
Where forever I will praise*

Where would I be Lord without Your strength?
Without Your cross or Your never-ending grace

Oh Lord where would I be?

John 15:5

*I am the vine, you are the branches. He who abides in
Me and I in him, bears much fruit, for without Me you
can do nothing.*

Do You Know My Jesus?

Do You know my Jesus? Who gave all for your sin
Do You know my Jesus? He is so ready to forgive

Do You know Jesus? The Savior of my soul
Do You my Jesus? The only One you need to know

For He's the One Who takes away my heart's hurt
He's the One Who has given my soul peace
He's the One Who stands here right beside of me
Throughout all of my suffering
Do You know my Jesus?

Do You know my Jesus? The King of all kings
Do You know my Jesus? The Lord of all created things

Do You know my Jesus? The Healer of my heart
Do You know my Jesus? He knows my every part

There will be a moment in your life
When you fall down to your knees
There will be a time in your life
When you ask, "Oh my Lord, oh my God please!"

For He's the One Who takes away my heart's hurt
He's the One Who has given my soul peace
He's the One Who stands here right beside of me
Throughout all of my suffering
Do You know my Jesus?

Do You know Jesus? The Savior of my soul
Do You my Jesus? The only One you need to know

1 John 2:3-6

Now by this we know that we know Him, if we Keep His
commandments. He who says, "I know Him," and does not
keep His commandments, is a liar and the truth is not in him.
But whoever keeps His word, truly the love of God is perfected
in him. By this we know that we are in Him. He who says he
abides in Him ought himself also to walk just as He walked.

With Nothing Less

I will always believe in You, I will always love You
With all that I am, with all of my heart

I will always worship You, I will always praise You
With all that I am, with all of my heart

**With nothing less than all I have to give
My whole life, every moment that I live
I place my sin at Your cross, with nothing less**

I will always honor You, I will always adore You
With all that I am, with all of my heart

*With all my soul, all my love and all of my faith
With all my hope, all my breath and all of my strength
With nothing less, with nothing less*

I will always follow You, I will always seek You
With all that I am, with all of my heart

**So with nothing less than all I have to give
My whole life, every moment that I live
I place my sin at Your cross, with nothing less
With nothing less**

Matthew 22:37-40

*Jesus said to him, "You shall love the Lord your God with all
your heart, with all your soul and with all your mind." This is
the first and great commandment and the second is like it,
"You shall love your neighbor as yourself, on these two
commandments hang all the Law and the prophets."*

Lord Have Mercy On My Soul

Lord I am sorry for just who I am
Lord I am sorry for the way that I have been
Lord I am sorry for the things I've said
Lord I am sorry for what I've done

**Oh my Lord, have mercy on me
Oh my Lord have mercy on my soul**

Lord I'm sorry for the path I choose
Lord I'm sorry for the life I've led
Lord I'm sorry for the words I've used
Lord I'm sorry for the thoughts in my head

**Oh my Lord, have mercy on me
Oh my Lord have mercy on my soul**

*From the times that I've failed and just did not care
To all the lost prayers, that we could have shared
From the hurt I've caused, to the ones I love
To the sins I've sinned, before Heaven above*

**Oh my Lord, have mercy on me
Oh my Lord have mercy on my soul**

When I fail, time and time again
My God is with me as a Friend
And when I fall down upon my knees
My God is kneeling right here next to me
Hearing my every prayer, hearing my every plea

**Oh my Lord, have mercy on me
Oh my Lord have mercy on my soul**

Psalm 6:2-4

*Have mercy on me, O' Lord, for I am weak O' Lord, heal me,
for my bones are troubled, my soul also is greatly troubled.
But You, O' Lord how long? Return, O' Lord deliver me!
Oh save me for Your mercies sake.*

My Lord Hear My Prayer

I am reaching, my arms now for You Lord
I'm searching for You
Lord I'm searching for You

I am lifting, my eyes now to You Lord
I'm searching for You
Lord I'm searching for You

I feel alone, I feel so broken
My Lord hear my prayer
I feel afraid, I feel so shaken
My Lord hear my prayer

Lord I am here and Lord You are there
Lord I feel, so separated
Lord I am lost and Lord please find me
Here upon my knees, asking of You please

I feel alone, I feel so broken
My Lord hear my prayer
I feel afraid, I feel so shaken
My Lord hear my prayer

So I am crying, all my prayers out to You Lord
I'm searching for You
Lord I'm searching for You

This song was written as an unspoken dedication
Always praying the for the healing of hearts

Psalm 39:12-13

*Hear my prayer, O' Lord and give ear to my cry, do not
be silent at my tears, for I am a stranger with You, a
sojourner, as all my fathers were. Remove Your
gaze from me, that I may regain strength,
before I go away and am no more.*

Until The End

Know when you're hurting, that God is working
Upon your heart and in your life
Know when you're crying, that God is drying
Your every tear now from your eyes

**Know He is beside you
Closer than a friend
Know He is within you
All the way until the end, until the end**

Know when you're searching, that God is finding
Wherever you are, you are never lost
Know when you're falling, that God is lifting
You into His arms and to the cross

***For you are never, you're never left alone
For you are never, ever too far from home***

**Know He is beside you
Closer than a friend
Know He is within you
All the way until the end, until the end**

Know when you're hurting, that God is working

Isaiah 41:10

*Fear not, for I am with you, be not dismayed, for
I am your God. I will strengthen you, yes I will help
you, I will uphold you with My righteous right hand.*

We've All Just Got To Believe

To hear your words today, well they just broke my heart
To hear that your whole world, is now just falling apart

But don't lose faith, don't give up on hope
Know you are loved, far more than you know

We've all just got to believe, in something greater
Than what our eyes may see
We've all just got to believe, in something better
Than what our lives can be, we all just got to believe

To hear you cry today, that you feel so empty inside
To hear your hurt won't go away
And it's something you just can't hide

But don't lose faith, don't give up on hope
Know you are loved, far more than you know

For nothing in this world, will show you all you seek
For nothing on this earth, will give you all you need
I am not trying to tell you, that all your pain will all disappear
All that I am praying for, is that someday you will draw near
And believe and believe

We've all just got to believe, in something greater
Than what our eyes may see
We've all just got to believe, in something better
Than what our lives can be, we all just got to believe
We've all just got to believe

Deuteronomy 31:6

Be strong and of good courage, do not fear nor be afraid
of them, for the Lord your God, He is the One Who goes
with you. He will not leave you nor forsake you.

For This Is Not Who I Am

I will not stop loving you or holding your hand
I will not stop lifting you or helping you stand

**For this is not Who I am, for this is not what I died for
For this is not Who I am, that's not why I shed My blood
For this is not Who I am**

I will not stop leading you or guiding your soul
I will not stop holding you or giving you hope

*Know that I am always there for you
In everything that you will go through
Know that I am always beside of you
In everything that you now do
Know that I am there for you*

I will not stop forgiving you or changing your life
I will not stop believing you or showing you light

**For this is not Who I am, for this is not what I died for
For this is not Who I am, that's not why I shed My blood
For this is not Who I am**

*For no matter who you are, or what you have done
My grace it is yours and your victory it is won!*

I will not stop searching for you or whispering your name
I will not stop healing you or hearing you pray

**For this is not Who I am, for this is not what I died for
For this is not Who I am, that's not why I shed My blood
For this is not Who I am**

Zephaniah 3:17

*The Lord your God in your midst
The Mighty One will save
He will rejoice over you with gladness
He will quiet you with His love
He will rejoice over you with singing.*

For Only Jesus

Only Jesus gave His life for me
For Jesus walked the road to Calvary
Only Jesus has set my lost soul free
For Jesus let my blind eyes see

Only Jesus has forgiven my sin
For Jesus opened Heaven to let me in
Only Jesus suffered, died and rose again
For Jesus calls me beloved, calls me His friend

**For only Jesus sacrificed His all
So that one day I would be called home
For only Jesus surrendered His all
So that on that day, He would call me His own**

Only Jesus made a way for the lost
For Jesus shed His blood upon the cross
Only Jesus paid the ultimate cost
For Jesus felt the pain, Jesus felt the loss

*There's no other name that speaks to my heart
There's no other name that sings to my soul
For there's no other name that cries for my sin
No other name that for me will ever forgive
No other name, no other name, loves me the same*

**For only Jesus sacrificed His all
So that one day I would be called home
For only Jesus surrendered His all
So that on that day He could call me His own
For only Jesus**

John 1:1-5

*In the beginning was the Word and the Word was with God
and the Word was God. He was in the beginning with God.
All things were made through Him and without Him nothing
was made that was made. In Him was life, and the life was
the light of men. And the light shines in the darkness,
and the darkness did not comprehend it.*

I'm Here Reaching Out For You

I know you've been searching, I know you've been hurting
I know you've been seeking
You're looking for something to change
I know you've been crying, I know you've been trying
I know you've been hoping
You're praying for something to change

Well I am here now, I'm calling out to you
With everything that I know, all I know how to do
And with My arms now open wide, all to invite you inside
I'm here reaching out for you

I know you've been dreaming, I know you've been screaming
I know you've been longing
You're asking for something to change
I know you've been doubting, I know you've been shouting
I know you've been listening
You're waiting for something to change

Please know you are a miracle, every time that you breathe
My child you are My miracle and above all of this
This I need you to know, all of this I need you to know

Well I am here now, I'm calling out to you
With everything that I know, all I know how to do
And with My arms now open wide, all to invite you inside
I'm here reaching out for you

Matthew 8:1-3

When He had come down from the mountain, great multitudes
followed Him. And behold, a leper came and worshiped Him,
saying, "Lord, If You are willing, You can make me clean."
Then Jesus put out His hand and touched him, saying, "I am
willing, be cleansed." Immediately his leprosy was cleansed.

One Prayer Away

Your soul feels like it's drowning in the ocean
Your heart feels like it's been nothing but broken
Your life feels like it's driving in the slow lane
Your faith feels like it's been nothing but sin and shame

**What if I told you, what if I showed you
That you are only one prayer away?
From salvation, reconciliation, Who loves you more
From communion, from celebration
With the Son Who is knocking at your door
Who loves you more**

Your walk feels like your falling and you can't stand up
Your strength feels like it's failing and you've had about enough

**What if I told you, what if I showed you
That you are only one prayer away?
From salvation, reconciliation, Who loves you more
From communion, from celebration
With the Son Who is knocking at your door
Who loves you more**

Your soul feels like it's drowning in the ocean

1 Timothy 2:5

*For there is one God and one Mediator
between God and men, the Man Christ Jesus.*

Just Reach Out Your Heart

I don't want you to know any more tears
I don't want you to know any more hurt
I don't ever want you to feel afraid

I don't want you to know any more fear
I don't want you to know any more doubt
I don't ever want you to feel alone

**I want you to feel My love
Love like you've never known
I want you to know My hope
Love like you've never been shown
That it's all right here
For you right here in My arms
Yes that it's all right here for you
If just reach out your heart**

I don't want you to know any more loss
I don't want you to know any more pain
I don't ever want you to feel afraid

I don't want you to know any more regret
I don't want you to know any more trials
I don't ever want you to feel alone

*And find My peace within the storm
Find My strength here in your weakness
And to know I am always here for you
And find My voice high above the roar
Find My light here in your darkness
And to know I am always here for you*

I don't want you to know any more tears

3 John 1:4

*I have no greater joy than to hear
that My children walk in truth.*

May We Always Lift You Up

Lord as we leave this church today
We pray for Your grace
Here along our way

Lord as we leave this church today
We pray for Your peace
Here in the words we say

In every step that we take
In every choice that we make
In everywhere that we go
In every side that we choose to show
May it always be in prayer
May it always be in prayer

May we always lift You up
May You always be enough for us
Our Lord Jesus

For Lord You know our hearts
You know just who we are
Everything that we are made of
Lord You know just what we'll say
All the mistakes that we'll make
Lord may Your love, now guide us

May we always lift You up
May You always be enough for us
Our Lord Jesus

John 8:28-32

Then Jesus said to them, "When you lift up the Son of Man, then you will know that I am He and that I do nothing of Myself, but as My Father taught Me, I speak these things. And He Who sent Me is with Me. The Father has not left Me alone, for I always do those things that please Him." As He spoke these words, many believed in Him. Then Jesus said to those Jews who believed Him, "If you abide in My word, you are My disciples indeed. And you shall know the truth, and the truth shall make you free."

June 24TH

Take Me Home

Lord take me home now into Your arms
Lord take me home, where I will know no harm

Where I'll know only love
With no more tears, yes only love

Lord lead me home now into Your keep
Lord lead me home, where my soul will be set free

Where I'll know only love
With no more tears, yes only love

Only love, home at last
Only love, where I am blessed

Lord bring me home now into Your love
Lord bring me home
Where we will share all of Heaven above

Where I'll know, where I will know
No more tears, yes only love
Where I will know
No more tears, yes only love

John 11:26

And whoever lives and believes in Me shall never die.
Do you believe this?

Right Here At My Side

When I look back, upon all I have done
All the battles lost and all the wars won
You've always been there, right at my side

As I look ahead, upon all I will do
Each and every trial, that I will go through
You will always be there, right at my side

**I'd never change a minute of one day
I wouldn't have it any other way
Than to have You here along for the ride
Right here at my side**

*Each and every step and each and every mile
Each and every tear and each and every smile
Each and every joy and each and every hurt
Each and every moment
And each and every lesson learned*

**I'd never change a minute of one day
I wouldn't have it any other way
Than to have You here along for the ride
Right here at my side**

Psalm 16:7-9

I will bless the Lord Who has given me counsel, My heart also instructs me in the night seasons. I have set the Lord always before me, because He is at my right hand I shall not be moved. Therefore my heart is glad, and my glory rejoices, my flesh also will rest in hope.

Only My Lord Jesus

We shall call Him Savior
He's our Deliverer and Friend
We shall call Him Redeemer
He's our Beginning and our End

We shall call Him Wonderful
He's our Light of the world
We shall call Him Merciful
He's our Hope for all the earth

We shall call Him Precious
Our Bright and Morning Star
We shall call Him Messiah
For He is our Great Thou Art!
Only my Lord Jesus

We shall call Him Worthy
He's our Shelter in the storm
We shall call Him Holy
He's our Lord of all!

We shall call Him Glorious
Our Shelter in our storm
We shall call Him Victorious
For He is our Holy One!
Only my Lord Jesus

For He is our Beloved, our Everlasting
He is our Almighty, our Prince of Peace
For He is our Victory, our Majesty
He is our Wonderful, our King of kings
Only my, only my Lord Jesus

I Corinthians 5:4

In the name of our Lord Jesus Christ, when you are gathered together, along with My spirit, with the power of our Lord Jesus Christ.

Love Will Change

Love will change just who you are
Love will change your very heart
Love will change all that you know
Love will change your very soul

**Lord I want to go, where You want me to go
Lord I want to be, just who You want me to be**

Love will change everything you believe
Love will change all that your eyes perceive
Love will change the very words you speak
Love will change this life you seek

**Lord I want to go, where You want me to go
Lord I want to be, just who You want me to be**

*Lord I want to walk, where You want me to walk
Lord I want to see, all You want me to see
I've tried living my life on my own
I've tried hoping all that I can hope
I've tried believing with all of my soul
I've tried going as far as I could go*

Love will change just how you pray
Love will change your life this very day

Jeremiah 24:7

*Then I will give them a heart to know Me, that I am the Lord
and they shall be My people and I will be their God, for
they shall return to Me with their whole heart.*

For It Is Then

I pray for My hope, now to fill your heart
To find you there just where you are

I pray for My light, now to shine in your life
When the darkness seems so dark

For it is then, that I am there all around you
For it is then, that I am there surrounding you
I am always holding on to you, for it is then

I pray for My strength, now to lift you up
Up off of the ground from where you've fallen

I pray for My love, now to dry your tears
And to keep them away, please know you are forgiven

It may seem, that you are on your own
But it only seems that way
For I am with you, in every prayer you pray
It may seem, that you are all alone
But it only seems that way
For I am with you in every moment of every day

I pray for My truth now to guide your faith
And to have all of your doubt all to be washed away

I pray for My grace, now to be your forgiveness
And to have all your sin, now to be worthless

For it is then, that I am there all around you
For it is then, that I am there surrounding you
I am always holding on to you
For it is then

Ephesians 4:6

One God and Father of all, Who is above
all and through all and in you all.

—186—

Come Now Father

Come now Father to my side
Draw near to me this very night
Come now Father as I pray
Kneel down beside me closer every day

You told us to ask You in Your name
You said it's the reason, the very reason You came
The reason You lived, the very reason You died
The reason You suffered, it was all for me to survive

Come now Father to my side
Draw near to me this very night
Come now Father as I pray
Kneel down beside me closer every day

You showed us how to follow in Your way
You said it's the purpose, the very purpose of Your pain
The reason You lived, the very reason You died
The reason You suffered, it was all for me to survive

Nearer than You've ever been
Than I can remember when
Closer to my broken heart
So You can heal my every part
Every broken part

Come now Father to my side
Draw near to me this very night
Come now Father as I pray
Kneel down beside me closer every day

John 14:23

Jesus answered and said to him, "If anyone loves Me,
he will keep My word and My Father will love him and
we will come to him and make Our home with him."

I Will Rise

When He shall come with a trumpet sound
Here upon my knees Lord, I pray that I'll be found
And when through the clouds my Savior flies
There I'll meet Him in the sky

And I will rise, with hands both raised
I will rise, singing all of my praise
And I will rise, Lord I will rise
And I will meet You eye to eye
Lord I will rise

For my hope it is built upon solid rock
For my hope it is built, upon nothing less
Upon Jesus's blood and His righteousness
Upon Jesus's love and His forgiveness
For my hope it is built, upon nothing less

Yes I will rise, with hands both raised
I will rise, singing all of my praise
And I will rise, Lord I will rise
And I will meet You eye to eye
Lord I will rise

On Jesus Christ the Solid Rock I'll stand
For all other ground, it is sinking sand
For all other ground, it is sinking sand

1 Thessalonians 4:14-17

*For if we believe that Jesus died and rose again, even so God
will bring with Him those who sleep in Jesus. For this we say to
you by the word of the Lord, that we who are alive and remain
until the coming of the Lord will by no means precede those who
are asleep. For the Lord Himself will descend from Heaven with
a shout, with the voice of an archangel and with the trumpet
of God and the dead in Christ will rise first. Then we who are
alive and remain shall be caught up together with them in
the clouds to meet the Lord in the air and thus we
shall always be with the Lord.*

July

Let Him In

July 1ST

Let Him In

God blesses those who are humble
God blesses those who are beaten down
God blesses those who forgive the unforgivable
So God can forgive you right now

God blesses those who fall to their knees
God blesses those who are hurt and lost
God blesses those who doubt and yet believe
God blesses those who are searching for the cross

**For no matter what you've done
For no matter what you've said
For no matter who you really are
And no matter who you've been
God awakes every morning
Knocking on the door to your heart
Today might be a great day to start
So let Him in, let Him in**

*So open up your heart and let the Lord inside
Be glad for every moment that's He's along for the ride
So let Him in, please let Him in*

**For no matter what you've done
For no matter what you've said
For no matter who you really are
And no matter who you've been
God awakes every morning
Knocking on the door to your heart
Today might be a great day to start
So let Him in, let Him in**

Revelation 3:20

*Behold, I stand at the door and knock. If anyone hears
My voice and opens the door, I will come into him
and dine with him and he with Me.*

Hosanna Hallelujah

Lord to stand in Your presence
To fall down at Your feet
To pray with all the faithful
To sing for all eternity
Hosanna, hallelujah

Lord to see You in all Your beauty
To hold Your nail scarred hands
To join with all Your children
To shout our love across the land
Hosanna, hallelujah

All honor and praise to the Lord
All honor and praise to the Lord
All honor and praise, all glory to Your name
All honor and praise to the Lord

Lord to be with You forever
To walk along the glassy sea
To join with all the nations
Upon our bended knee

Hosanna, hallelujah, hosanna, hallelujah amen!

All honor and praise to the Lord
All honor and praise to the Lord
All honor and praise to the Lord, to the Lord
Hosanna, hallelujah

Matthew 21:9

Then the multitudes who went before and those who followed cried out, saying, "Hosanna to the Son of David! Blessed is He who comes in the name of the Lord! Hosanna in the highest!"

July 3ʳᵈ

A Prayer For A Brother

I pray now that the Lord
Shines for you His light
That right now you need to see

And I pray now that the Lord
Shares for you His love
That right now you need to believe

**For only God's light
Will ever break through the darkness
Lord shine for him Your light
For only God's love
Will ever hold you in your loneliness
Lord hold him in Your love**

I pray now that the Lord
Shows to you His hope
That right now you need to feel

And I pray now that the Lord
Gives to you His peace
That right now you need to let it in

**For only God's hope
Will ever see you through the lovelessness
For only God's peace
Will ever hold you in your emptiness**

I pray now that the Lord
Shines for you His light

1 Corinthians 2:9

*But as it is written, "Eye has not seen, nor ear heard,
nor have entered into the heart of man the things
which God has prepared for those who love Him."*

Lord Thank You For America

Lord thank You for America
And everything that it means
For Your love it shines upon us
From sea to shining sea
Lord thank You for America
Let us now raise up our hands
For Your hope it holds this nation
Every child, woman and man

**For no matter where we've come from
For no matter what we believe
We are all one nation, only under God do we breathe
For no matter all we've suffered
For no matter what heights we reach
We are all one nation, only under God do we breathe**

On fields across this country
They have fought and they have died
On fields of many nations
They have bled and they have cried
All for me, and for you, and for the red
And for the white, all for the blue

So Lord thank You for America
We remember their sacrifice
It's their courage we now honor
Every soul who gave their life
From a revolution in New England
To dark deserts in Afghanistan
It's for every soldier that we now salute
And now we stand!

**For no matter where we've come from
For no matter what we believe
We are all one nation, only under God do we breathe
For no matter all we've suffered
For no matter what heights we reach
We are all one nation, only under God do we breathe
Lord thank You for America**

2 Corinthians 3:17

*Now the Lord is the Spirit and where
the Spirit of the Lord is, there is liberty.*

— 193 —

The All Of The Lord

We all need, all of His grace
All of His love from Heaven above
We all need, all of His strength
All of His hope from Heaven alone

**For we all need the all of God
We all seek the all of the Lord
For we all need the all of God
We all seek the all of the Lord**

*We need every word and we need every breath
We need every bit of His love
We need every prayer and we need every truth
We need every drop of His blood*

We all need, all of His grace
All of His love from Heaven above
We all need, all of His strength
All of His hope from Heaven alone
All of His hope from Heaven alone

**For we all need the all of God
We all seek the all of the Lord
For we all need the all of God
We all seek the all of the Lord**

We all need, all of His grace
All of His love from Heaven above

2 Corinthians 1:20-22

*For all the promises of God in Him are Yes and in Him Amen,
to the glory of God through us. Now He Who establishes us
with you in Christ and has anointed us is God, Who also has
sealed us and given us the Spirit in our hearts as a guarantee.*

All Before You Know

There are those who will be right
There are those who'll be so wrong
But don't take, don't take too long

There are those who won't decide
There are those who can't make up their mind
But don't take, don't take too much time

**For the moment it will come and the moment it will go
All before, all before you know**

There are those who will doubt
There are those who'll be so sure
But don't be, don't be too assured

*For in the blink of an eye
In a star shooting across the sky
He will come, the Lord He will come
For in the beat of a heart
In the place wherever you are
He will come, the Lord He will come*

There are those who will choose
There are those who will still wait
But please don't, please don't hesitate

There are those who just will not believe
There are those who'll give their everything
But don't to, don't to this world cling

**For the moment it will come and the moment it will go
All before, all before you know**

1 Corinthians 15:52

*In a moment, in the twinkling of an eye, at the last
trumpet. For the trumpet will sound and the dead
will be raised incorruptible and we shall be changed.*

July 7TH

If It Be Your Will

Lord take away all of my pain
All of my loneliness
Lord wipe away all of my tears
All of my emptiness

Lord take away all of my shame
All of my lovelessness
Lord wipe away all of my sin
All of my righteousness

If it be Your will, please make it so
If it be Your will, please let me know
Where I am to go, where I am to stay
Who I am to be, what I am to pray
If it be Your will

Lord find me still, here upon my knees
With my arms raised high, reaching up to the sky
For Lord there's so much here to be done

So many souls here to be won!
And it's true, there's only so much I can do
But what I have I want to give my all to you

If it be Your will

Ephesians 5:17

Therefore do not be unwise, but understand
what the will of the Lord is.

He Watches Me

When I fail, when I fall
He is here, throughout it all always beside of me

Where I am, where I'll go
He is here, this I know always nearby me

**For His eyes they are upon me
For His eyes they never leave me
He watches me in all I do, in all that I go through
He watches me, my Lord watches me**

*He never turns away, to leave me here alone
He never looks away, to have me be here on my own*

So when I'm lost, when I'm found
He is here, all around always surrounding me

When I kneel, when I pray
He is here, every day always a part of me

**For His eyes they are upon me
For His eyes they never leave me
He watches me in all I do, in all that I go through
He watches me, my Lord watches me**

*He never turns away, to leave me here alone
He never looks away, to have me be here on my own
He watches me*

When I fail, when I fall
He is here, throughout it all always beside of me

Psalm 146:9

*The Lord watches over the strangers, He relieves
the fatherless and widow, but the way of the
wicked He turns upside down.*

July 9TH

Here In Your Prayers

Our prayer is the only way, that we speak with our Lord
Our prayer is the only way, that we speak with our God

Let Him hear what is in your heart
Tell Him everything
Let Him see what is in your soul
Tell Him everything, here in your prayers

Our prayer is the only way, that we speak with our King
Our prayer is the only way, that we speak with our Friend

Let Him hear what is in your heart
Tell Him everything
Let Him see what is in your soul
Tell Him everything, here in your prayers

For there's now a peace here in your prayers
Here in your prayers
For there's now a power here in your prayers
Here in your prayers

Let Him hear what is in your heart
Tell Him everything
Let Him see what is in your soul
Tell Him everything, here in your prayers

Tell Him everything, tell Him everything
Here in your prayers

Our prayer is the only way, that we speak with our Lord

Acts 16:25-26

But at midnight Paul and Silas were praying and singing hymns to God and the prisoners were listening to them. Suddenly there was a great earthquake, so that the foundations of the prison were shaken and immediately all the doors were opened and everyone's chains were loosed.

Even Now

Jesus speak to my heart, in this hour of my need
Jesus speak to my heart, for it is Your grace that I seek

**Lord through these tears that I now cry
Sing Your song to my soul
Lord through these prayers that I lift high
May Your love come alive
Right now, even now**

Jesus speak to my heart, in this hour of my need
Jesus speak to my heart, for it is Your grace that I seek

*Surround me and be all around me now
Surround me with Your love
Surround me and be all around me now
Surround me with Your love*

**Lord through these tears that I now cry
Sing Your song to my soul
Lord through these prayers that I lift high
May Your love come alive
Right now, even now**

**May Your love come alive
Right now, even now**

John 11:22-24

*But even now I know that whatever You ask of God, God
will give You Jesus said to her, "Your brother will rise again."
Martha said to Him, "I know that he will rise again in the
resurrection at the last day."*

Please Invite Me Inside

Lord Your love I know it is mine
For Your light it forever shines
Lord Your grace it is always enough
For Your hope it is my only hope

For I am here Lord, just as I am
For I am here Lord, I come as a broken man
For I am here Lord, with my arms open wide
For I am here Lord, please invite me inside

Lord Your peace it is all that I need
Lord Your cross is where I fall to my knees
For Your song it is a gift to my soul
For Your hope it is my only hope

For I am here Lord, just as I am
For I am here Lord, I come as a broken man
For I am here Lord, with my arms open wide
For I am here Lord, please invite me inside

For so long I've stood outside Your door
Wanting so much more
For too long I've prayed for a way in
To be forgiven, oh Lord please invite me in

For I am here Lord, just as I am
For I am here Lord, I come as a broken man
For I am here Lord, with my arms open wide
For I am here Lord, please invite me inside

Lord Your love I know it is mine

John 6:37

All that the Father giveth Me shall come to Me, and
him that cometh to Me I will in no wise cast out.

Grace

If you'll turn away from all your sinful ways
And follow Me for the rest of your days
I will heal your broken heart
I will save your wounded soul

If you leave all of your past behind
And take up My cross, until the end of your time
I will heal your broken heart
I will save your wounded soul

**I will show you grace like you've never known
I will show you strength like you've never been shown
I'll show you grace, I will show you grace**

If you'll shake off the dust, all the dust of this world
And trust in My truth, each holy word
I will heal your broken heart
I will save your wounded soul

**I will show you grace like you've never known
I will show you strength like you've never been shown
I'll show you grace, I will show you grace**

So if you'll turn away, from all your sinful ways
And follow Me for the rest of your days
I will heal your broken heart
I will save your wounded soul

Numbers 6:24-26

*"The Lord bless you and keep you, the Lord make His
face shine upon you and be gracious to you, the Lord lift up
His countenance upon you and give you peace."*

So Much More Than Enough

Lord Your grace, it is my everything
Lord Your grace, it is my everlasting Lord
Your grace, Your grace it is, enough

Lord Your faith, it is so powerful
Lord Your faith, it is so merciful
Lord Your faith, Your faith it is, enough

Enough for my soul, enough for my life
Lord all that You are, is so much more than enough
Enough for my heart, enough for my sin
Lord all that You are, is so much more than enough

Lord Your love, it is so amazing
Lord Your love, it is my wellspring
Lord Your love, Your love it is, enough

Lord Your cross, it is so victorious
Lord Your cross, it is so glorious
Lord Your cross, Your cross it is, enough

Lord may Your glory reign, Lord may Your beauty shine
Lord may Your mercy fall, Lord may Your majesty rise

Lord may Your faithful sing, Lord may Your children pray
Lord may Your nations shout, Lord may Your beloved say

That You are Enough for our soul, enough for our life
Lord all that You are, is so much more than enough
Enough for our heart, enough for our sin
Lord all that You are, is so much more than enough

2 Corinthians 12:9-10

And He said to me, "My grace is sufficient for you, for My
strength is made perfect in weakness." Therefore most gladly
I will rather boast in my infirmities, that the power of Christ
may rest upon me. Therefore I take pleasure in infirmities, in
reproaches, in needs, in persecutions, in distresses, for Christ's
sake. For when I am weak, then I am strong.

From Heaven Above

Know God is with you, at this very hour
He's right there by your side
Know God is with you, He'll find you where you are
He'll wipe the tears that you've cried

So open up your hurting heart
Now feel all of His love
For it is raining down
Down from Heaven above

Know God is with you, this you must now know
In the midst of all your fear
Know God is with you, His mercy He will show
And right now He's drawing you near

So open up your hurting heart
Now feel all of His love
For it is raining down
So open wide your healing heart
Now feel all of His love
For it is raining down
Down from Heaven above

For He is now holding you
He is now comforting you
His loving arms are now all around you
For He is now embracing you
He is now rejoicing with you
His loving arms are now surrounding you
Surrounding you from Heaven above

Psalm 57:5

Be exalted, O' God, above the Heavens,
let Your glory be above all the earth.

Lord Am I Worthy?

Lord am I worthy, worthy of Your love?
Am I worthy of Your sacrifice and Your grace?
Lord am I worthy, worthy of Your hope?
Am I worthy of Your salvation and Your faith?

**For on my own I'll never find my way back home
For on my own I'll never make it here alone, on my own**

Lord am I worthy, worthy of Your cross?
Am I worthy of Your suffering and Your loss?
Lord am I worthy, worthy of Your light?
Am I worthy of Your surrender and Your life?

*Lord I always do all the things I don't want to do
That lead me far away from You
Lord I want to be set free
From the chains that are holding me
Lord I want to be the man that You see here in me*

**For on my own I'll never find my way back home
For on my own I'll never make it here alone, on my own**

So Lord am I worthy, worthy of Your love?
Am I worthy of Your sacrifice and Your grace?

Colossians 1:10

*That you may walk worthy of the Lord, fully
pleasing Him, being fruitful in every good work and
increasing in the knowledge of God.*

A Better Man

Every day I get on my knees and I pray
Every night I ask You to be my guide
Every day I do my best just to make my way
Every night I thank You as I turn off the light

**Lord please give me Your hand
Help my heart understand
Lord I want to be, a better man**

Every day I search Your words, for the words to say
Every night I ask You, to choose what's right
Every day I try hard not to fall away
Every night I ask You for another reason to try

*Lord Your love brings to me love
And Your faith brings to me faith
Lord Your love brings to me love
And Your strength brings to me strength
Lord it brings to me strength*

**Lord please give me Your hand
Help my heart understand
Lord I want to be, a better man**

Every day I get on my knees and I pray
Every night I thank You as I turn off the light

Proverbs 21:1-3

The king's heart is in the hand of the Lord, like the rivers of water, he turns it wherever he wishes. Every way of a man is right in his own eyes, But the Lord weighs the hearts. To do righteousness and justice Is more acceptable to the Lord than sacrifice.

When I Think Of Heaven

When I think of Heaven and all that will be
I think of Your glory and how You will welcome me
When I think of Heaven and all I will see
I think of Your beauty and how we'll spend eternity

**Lord I want to see Your face
And to hold Your nailed scarred hands
Lord I want to sing Your praise
And to be a part of all You've planned
And to be a part of all You've planned**

When I think of Heaven and all we will share
I think of Your story and how much I want to be there
When I think of Heaven and how I'll finally be home
I think of Your mercy and Your great sacrifice alone

**Lord I want to see Your face
And to hold Your nailed scarred hands
Lord I want to sing Your praise
And to be a part of all You've planned
And to be a part of all You've planned**

When I think of Heaven and all I will see
I think of Your beauty and how we'll spend eternity

Psalm 8:3-5

When I consider Your Heavens, the work of Your fingers, the moon and the stars, which You have ordained, What is man that You are mindful of him and the Son of Man that You visit Him? For You have made Him a little lower than the angels and You have crowned Him with glory and honor.

He Will Speak To Your Heart

Do you hear His voice? He's now calling out to you
Have you made your choice? Is it your time to follow through?
And to know His love, and to know His love

Do you hear His cry? He's now whispering in your ear
Have you waited your whole life? Couldn't it be any more clear?
And to hear His song, and to hear His song

**So be still and hear Him sing, for He will speak to your heart
Be still and listening, for He will speak to your heart
Don't wait much longer, for He wants you to draw nearer
So be still and listening, He will speak to your heart**

Do you hear His plea? He's now reaching out for your hand
Are your eyes open to see? Have you laid out your plan?
And to feel His strength, and to feel His strength

So do you hear His shout? He's now bursting through the clouds
What are you waiting for? Do you hear His trumpet sound?
And you hear His song, and you hear His song

***Know the world is trying to drown Him out
Know the world is just too loud
Know the world is lying about His truth
Know the world is wrong and right on cue***

**So be still and hear Him sing, for He will speak to your heart
Be still and listening, for He will speak to your heart
Don't wait much longer, for He wants you to draw nearer
So be still and listening, He will speak to your heart**

So how about you? Will you be still and hear Him sing?
So will you be still and listening?

Psalm 139:23-24

*Search me, O' God and know my heart, try me and know
my anxieties and see if there is any wicked way in me and
lead me in the way everlasting.*

July 19TH

A Little More Patient And Kind

I know I've said these words before
Maybe over a thousand times
Even wrote them down in a song
Making sure that each one rhymes

I know I've written them all on a card
Leaving them for you to read
Even said them right out loud
Praying that you would believe

But this time you'll find that I'll try, yes I'll try
To be a little more patient and kind

It's all about the patience I don't show
About the kindness that can grow
About the love that you deserve
All about the God that we both serve
And being a little more patient and kind

For our words can lift you up, for they can tear you down
For our words can break your heart
They can turn you around or can make you smile
They can heal your soul, or can speak the truth
They can lead you home, they will lead you home

It's all about the patience I don't show
About the kindness that can grow
About the love that you deserve
All about the God that we both serve
And being a little more patient and kind

A little more patient and kind

1 Corinthians 13:4-8

Love suffers long and is kind, love does not envy, love does
not parade itself, is not puffed up, does not behave rudely,
does not seek its own, is not provoked, thinks no evil, does
not rejoice in iniquity, but rejoices in the truth, bears all
things, believes all things, love all things, endures all things.
Love never fails.

Right Beside Of You

When your heart it is broken
Know that I will heal it
When your last prayer is spoken
Know that I will hear it

And when you are lonely
Know that I am by your side
And when you cry, know that I will dry
Every tear from your eye

**Know that I will love you
That I'll take care of you
For in whatever trial
You may go through
Know that I am here
Know that I am always near
Right beside of you**

**So when your walls
They come crashing down
And in the silence
You just can't hear a sound
Know that I'll be found
Right beside of you
Know that I'll be found
Right beside of you**

When your heart it is broken
Know that I will heal it
When your last prayer is spoken
Know that I will hear it

Matthew 17:20

*So Jesus said to them, "Because of your unbelief, for
assuredly I say to you, if you have faith as a mustard seed,
you will say to this mountain, 'Move from here to there,' and
it will move and nothing will be impossible for you.*

Lord Take Away Our Hurt

Lord my heart it is healing now
For only You have healed me by Your love
Lord my life it is changing now
For only You have changed me by Your love

**So Lord here in this place, fill our hearts with Your grace
Lord here in this church, take away our hurt**

Lord my soul it is searching now
For only You have searched me by Your love
Lord my sin it is forgiven now
For only You forgave me by Your love

So Lord here in this place, fill our hearts with Your grace
Lord here in this church, take away our hurt

*For Lord You know my heart, even the deepest part
Lord You know my soul and every secret that it holds
For Lord You know my life, the dark and the light
Lord You know my heart, just who I am, just who I'm not*

Lord my soul it is searching now
For only You have searched me by Your love
Lord my sin it is forgiven now
For only You forgave me by Your love

Romans 8:18

*For I consider that the sufferings of this present
time are not worth to be compared with the glory
which shall be revealed in us.*

Lord I've Been Praying

I've been praying a lot lately about my life
Been praying about all the wrong and all the right
I've been praying a lot lately about all I've done
Been praying about all the moments I took too long

**Some were good and some were bad
Some were happy and some were sad
I'm so sorry, about all of my weakness
With all the winning and the losing
All of the hurting and all the healing
All the sinning and the asking for forgiveness
Lord I've been praying**

I've been praying a lot lately about my faith
I've been praying about the times I lacked the strength
I've been praying a lot lately about my hope
I've been praying about the very depths of my soul

*Where I've been, where I'm going
What I'm hiding and what I am showing
Who I am, who I'll be, what I doubt and just what I believe*

**Some were good and some were bad
Some were happy and some were sad
I'm so sorry, about all of my weakness
With all the winning and the losing
All of the hurting and all the healing
All the sinning and the asking for forgiveness
Lord I've been praying**

I've been praying a lot lately

James 5:15-16

*And the prayer of faith will save the sick and the Lord will raise
him up. And if he has committed sins, he will be forgiven. Confess
your trespasses to one another and pray for one another, that
you may be healed. The effective, fervent prayer of a righteous
man avails much*

And So Believe

I am the Bread of Life, I am the Song to your soul
I am the Holy Light, that will guide you home

I am the Lamb of God, I am the love to your heart
I am the Holy Light, that will find you where you are

And so believe in all I say, so believe in all I've done
Know that it was all just for you
That My victory it was won

I am the Son of God, I am the Love of your life
I am the Holy Light, that will lead you to My side

I am the Morning Star, I am the Promise of your prayers
I am the Holy Light, that will take you far from here

And when I gave My final tear
It was all just to draw you near
And when I gave My final breath
It was all the life I had left
Yes I cried for you, yes I died for you

And so believe in all I say, so believe in all I've done
Know that it was all just for you
That My victory it was won

I am the Son of God, I am the Love of your life
I am the Holy Light, that will lead you to My side
I will lead you to My side

When you need Jesus the very most, please read these words
and know what the Lord is to you, please never forget this!

Romans 1:16-17

For I am not ashamed of the gospel of Christ, for it is the
power of God to salvation for everyone who believes, for the
Jew first and also for the Greek. For in it the righteousness of
God is revealed from faith to faith, as it is written,
"The just shall live by faith."

The Dark And The Light

Father You taught the rains to dance
Placed forests to stand tall

Father You willed the winds to sing
And gave thunder, to roar above them all

**And the dark to be night
And the day to be light**

Father You fashioned the oceans deep
Loosed lightning across the sky

Father You formed the mountains strong
And poised the eagle, ready to take flight

**And the dark to be night
And the day to be light**

***And like the wind
That now moves upon the water
Lord You breathe
Your life into this life***

***And like the dew
That now rests upon the flower
Lord You breathe
Your life into this life***

**And the dark to be night
And the day to be light**

Genesis 1:1-5

*In the beginning God created the Heavens and the earth.
The earth was without form and void and darkness was on
the face of the deep and the Spirit of God was hovering over
the face of the waters. Then God said, "Let there be light",
and there was light and God saw the light, that it was good
and God the light from the darkness. God called the
light Day and the darkness He called Night. So the evening
and the morning were the first day.*

All My Soul Needs

Lord I have a blessed assurance
Yes I have an amazing grace
I have all that my soul needs
To one day look upon Your Face

Lord I have an old rugged cross
I have a closer walk with Thee
I have all that my soul needs
To one day worship at Your feet

Lord I have a Mighty Fortress
I have power in the blood
I have all that my soul needs
To one day be washed within the flood

Lord I have a wonderful peace
I have a Shelter in the storm
I have all that my soul needs
To one day forever praise the Holy One

Lord I have a victory in Jesus
I have a Lover of my soul
I have all that my soul needs
To one day enter Your Heavenly home

Lord I have a blessed assurance
Yes I have an amazing grace
I have all that my soul needs
To one day look upon Your face

2 Corinthians 13:14

The grace of the Lord Jesus Christ and the love of God and
the communion of the Holy Spirit be with you all. Amen!

Here You Are Again

You've tried to keep inside
Every one of your tears
Tried so hard to hide
Every one of your fears

You've tried to break free
With nothing holding you down
Tried so hard to believe
With nothing but your doubt

**And here you are again
Between your faith and your sin
Here you are again
So ready to be forgiven
Here you are again**

You've tried to run away
Your feet didn't get you very far
Tried so hard pray
You just didn't how to start

So you fell to your knees
And you looked up to the sky
Tried so hard to be strong
Without ever knowing why

**And here you are again
Between your faith and your sin
Here you are again
So ready to be forgiven
Here you are again**

Hebrews 4:13

*And there is no creature hidden from His sight, but
all things are naked and open to the eyes of Him to
whom we must give account.*

In The Silence Of A Prayer

I must say a thousand times a day, why, God, why?
Why must my heart still cry?

I must pray a thousand times a day, when, God, when?
When will I ever smile again?

And then here, in the silence of a prayer
In the quiet of a moment, You speak to me
Then here, in the stillness of the night
In the calm before dawn, You whisper to me
In the silence of a prayer

I must say a thousand times a day, how, God, how?
How will I ever make it now?

I must pray a thousand times a day, where, God, where?
Where does my soul go from here?

Only when I am still and I am all alone
You make Yourself known

Only when I am still, when I am down upon my knees
You put my lost soul at ease, in the silence of a prayer

I must say a thousand times a day, who, God, who?
Who can I now reach for You?

And then here, in the silence of a prayer
In the quiet of a moment, You speak to me
Then here, in the stillness of the night
In the calm before dawn, You whisper to me
In the silence of a prayer

Matthew 6:6

But you, when you pray, go into your room and when you have
shut your door, pray to your Father Who is in the secret place
and your Father Who sees in secret will reward you openly.

All You've Done For Me

You showed to me strength and I chose my weakness
You showed to me light and I chose the darkness
Still You stood by me, never left my side

You showed to me joy and I chose my sadness
You showed to me love and I chose the loneliness
Still You stood by me, never left my side

You held on and You never let me go
You stayed strong so that I would always know
All You've done for me, all You've done for me

You showed to me sight and I chose my blindness
You showed to me truth and I chose the madness
Still You stood by me, never left my side

You showed me grace and I chose my sinfulness
You showed me love and I chose the emptiness
Again and again

You showed to me strength and I chose my weakness
You showed to me light and I chose the darkness
Still You stood by me, never left my side

You held on and You never let me go
You stayed strong so that I would always know
All You've done for me, all You've done for me

Matthew 25:40

*And the King will answer and say to them, "Assuredly, I say
to you, in as much as you did it to one of the least of these
My brethren, you did it to Me."*

Far Apart

How can I make them see
To have them believe?
Lord what can I ever do
Just to somehow break through?

How can I let them hear
To have them draw now near?
Lord what can I ever say
Just to find a way?

To open up their eyes
Let them know that You're there by their side
To open up their hearts
Let them know that You've set their soul apart, far apart

How can I change their minds
To have them feel a little more alive?
Lord what can I ever explain
Just to make sure that they know?

How can I lead them home
To have them never walk alone?
Lord what can I ever show
Just to make sure that they all know?

To touch theirs lives, to reach deep inside
To pray with them a little prayer

To help them stand, to hold their trembling hands
To pray with them a little prayer, to pray a little prayer

To open up their eyes
Let them know that You're there by their side
To open up their hearts
Let them know that You've set their soul apart, far apart

James 4:8

Draw near to God and He will draw near to you. Cleanse your
hands, you sinners and purify your hearts, you double-minded.

Stand With Jesus

Stand with Jesus, right by His side
Stand with the Lord for your faith, for your life

Stand with Jesus, lean on His strength
Stand with the Lord for your hope, for your grace

So hold onto His perfect plan
Hold onto His mighty hands
For you, in all you do, in all you go through

Stand with Jesus, give Him all your praise
Stand with the Lord for your peace, for your prayers

Stand with Jesus, share your very soul
Stand with the Lord, for your love, for your all

So hold onto His perfect plan
Hold onto His mighty hands
For you, in all you do, in all you go through

Stand with Jesus, He'll hold you in His arms
Stand with Jesus, He'll keep you safe from all harm
Stand with Jesus, He'll show you your way home
Stand with Jesus, He'll show you all that needs to be shown

So hold onto His perfect plan
Hold onto His mighty hands
For you, in all you do, in all you go through

Stand with Jesus, right by His side

Galatians 5:1

Stand fast therefore in the liberty by which Christ
has made us free and do not be entangled again
with a yoke of bondage.

Good Morning Lord

Good morning Lord
There's no better way, to greet the day
There's no better way

Good morning Lord
I just want to say, I love You in every way
I just want to say

I want to live all of my life for You
I want to live my life just for You
That I want to give all of my love to You
I want to give my love just to You
Good morning Lord

Good morning Lord
I'm glad You're here today, can we kneel and pray?
I'm glad You're here today

Good morning Lord
I just want to say, I never want You to go away
I just want to say

Let the sun now meet the morning
May the first light now greet the dawn
Let the winds now sing across the valley
May the blue skies now touch the 'morn
Good morning Lord, oh good morning Lord

There's no better way, to greet the day
I just want to say, I love You in every way
I'm glad You're here today, can we kneel and pray?
I just want to say, I never want You to go away

Good morning Lord, good morning Lord

Psalm 5:3

My voice You shall hear in the morning, O' Lord, in
the morning I will direct it to You and I will look up.

August

What Do You Believe?

August 1ST

What Do You Believe?

What do you believe way down deep in your soul?
If tonight you were to close your eyes
Where do you think you'd go?
What do you believe down deep in your soul?

What do you believe deep within your heart?
If tonight you were to take your last breath
And we would be apart
What do you believe deep within your heart?

**Do you believe that there's a Savior
Who died for your sins?
Do you believe that there's a Father
Who is ready to forgive?
Right here, right now
What do you believe?**

What do you believe way down deep in your mind?
If tonight your road came to an end
And you ran out of time
What do you believe way down deep in your mind?

What do you believe way down in your life?
If tonight death would come
And you began to head towards the light
What do you believe down deep in your life?

**So do you believe that there's a Savior
Who died for your sins?
Do you believe that there's a Father
Who is ready to forgive?
Right here, right now
What do you believe?**

Matthew 21:22

And whatever things you ask in prayer, believing, you will receive

— 222 —

If You Pray

So today there is rain
Tomorrow the skies will clear again
So today there is hurt
Tomorrow your heart will feel joy again
Tomorrow there'll be no more rain
Tomorrow there'll be no more hurt

If you pray faith will win the day
If you pray love will find a way
Into your heart, into your soul
Into your life, if you pray

So today there are storms
Tomorrow the seas will calm again
So today there is doubt
Tomorrow your hope will rise again
Tomorrow there'll be no more storms
Tomorrow there'll be no more doubt

Kneeling down, all alone
Giving all, all you own, if you pray

If you pray faith will win the day
If you pray love will find a way
Into your heart, into your soul
Into your life, if you pray

1 John 5:14

Now this is the confidence that we have in Him, that
If we ask anything according to His will, He hears us.

My Very Soul Lord Is Yours

Lord open up my eyes, Lord open up my heart
Lord have, my soul, be still

Lord open up my hands, Lord open up my arms
Lord have, it be, Your will

**For my salvation is only by Your grace
For my forgiveness is only through Your grace
My very soul Lord is Yours**

Lord open up my eyes, Lord open up my heart
Lord have, my soul, be still

Lord open up my hands, Lord open up my arms
Lord have, it be, Your will

***All I am I lay down at Your feet
My every victory, my every defeat
All I have I bring now to Your cross
My every hope and dream, my every gain and loss
All to Your cross, all to Your cross***

**For my salvation is only by Your grace
For my forgiveness is only through Your grace
My very soul Lord is Yours**

Lord open up my eyes, Lord open up my heart
Lord have, my soul, be still

Psalm 130:1-8

*Out of the depths I have cried to You, "O' Lord hear my voice!
Let Your ears be attentive to the voice of my supplications. If You,
Lord should mark iniquities, O' Lord, who could stand? But there
is forgiveness with You, That You may be feared. If I wait for the
Lord, my soul waits and in His word I do hope. My soul waits for
the Lord more than those who watch for the morning, yes, more
than those who watch for the morning. O' Israel, hope in the
Lord, for with the Lord there is mercy and with Him is abundant
redemption. And He shall redeem Israel from all his iniquities."*

By His Faith In Me

The grave once held me, it once held me down
Now I am free, I am free to fly away

My sins once bound me, they once kept me in the ground
Now I am free, I am free to now say

**That I have been saved, I've been saved by my Savior
That I have been healed, I've been healed by my Healer
By His strength, by His grace, by His name and by His faith
By His faith in me**

My hurt once broke my heart, it once separated us
Now I am free, I am free to spread my wings
My doubt once kept up apart, then I was found here by Jesus
Now I am free, I am free to dance and sing

*For only Jesus can save your soul
When your soul it needs saving
For only Jesus can heal your heart
When your heart it needs healing*

*So I will sing of my love, I will lift my hands high
All to Heaven above, until the day that I die
All to my Jesus, all for my Jesus*

**For I have been saved, I've been saved by my Savior
For I have been healed, I've been healed by my Healer
By His strength, by His grace, by His name and by His faith
By His faith in me**

Mark 11:22-23

*So Jesus answered and said to them, "Have faith in God.
For assuredly, I say to you, whoever says to this mountain,
'Be removed and be cast into the sea,' and does not
doubt in his heart, but believes that those things he says
will be done, he will have whatever he says.*

It's Alright!

It's alright if raise your hands, lift your praise to the Lord
It's alright if you reach up high, lift your hopes to the Lord

It's alright, it's alright!

It's alright if you feel afraid, give your fears to the Lord
It's alright now if you cry, give your tears to the Lord

It's alright, it's alright!

It's alright to give Him all you can
It's alright if your hurt, He will understand
It's alright He's got a plan, it's alright, it's alright!

It's alright when you look to the sky, lift your soul to the Lord
It's alright as you open your heart, lift up your life to the Lord

It's alright, it's alright!

It's alright as you now kneel, give your prayers to the Lord
It's alright, as you close your eyes, give your cares to the Lord

It's alright to give Him all you can
It's alright if your hurt, He will understand
It's alright He's got a plan
It's alright, it's alright!

Psalm 29:1-4

Give unto the Lord, O' you mighty ones
Give unto the Lord glory and strength
Give unto the Lord the glory due to His name
Worship the Lord in the beauty of holiness
The voice of the Lord is over the waters
The God of glory thunders
The Lord is over many waters
The voice of the Lord is powerful
The voice of the Lord is full of majesty

When There Is Faith

Tears dry, hurt is healed
When there is faith
Mountains move, truth is revealed
When there is faith

When there is faith
You'll believe the unbelievable
When there is faith
You'll reach the unreachable
When there is faith

Doubts fade, hope is raised
When there is faith
Hearts sing, souls saved
When there is faith
Your soul will sing a new song
When there is faith

Your soul will find its home
You will never again be alone
When there is faith

Tears dry, hurt is healed
When there is faith
Mountains move, truth is revealed
When there is faith

James 2:19

You believe that there is one God. You do well.
Even the demons believe and tremble!

August 7TH

Bring Me Closer Today

How do You know my name?
How do You hear me cry?
How do You feel my hurt?
How do You know what's deep inside?
When I'm all alone, when nothing I show

How do You know my heart?
How do You hear my prayers?
How do You feel my pain?
How do You know what's hidden here?
When I'm all alone, when nothing I show

When I am so far away
Much farther than just yesterday
To bring me near is what I pray
Closer today, bring me closer today

How do You know my soul?
How do You hear my plea?
How do You feel my hope?
How do You know what's deep inside of me?
When I'm all alone, when nothing I show

Yeah when I'm all alone, when nothing I show

When I am so far away
Much farther than just yesterday
To bring me near is what I pray
Closer today, bring me closer today
Bring me closer today

Matthew 5:8

Blessed are the pure in heart, for they shall see God.

He Never Fails Me

As I fail, I fall and I lie
As I sin, I doubt and I cry

**My Lord and my God and my King
My Savior and Friend and my Everything
He never fails me**

As I run, I hurt and I hide
As I weep, I grieve and I ask why

*For He holds me close
He never lets me go
He keeps me safe
So I always know
For He draws me near
He never leaves my side
He takes my hand
And He helps me to rise, to rise*

**My Lord and my God and my King
My Savior and Friend and my Everything
He never fails me**

As I fail, I fall and I lie
As I sin, I doubt and I cry
He never fails me!

Jeremiah 17:7-8

*Blessed is the man who trusts in the Lord and whose love
Is the Lord. For he shall be like a tree planted by the waters,
which spreads out its roots by the river and will not fear when
heat comes, but it's leaf will be green and will not be anxious
in the year of drought, nor will cease from yielding fruit.*

August 9TH

All Because Of You

Some may say that I'm saved
That I've found my forgiveness and my grace
It's all because of You, it's all because of You

Some may say that I've changed
That nothing about me is the same
It's all because of You, it's all because of You

From where there was doubt, now there is faith
From where there was sin, now there is strength
And now all that I do, yes now all that I do
It's all because of You

Well some may say that I'm blessed
That now in Your loving arms is where I rest
It's all because of You, it's all because of You

Still some may say that I am free
That by faith my soul, it now believes
It's all because of You, it's all because of You

From where there was doubt, now there is faith
From where there was sin, now there is strength
And now all that I do, yes now all that I do
It's all because of You

Some may say that I'm saved
That I've found my forgiveness and my grace
It's all because of You Lord, it's all because of You

From where there was doubt, now there is faith
From where there was sin, now there is strength
And now all that I do, yes now all that I do
It's all because of You

Psalm 63:3-4

Because Your lovingkindness is better than life, my lips
shall praise You. Thus I will bless You while I live, I will
lift up my hands in Your name.

Lord You Are There

There's a place where my soul can go
There's a place that blesses my soul
For there's a place where I'm safe I know
And Lord You are there

There's a place deep in my heart
There's a place where I know that You are
For there's a place where we'll never part
And Lord You are there

Where I am Yours and You are mine
Where all is right and peace I find
Where my prayers are spoken and my faith is awoken
And Lord You are there

There's a place where I pray
There's a place where on my knees I'll stay
For there's a place where I'm never afraid
And Lord You are there

Where there is hope not hurt, there is love not lies
Where there is truth not tears, there is faith not fears
There's a place where we both now draw near
And Lord You are there

There's a place, where I am home
There's a place where I'm never on my own
For there's a place where I'll never walk this world alone
And Lord You are there

Mark 4:38-39

But He was in the stern, asleep on a pillow. And they awoke Him and said to Him, "Teacher, do You not care that we are perishing?" Then He arose and rebuked the wind, said to the sea, "Peace, be still!" And the wind ceased and there was a great calm.

Always Praying

Lord I need to be, Lord I want to be
Lord I should now be
Praying and asking of You please

Lord I need to be, Lord I want to be
Lord I should now be
Staying and falling to my knees

Always praying, pleading for Your will
Always staying, needing to be still
To be always praying, always praying

There really is no time
To waste any time
We don't have the time
To give away any time
When every second counts
Every moment is so precious
There is no time, to give away any time

When we need to be
Always praying, pleading for Your will
Always staying, needing to be still
To be always praying, always praying

Lord I need to be, Lord I want to be
Lord I should now be
Praying and asking of You please

I Thessalonians 5:16-18

Rejoice always, pray without ceasing, in everything give
thanks, for this is the will of God in Christ Jesus for you.

Jesus Where I Would Be?

Have You the strength that strengthens my weakness?
Have You the light that lights up the darkness?

Have You the hope that takes away all my fears?
Have You the love that will dry my every tear?

**For on my own, if it were left up to me
Lord I just don't know
Jesus where I would be?**

*I need to have my lessons learned
By living out Your holy word
I need to have my soul be still
By always praying for Your will*

Have You the prayers that will pray for all my sin?
Have You the grace that for my soul will forgive?

Have You the will to be just Who You are?
Have You the faith enough faith to heal this heart?

**For on my own, if it were left up to me
Lord I just don't know
Jesus where I would be?**

*For You are my Rock here within the storm
For You are my Strength when I cannot go on
For You are my Hope when all hope is gone
For You are my Keep when I'm here alone*

Have You the strength that strengthens my weakness?

John 15:4-6

Abide in Me and I in you. As the branch cannot bear fruit of itself, unless It abides in the vine, neither can you, unless you abide in Me. "I am the vine, you are the branches. He who abides in Me and I in him, bears much fruit, for without Me you can do nothing. If anyone does not abide in Me, he is cast out as a branch and is withered and they gather them and throw them into the fire and they are burned.

To Be Found In Faith

We all need to pray just a little more
And lift our eyes high up towards Heaven's door

We all need to hope just a little more
And lift our hearts high and to have our spirits soar

And to step out into this world in faith

And to be found, to be found in grace
Just as a child to be found in faith
To be found in faith

We all need to cry just a little more
And lift our eyes high and to forget what was before

We all need to believe just a little more
And lift our faith higher than we've ever lifted it before

And to step out into this world in faith

And to be found, to be found in grace
Just as a child to be found in faith
To be found in faith

We all need to pray just a little more
And lift our eyes high up towards Heaven's door

And to step out into this world in faith

Mark 10:14-15

But when Jesus saw it, He was greatly displeased and said to them, "Let the little children come to Me and do not forbid them, for of such is the Kingdom of God. Assuredly, I say to you, whoever does not receive the Kingdom of God as a little child will by no means enter it."

It Means Everything

What does it mean to have You here in my life?
Always guiding my way, with Your Heavenly light

What does it mean to have You here in my heart?
Always leading me home, right to where You are

Well it means everything, everything to me
Well it means everything, everything I believe
All of my faith, all of my hope it rests within Your arms
All of my strength and all of my soul
Lord it rests within Your arms
It means everything

What does it mean to have You here in my prayers?
Always kneeling with me, for You are always near

What does it mean to have You here as my own?
Always holding me close, for I am never here alone

Nothing is the same, nothing remains of who I was
Everything has changed, nothing remains all because
All because it means everything!

Well it means everything, everything to me
Well it means everything, everything I believe
All of my faith, all of my hope it rests within Your arms
All of my strength and all of my soul
Lord it rests within Your arms
It means everything

What does it mean to have You here in my life?
Always guiding my way, with Your Heavenly light
Your Heavenly light

Hebrews 4:15-16

For we do not have a High Priest Who cannot sympathize with our
weaknesses, but was in all points tempted as we are, yet without
sin. Let us therefore come boldly to the throne of grace, that we
may obtain mercy and find grace to help in time of need.

You Will See A Victory

What if I told you, your tears will stop?
That your crying will end
What if I told you, you were never again to sin?
That a new life will begin

**For you will see a victory
For you will shout hallelujah
For you will claim His victory
And will cry out His name forever
For you will see a victory**

What if I told you, there'll be no more hurting?
That there is no more suffering
What if I told you, your soul survives?
That forever you are alive

*You will see all of His glory
You will know that He is holy
You will feel all of His mercy
And you will tell of His wonderful story*

**For you will see a victory
For you will shout hallelujah
For you will claim His victory
We will cry out His name forever
For you will see a victory!**

1 Corinthians 15:55-57

*"O' Death, where is your sting? O' Hades, where is your
victory?" The sting of death is sin and the strength of sin
is the law. But thanks be to God, Who gives us the victory
through our Lord Jesus Christ.*

Matthew 5:9

*Blessed are the peacemakers,
for they shall be called sons of God.*

Jesus I Believe In You

I've got to do better, I've got to be stronger
I can't give up, I can't give in any longer
I've got to try harder, I've got to draw nearer
I can't run and hide, I can't run away any further

**I've got to stay right here, I've got to make it very clear
I've got to prove my love for You
I want to have You see that my soul believes
No matter what I'm going through, Jesus I believe in You**

*Jesus I'm holding on
When all my strength is gone
Jesus I'm holding on
When all my hope wants to move on
When my life is at a loss
I will always turn to Your cross
Jesus I believe in You*

*I'm holding on, I'm holding on to You
Jesus, I'm holding on, I'm holding on to You*

I can do better, I can be stronger
I won't give up, I won't give in any longer
I can try harder, I can draw nearer
I won't run and hide, I won't run away any further

**I've got to stay right here, I've got to make it very clear
I've got to prove my love for You
I want to have You see that my soul believes
No matter what I'm going through, Jesus I believe in You
Jesus I believe in You**

John 5:24

*Most assuredly, I say to you, he who hears My word and
believes in Him Who sent Me has everlasting life and shall not
come into judgment but has passed from death into life.*

August 17TH

A First Step Of Faith

There's a road that leads you ahead
There's a road where your Savior bled
There's a road that leads you home
There's a road where you're never alone

**So take that first step and reach out in faith
Lay down all of your sin and know all of His grace
So take that first step of faith
A first step of faith**

There's a road that's never-ending
There's a road where your heart it is heading
There's a road that where Heaven awaits
There's a road where your soul is safe

*Falling to your knees, lifting now all your prayers
Raising up your arms, casting now your eyes
High up to the sky, your all to Heaven tonight*

**So take that first step, a first step of faith
Just lay down all of your sin and know all of His grace
So take that first step of faith
A first step of faith**

Psalm 40:1-3

*I waited patiently for the Lord and He inclined to me and
heard my cry. He also brought me up out of a horrible pit, out
of the miry clay and set my feet upon a rock and established
my steps. He has put a new song in my mouth, praise to our
God, many will see it and fear and will trust in the Lord.*

Lord Reach Down

Lord reach down and lift my soul
My Lord reach down and make me whole
Lord reach down and dry my tears
My Lord reach down and calm my fears

**And from where You are, Lord reach down
And from where You are, my Lord reach down!**

Lord reach down and hold my heart
My Lord reach down and set me apart
Lord reach down and hear my prayers
My Lord reach down and find me here

*I want to be where You are, no matter how far
I want to be there, Lord I want to be there
I want to be by Your side, no matter the divide
I want to be there, Lord I want to be there*

So Lord reach down and speak my name
My Lord reach down and bear my blame
Lord reach down and take me home
My Lord reach down and make me Your own

**And from where You are, Lord reach down
And from where You are, my Lord reach down!**

Psalm 18:16-19

*He sent from above, He took me, He drew me out of many
waters. He delivered me from my strong enemy, From those who
hated me, for they were too strong for me. They confronted me in
the day of my calamity, But the Lord was my support. He also
brought me out into a broad place, He delivered me because
He delighted in me.*

You Have Made Me Brand New

We need to feel all of Your joy
We need to know all of Your happiness
Like we've never known before
Like we've never known before

We need to feel all of Your grace
We need to know all of Your forgiveness
Like we've never known before
Like we've never known before

Lord You have changed me from the inside out
You have made me brand new
Lord You have moved me from where I was
Like we've never known before
Like we've never known before

We need to feel all of Your love
We need to know all of Your salvation
Like we've never known before
Like we've never known before

We need to feel all of Your love
We need to know all of Your redemption
Like we've never known before
Like we've never known before

Lord You have changed me from the inside out
You have made me brand new
Lord You have moved me from where I was
Like we've never known before
Like we've never known before

Romans 8:31

What then shall we say to these things?
If God is for us, who can be against us?

Nothing Remains

Take my heart and free my soul
Lord take all, You need from me
Take my sin and make me whole
Lord show me all, You want me to be

Lord take my life and make it Yours
Lord It is no longer mine to live
Take my fears and make me strong
Lord it's all I have left to give

**For who I was, who I was before
I'm no longer now, I'm no longer now
For where I walked before I'm no longer found
I'm no longer found, nothing remains**

So take my pain and dry my tears
Lord get me through another day
Take my hand and calm my fears
Lord here in Your keep I'll stay

Take my faith and set it free to fly
Lord give me wings now to soar
Take my soul and change what's inside
Lord to become now something more

**For who I was, who I was before
I'm no longer now, I'm no longer now
For where I walked before I'm no longer found
I'm no longer found, nothing remains**

Mark 4:22-24

*For there is nothing hidden which will not be revealed,
nor has anything been kept secret but that it should
come to light. If anyone has ears to hear, let him hear."
Then He said to them, "Take heed what you hear. With
the same measure you use, it will be measured to you
and to you who hear, more will be given."*

All Of You

You've forgiven me of all my sin
You've accepted me of all I have been

**I want to pray with You, to stay with You
To hold on now to You
To walk with You, to talk with You
Be now a part of all of You, all of You**

You've remembered me in my times alone
You've invited me, to share Your Heavenly home

*Now as I breathe, now as I awake
Now as I choose and I make my mistakes
Now as I speak, now as I lie
Now as I fail and now as I try, now as I try*

**I want to pray with You, to stay with You
To hold on now to You
To walk with You, to talk with You
Be now a part of all of You, all of You**

You've forgiven me of all my sin
You've accepted me of all I have been

Romans 8:26

*Likewise the Spirit also helps in our weaknesses. For we
do not know what we should pray for as we ought, but
the Spirit Himself makes intercession for us with
groanings which cannot be uttered.*

Only For Today

Lord I'll pray for this day
For every trial that I'll pass through

Lord I'll pray just for today
For every step that I'll walk with You

**Lord I'll pray not for tomorrow
Lord I'll pray not for yesterday
Not for what's to come, not for what has been
Lord I'll pray only for today**

Lord I'll pray just for today
For every tear, that I'll cry in shame

Lord I'll pray for this day
For every word that I'll speak in vain

*Lord I'll pray that Your will be done
To one day walk together just as one*

*Lord I'll pray that Your will be done
To one day walk with You along streets of gold
Along the streets of gold*

Lord I'll pray for this day
For every time that I'll walk away

Lord I'll pray just for today
For every promise that I'll break

**Lord I'll pray not for tomorrow
Lord I'll pray not for yesterday
Not for what's to come, not for what has been
Lord I'll pray only for today**

Matthew 6:34

*Therefore do not worry about tomorrow, for
tomorrow will worry about its own things.
Sufficient for the day is its own trouble.*

Every One Of His Tears

You think you don't deserve
You think yourself unworthy
You think with all You've done
That He will turn His eyes away and run

**But you don't know His grace
The depths of His mercy
His love, forgiveness for you
But you don't know
You don't know His grace
The depths of His mercy
His love, forgiveness for you**

*For you He bled and died
For your life He cried, every one of His tears
For you He knelt and prayed
For your life He gave, every one of His tears*

**But you don't know His grace
The depths of His mercy
His love, forgiveness for you
But you don't know
You don't know His grace
The depths of His mercy
His love, forgiveness for you**

So you think you don't deserve
You think yourself unworthy

John 11:35

Jesus wept.

Jesus, Savior, Son

Do you need a little more hope for your hope?
Need a little more love for your love?
Then I've got a Savior, I've got a Savior for you

Do you need a little more faith for your faith?
Need a little more grace for your grace?
Then I've got a Savior, I've got a Savior for you

**For your heart, He will heal all your hurt
And for your life, He will lead you by His love
And for your tears, He will dry each and every one
Jesus, Savior, Son, Jesus, Savior, Son**

Do you need a little more peace for your peace?
Need a little more truth for your truth?
Then I've got a Savior, I've got a Savior for you

*Holy are You Lord, so merciful and kind
You are our forgiveness
Glory You are Lord, so beautiful and mine
You are our salvation, Lord You are our salvation*

**For your heart, He will heal all your hurt
And for your life, He will lead you by His love
And for your tears, He will dry each and every one
Jesus, Savior, Son, Jesus, Savior, Son**

Do you need a little more strength for your strength?
Need a little more hope for your love?
Then I've got a Savior, I've got a Savior for you
Then I've got a Savior for you

1 John 4:14

*And we have seen and testify that the Father
has sent His Son to be the Savior of the world.*

Will There Ever Come a Day?

Lord will my prayers ever be heard on high?
And Lord will my tears ever be wiped dry?

Lord will my faith ever be deep enough?
And Lord will my praise ever lift You up?

**And Lord will there ever come
Will there ever come a day?
When I'll find the right prayers to pray?
Lord will there ever come
Will there ever come a day?**

Lord will my life ever be lived for You?
And Lord will my lies ever know Your truth?

Lord will my prayers ever be heard on high?
And Lord will my tears ever be wiped dry?

**And Lord will there ever come
Will there ever come a day?
When I'll find the right prayers to pray?
Lord will there ever come
Will there ever come a day?**

Revelation 21:4-7

*And God will wipe away every tear from their eyes, there shall be
no more death, nor sorrow, nor crying. There shall be no more
pain for the former things have passed away." Then He Who sat
on throne said, "Behold, I make all things new." And He said
to me, "Write, for these words are true and faithful." And He said
to me, "It is done! I am the Alpha and the Omega, the Beginning
and the End. I will give of the fountain of the water of life freely to
him who thirsts. He who overcomes shall inherit all things and I
will be his God and he shall be My son."*

Until The Day That I Die

I am washed by the blood of Jesus Christ
Resurrected and raised to new life
I am saved by the grace of Jesus Christ
Forgiven and free and now lifted to new heights

**For Lord You loved me before my first cry
And Lord You'll hold me until the day that I die
You'll never leave me, leave me alone
For Lord You'll always lead me, lead me home**

I am strong in the strength of Jesus Christ
Delivered from death by the perfect Spotless Lamb
I am alive in the hope of Jesus Christ
Restored and redeemed now by the Great I Am

*For You've never broken one promise You've made
You've never forsaken one child Your love has saved
You've never not forgiven one sin by Your grace
You've never forbidden one soul who comes to pray*

I have rest in the arms of Jesus Christ
Surrendered and sure and now changed by His love
I have peace in the words of Jesus Christ
Salvation and song are my gifts from Heaven above

**For Lord You loved me before my first cry
And Lord You'll hold me until the day that I die
You'll never leave me, leave me alone
For Lord You'll always lead me, lead me home**

And I am washed by the blood of Jesus Christ

Philippians 4:8-9

*Finally, brethren, whatever things are true, whatever things
are noble, whatever things are just, whatever things are pure,
whatever things are lovely, whatever things are of good report
if there is any virtue and if there is anything praiseworthy,
meditate on these things. The things which you learned and
received and heard and saw in me, these do and the God of
peace will be with you.*

I Fear No More

I fear no more, no longer am I afraid
For I am sure, that in Your arms I'll stay

For my soul now it now has a home
For my heart it now is Your very own

And nothing can ever separate our love
And nothing will ever break us apart
And nothing may ever come between us now
And nothing will ever change the way we are

I fear no more, no longer am I forsaken
For I can endure, for I am now forgiven

For my soul now it now has a home
For my heart it now is Your very own

And nothing can ever separate our love
And nothing will ever break us apart
And nothing may ever come between us now
And nothing will ever change the way we are

I fear no more

Psalm 56:3-4

In God I will praise His word, in God I have put my trust, I will not fear what flesh can do unto me.

I've Turned Away From You

Open wide my eyes to see Your glory
Open wide my heart to feel Your love
Open wide my soul to know Your mercy
Open wide my life, to share Heaven above

Open wide my faith to tell Your story
Open wide my doubt to believe all of You
Open wide my praise, to shout "You are worthy!"
Open wide my words to speak Your truth

For so long I've turned You away
For too long I've turned away, from You

I've kept You far from my heart, so far apart
I've kept You there at a distance
Kept You so far at bay, so far away

I've kept You there at a distance
When all I needed, all I ever waanntted
Was Your love and grace
Forgiveness and strength

When all I searched for, all I ever hoped for
Was Your cross and truth
Your loving kindness and all of You

For so long I've turned You away
For too long I've turned away, from You

James 4:7

Submit yourselves therefore to God.
Resist the devil and he will flee from you.

No Never Again

How do I find my way?
To have the right words to say, to find a quiet place to pray

How am I to change my mind?
To now take the time, to leave my every sin behind

How am I to let go?
Of all that I know, of all I ever was before

How am I to hold onto?
To all these things new and keep my eyes only on You

**And never again to turn away from You my Friend
And never again to lose my way from You my Friend
No never again!**

How do I see the light?
To always know what's right, to hold You here in my sight

How can I not go wrong?
To never take too long and to find the strength to be strong

***Then I'm to step out in faith
To stand up in praise and my arms I raise
Then I'm to lift up my eyes
To cast my cares to the sky, never will we say goodbye***

**And never again to turn away from You my Friend
And never again to lose my way from You my Friend
No never again!**

1 Peter 3:11-12

*Let him turn away from evil and do good, let him seek
peace and pursue it. For the eyes of the Lord are on the
righteous and His ears are open to their prayers, but the
face of the Lord is against those who do evil.*

My Prayer

Lord I pray for Your hope
Lord I pray for Your grace
Lord I pray for Your love
I pray for Your strength

**For Your forgiveness for my sins
For Your salvation for my soul
For Your mercy for my mistakes
For Your healing, for my broken heart
This is my prayer**

Lord I pray for Your truth
Lord I pray for Your light
Lord I pray for Your will
I pray for Your new life

***For Your will for my life
Your song for my soul
For Your hope for my heart
Your truth that I will always know***

**For Your forgiveness for my sins
For Your salvation for my soul
For Your mercy for my mistakes
For Your healing, for my broken heart
This is my prayer**

Philippians 1:9-11

And this I pray, that your love may abound still more and more in knowledge and all discernment, that you may approve the things that are excellent, that you may be sincere and without offense till the day of Christ, being filled with the fruits of righteousness which are by Jesus Christ, to the glory and praise of God.

He Will Heal All Our Land

If we pray, if we fall down before Him
If we fall to our knees
If we pray, lift our eyes up to Heaven
If we lift our eyes to see

**The Lord He will heal all our land
The Lord He will reach out His mighty hand
He will heal all our land**

*And if with all our heart and with all our might
If we all return to Him, He will heal all our land*

If we pray, if His sons and His daughters
Give to Him all that we have
If we pray, if we gather around Him
And share with Him all that we are

**The Lord He will heal all our land
The Lord He will reach out His mighty hand
He will heal all our land**

*And if with all our heart and with all our might
If we all return to Him, He will heal all our land*

**And if with all our hope and with all our life
If we return to Him, if we return to Him
If we return to Him, He will heal our land**

2 Chronicles 7:14

*If My people who are called by My name will humble
themselves and pray and seek My face and turn from
their wicked ways, then I will hear from Heaven and
will forgive their sin and heal their land.*

September

Fall In Love With Jesus

Fall In Love With Jesus

Fall in love with Jesus
Serve Him with all your heart, all of your heart
Trust in the Lord Jesus
Give to Him all you are, all that you are

**And before His throne
Lay down all you own, all that you own
And now at His feet
Lay down your life, your very life
For He will make everything right
He will make everything right**

So fall in love with Jesus
Serve Him with all your heart, all of your heart
Trust in the Lord Jesus
Give to Him all you are, all that you are

**And before His throne
Lay down all you own, all that you own
And now at His feet
Lay down your life, your very life
For He will make everything right
He will make everything right
Fall in love, fall in love
Fall in love with Jesus**

John 15:9

*As the Father loved Me, I also have
loved you, abide in My love.*

Count Your All As Loss

I pray that you know all God's love
I pray you look to Heaven above
I pray that you need all Gods strength
I pray you share all of Gods faith

**I pray that you cry out His name
I pray that you sing out all of your praise
I pray that you fall down at His cross
And you count your all, your all as loss**

I pray that you feel all God's grace
I pray you seek His holy word
I pray that you give to Him your all
I pray it is His name you call

**I pray that you cry out His name
I pray that you sing out all of your praise
I pray that you fall down at His cross
And you count your all, your all as loss**

*I pray that you search for all of Gods truth
I pray that He finds you right where you are
I pray that you know all of Gods will
And that one day you lay your down heart*

I pray that you find you way home
I pray you are His and His alone
I pray that you know all God's love
I pray you look to Heaven above

Oh Lord I pray

Philippians 3:9-10

*And be found in Him, not having my own righteousness,
which is from the law, but that which is through faith in Christ,
the righteousness, which is from God by faith, that I may know
Him and the power of His resurrection and the fellowship of
His sufferings, being conformed to His death.*

My First Love

**Come back into my life Jesus
Come home again my First Love
Come back into my heart Jesus
Come home my friend, my First Love**

Take Your place at the head of the table
I will celebrate at Your return
Take Your place here at my table
I will rejoice at Your return

***You've been gone, for far too long
I don't want You to ever go away again, never again!***

**Come back into my arms Jesus
Come home to stay my First Love
Come back into my faith Jesus
Come home to pray, my First Love**

Take Your place at the head of the table
I will sing and dance at Your return
Take Your place here in my heart
I will delight at Your return

***You've been gone, for far too long
I don't want You to ever go away again, never again!***

So come back into my life Jesus
Come home again my first love

Revelation 2:3-5

*And you have persevered and have patience and have
labored for My name's sake and have not become weary.
Nevertheless I have this against you, that you have left your
first love. Remember therefore from where you have fallen,
repent and do the first works, or else I will come to you
quickly and remove your lampstand
from its place, unless you repent.*

For You To Be Saved

Sometimes you just need to worship
Sometimes just praise
Sometimes you just need to cry out
And speak His holy word
Sometimes you just need to bow down
Sometimes just pray
Sometimes you just need to reach out
And hold on with all your faith

So however you can and wherever you are
For there's no time like right now
There's no day like today
For you to be saved

Sometimes you just need to listen
Sometimes just be still
Sometimes you just need to call out
And patiently wait for His wwwiiillllll
Sometimes you just need to be kneeling
Sometimes just be on your knees
Sometimes you just need to scream out
And shout out "Oh, my God please!"

For yesterday is gone and tomorrow may be too late
Today is here waiting and right now is the perfect date
For you to be saved

So however you can and wherever you are
For there's no time like right now
There's no day like today
For you to be saved

Acts 2:38

Then Peter said to them, "Repent and let every one of
you be baptized in the name of Jesus Christ for the
remission of sins and you shall receive the gift of the
Holy Spirit

Just Open Your Eyes

There is love, in the heart of the Lord
And there you'll find, you will find your love

Yes there is love, in the grace of the Lord
And there you'll find, you will find your love

There is rest, in the prayers of the Lord
And there you'll find, you will find your rest

Yes there is strength, in the arms of the Lord
And there you'll find, you will find your strength

**Just seek and you shall find, for you are no longer blind
Just open up, open up your eyes, open up your eyes**

There is peace, in the name of the Lord
And there you'll find, you will find your peace

Yes there is grace, in the cross of the Lord
And there you'll find, you will find your grace

There is truth, in the words of the Lord
And there you'll find, you will find your truth

There is joy, in the songs of the Lord
And there you'll find, you will find your joy

**Just seek and you shall find, for you are no longer blind
Just open up, open up your eyes, just open your eyes**

Psalm 119:18

*Open my eyes, that I may see wondrous
things from Your law.*

Do What You Will

In the end it is only His love, His great love
That will turn your life around

In the end it is only His hope, His great love
That will change the path you're on
Will change the path you're on

In the end it is only His faith, His great faith
That'll crush your heart of stone

In the end it is only His truth, His great truth
That will make a sinner His own
Will make a sinner His own

So Lord here is my heart do what You will
All my heart it is Yours, my soul it is still
Do what You will do what You will
All my heart it is Yours, my soul it is still

I will close my eyes and I will raise up my hands
I will look to the sky
And I will surrender here, right now where I stand
Right where I am

So Lord here is my heart do what You will
All my heart it is Yours, my soul it is still
Do what You will do what You will
All my heart it is Yours, my soul it is still

In the end it is only His love, His great love
That will turn your life around

John 6:38-40

For I have come down from Heaven, not to do My own will, but the will of Him Who sent Me. This is the will of the Father Who sent Me, that of all He has given Me I should lose nothing, but should raise it up at the last day. And this is the will of Him Who sent Me, that everyone who sees the Son and believes in Him may have everlasting life and I will raise him up at the last day.

September 7TH

Because He First Loved Me

I confess Jesus Christ as my Lord and Savior
And I will follow Him forevermore
I bow down to my God and my Risen King
And I will give to Him my everything

**For I am crucified in Christ
I am alive all because He died
I find my salvation in Christ
I am loved all because He first loved me**

*Lord it's Your forgiveness and Your grace
That is my hope and my strength
Lord it's Your mercy and Your Love
That is my gift from Heaven above
Lord it's Your love*

**For I am crucified in Christ
I am alive all because He died
I find my salvation in Christ
I am loved all because He first loved me**

I confess Jesus Christ as my Lord and Savior
And I will follow Him forevermore

1 John 4:20-21

*We love Him because He first loved us. If someone says,
"I love God," and hates his brother, he is a liar, for he
who does not love His brother whom he has seen, how
can he love God whom he has not seen? And this
commandment we have from Him, that he who loves
God must love his brother also.*

Forgiven

Lord by Your mercy I'm forgiven
Lord by Your grace I am redeemed
Lord by Your hands I'm delivered
Lord by Your blood I am washed clean
Lord I am washed clean

**Lord nothing I can do, here on my own
Can my works change
Lord nothing I can say, here all alone
Can my words change
Lord can I change, Lord can I change**

Lord by Your love I am ransomed
Lord by Your faith I'm all that I can be
Lord by Your words I'm spoken for
Lord by Your truth I am set free
Lord I am set free

**Lord nothing I can do, here on my own
Can my works change
Lord nothing I can say, here all alone
Can my words change
Lord can I change, Lord can I change**

Lord by Your love I am ransomed
Lord by Your faith I'm all that I can be
Lord by Your words I'm spoken for
Lord by Your truth I am set free
Lord I am set free

Ephesians 1:7

*In Him we have redemption through His blood, the
forgiveness of sins, according to the riches of His grace.*

September 9TH

If I Am Without You

Lord I need anything, that You can now give to me
All of Your grace, all of Your hope and all of Your mercy

Lord I want everything, that You can now show to me All of Your love, all
of Your strength and all of Your glory

For I am empty without You Lord
For I am a lost and wandering soul
Wandering this world alone
For I am broken without You Lord
For I am a hurt and suffering heart
Suffering through this life on my own
If I am without You

Lord I'll seek nothing, that Your word won't explain to me
Just Your truth, just Your will and just all of Your mercy

Lord I'll ask something, that You can now share with me
Just Your peace, just Your joy and just all of Your beauty

For here within the struggle, here within the storm
You are always fighting for me
For here during the battle, here during the war
You are always fighting for me
Your love it sings such a sweet melody, for me

For I am empty without You Lord
For I am a lost and wandering soul
Wandering this world alone
For I am broken without You Lord
For I am a hurt and suffering heart
Suffering through this life on my own
If I am without You

Lord I am believing, that You surrendered all for me
No more doubt, no more fear and Lord I am here faithfully

James 1:5

If any of you lacks wisdom, let him ask of God, Who gives to
all liberally and without reproach and it will be given to him.

Every Step Of The Way

Through all of the storms and all of the rain
Through all of my hurt and all of my pain
My Lord You walk with me every step of the way

Through all of the love and all of the hate
Through all of my doubt and all of my faith
My Lord You walk with me every step of the way

**You are the hand which I hold
You are my guide as I grow old
You are the hope of my heart
Lord I praise all that You are
You are my strength when I am weak
You are the Savior which that I seek
You are the hope of my heart
Lord I praise all that You are**

Through all of the day and all of the night
Through all of my wrong and all of my right
My Lord You walk with me every step of the way

**You are the hand which I hold
You are my guide as I grow old
You are the hope of my heart
Lord I praise all that You are
You are my strength when I am weak
You are the Savior which that I seek
You are the hope of my heart
Lord I praise all that You are**

*My Lord You walk with me every step of the way
Every step of the way*

Job 23:10-11

*But He knows the way that I take, when He has tested me,
I shall come forth as gold. My foot has held fast to His
steps, I have kept His way and not turned aside.*

All Across The Sky

I can feel His love now inside of me
I can feel His hope now surrounding me
I can feel the love of the Lord deep within me
So deep within me

I can feel His grace now forgiving me
I can feel His truth now defending me
I can feel the love of the Lord deep within me
So deep within me

Lord You've given me the wings, the wings now to fly
And I will write Your name all across the sky
Lord I'll write Your name all across the sky

I can feel His strength now protecting me
I can feel His faith now believing in me
I can feel the love of the Lord deep within me
So deep within me

I can feel His prayers now restoring me
I can feel His joy now rising up in me
I can feel the love of the Lord deep within me
So deep within me

Lord You've given me the wings, the wings now to fly
And I will write Your name all across the sky
Lord I'll write Your name all across the sky
All across the sky!

Amos 9:6

He Who builds His layers in the sky and has founded His strata
in the earth, Who calls for the waters of the sea and pours
them out on the face of the earth, the Lord is His name.

Fight For Your Love

So is it the world that you now hear?
Or is it God that you listen to?
So is it sin that draws you near?
Or is it God that will lead you through?
Can you tell the difference?
Can you see all the signs this time?

So is it the world that you now follow?
Or is it to God you kneel and pray?
So is it sin that holds your tomorrow?
Or is it God that will win the day?
Can you tell the difference?
Can you see all the signs this time?

Well it's time that you fight
It's time that you take a stand
It's time that you do battle
With all the strength that you can
It's time you look high above
It's time that you fight for your love

You cannot just turn away
From the love you need to feel
You cannot just turn aside
From the love you need to heal

Well it's time that you fight
It's time that you take a stand
It's time that you do battle
With all the strength that you can
It's time you look high above
It's time that you fight for your love

So is it the world that you now hear?
Or is it God that you listen to?

Exodus 14:14

The Lord will fight for you and you shall hold your peace.

September 13TH

Without You

The sun it will still rise and the moon will still shine
And the world will still turn, on and on

And the birds will still sing and the church bells will still ring
And the world will still turn on and on

And the sky, it will still be just as blue
As my heart it now breaks, without you
As my heart it now breaks, without you

And the waves they'll still crash upon the shore
And the wind through the mountains will still roar
And with the hours that now pass
Oh Lord I pray my hope will last

For I only seem, to now, miss you more
Yes I only seem, to now, miss you more

And the sky it will still be just as blue
As my heart it now breaks without you
As my heart it now breaks without you

The sun it will still rise and the moon will still shine
And the world will still turn on and on

For everyone we have ever loved and lost
May God bless their journey home!

Psalm 23:1-6

The Lord is my Shepherd, I shall not want. He makes me to lie down in green pastures, He leads me beside the still waters. He restores my soul, He leads me in the paths of righteousness for His name's sake. Yea, though I walk through the valley of the shadow of death, I will fear no evil, for You are with me, Your rod and Your staff, they comfort me.

You prepare a table before me in the presence of my enemies, You anoint my head with oil, my cup runs over. Surely goodness and mercy shall follow me all the days of my life and I will dwell in the house of the Lord forever.

Lord You Surround Me

Lord You surround me
When my battles they are hard
Lord You surround me
When my mistakes go too far
Lord You surround me
When I am shaking with fear
Lord You surround me
You're always holding me near

For I am never, ever left alone
For I am never, ever on my own
I'm never on my own

Lord You surround me
When I am lost and afraid
Lord You surround me
When all I know is my pain
Lord You surround me
When I am so full of despair
Lord You surround me
You're always drawing me near

For I am never, ever left alone
For I am never, ever on my own
I'm never on my own

Not for one minute am I ever out of Your reach
Not for one moment am I out of Your sight
Not for one minute am I ever out of Your keep
Not for one moment am I not by Your side

For I am never, ever left alone
For I am never, ever on my own
I'm never on my own

Lord You surround me
When I am lost and afraid

Psalm 19:14

Let the words of my mouth and the meditation of my heart be
acceptable in Thy sight, O' Lord, my Strength and my Redeemer.

Oh My Little Soul

Oh My little soul, how I pray for your life
In all that you will do

Oh My little soul, how I pray I'll be your light
In all that you'll go through, oh my little soul

**I pray that you will know
The reason I lived, the reason I died
I pray that you will know
The reason I came and will come back again
Oh My little soul**

Oh My little soul, how I hope you will find
All the love I have for you

Oh My little soul, how I hope that in time
That you will live out my truth, oh my little soul

**I pray that you will know
The reason I lived, the reason I died
I pray that you will know
The reason I came and will come back again
Oh My little soul**

Oh My little soul, I will hear your every prayer
When you fall upon your knees

Oh My little soul, how I'll always be right there
Right in the moment you need me, oh my little soul

1 Peter 3:15

*But sanctify the Lord God in your hearts and always be ready
to give a defense to everyone who asks you a reason for the
hope that is in you, with meekness and fear.*

My Lord Lives

My Lord lives here in my soul
My Lord's grace is my forgiveness and my hope
My Lord lives!

My Lord lives here in my heart
My Lord's love is my beginning and my start
My Lord lives!

**My Lord lives here deep inside of me
I'm wide open now for all the world to see
For I am not who I used to be, I have changed
My Lord lives!**

My Lord lives here in my life
My Lord's truth is my everything and my light
My Lord lives!

My Lord lives here in my faith
My Lord's cross is my salvation and mmyy strength
My Lord lives!

**My Lord lives here deep inside of me
I'm wide open now for all the world to see
For I am not who I used to be, I have changed
My Lord lives!**

My Lord lives here in my soul!

1 John 4:12

*No one has seen God at any time. If we love one another,
God abides in us and His love has been perfected in us.*

September 17TH

Over And Over Again

My chains have been broken, my soul it set free
For my eyes have awoken from their long and deep sleep

My hope has been restored, my doubt it erased
For my love has been reborn and my sins have found Your grace

**I've shared with You nothing but my shame
And You've given to me nothing but all of Your heart
I've brought to You nothing but my blame
And You've shown to me nothing but just Who You are
Over and over again**

My past has been forgiven, my life it washed clean
For my faith it was shaken, more than it's ever been

But my hope has been restored, my doubt it erased
For my love has been reborn and my sins have found Your grace

*Just when I should have been lifting up my prayers
I was doubting Your truth, I was doubting You
Just when I could have been believing Your holy word
I was denying Your will, I was denying You*

**I've shared with You, nothing but my shame
And You've given to me, nothing but all of Your heart
I've brought to You, nothing but my blame
And You've shown to me nothing but just Who You are
Over and over again**

Psalm 107:14-16

*He brought them out of darkness and the shadow of death
and broke their chains in pieces. Oh, that men would give
thanks to the Lord for His goodness and for His wonderful
works to the children of men! For He has broken the
gates of bronze and cut the bars of iron in two.*

Lord It's You

Lord it's in You that I love
And Lord it's in You that I will follow
For all of my days, in all of my praise
Lord it's in You that I love, it's in You that I love

Lord it's in You that I hope
And Lord it's in You that I believe
For all of my life, in all of my nights
Lord it's in You that I hope, it's in You that I love

And for my strength, Lord it's You
And for my faith, Lord it's You
And in Your mercy, Lord it's You
And in Your grace, Lord it's You, my Lord it's You!

Lord it's in You that I trust
And Lord it's in You that I'll remain
For all of my years, in all of my tears
Lord it's in You that I trust, it's in You that I trust

It's in You that I love, it's in You that I hope
It's in You that I trust, it's in You that I love
Lord it's You

And for my strength, Lord it's You
And for my faith, Lord it's You
And in Your mercy, Lord it's You
And in Your grace, Lord it's You, my Lord it's You!

Isaiah 25:1

O' Lord, You are my God. I will exalt You. I will praise
Your name, for You have done wonderful things, Your
counsels of old are faithfulness and truth.

My Hallelujah

Lord create in me the sweetest melody
One that I can sing for the whole world to hear
Lord compose in me the greatest symphony
One that I can bring so the whole world draws near

**For it will be a song of all my praise
For it will be a gift of all my faith
For it will be a song of Your great love and grace
It will be my hallelujah**

Lord arrange in me a perfect harmony
One that I can sing, so the whole world may share
Lord design in me a beautiful tapestry
One that I can bring to help the whole world to care

*Lord renew in me the hope in my heart
Lord restore in me the song in my soul
Lord revive in me the light of Your love
Lord reclaim in me the power of my prayer*

**For it will be a song of all my praise
For it will be a gift of all my faith
For it will be a song of Your great love
For it will be a song of Your great love
For it will be a song of Your great love and grace
It will be my hallelujah**

Lord awake in me Your glorious victory
One that I shout from every mountain top!

Colossians 3:10

*And have put on the new man who is renewed in
knowledge according to the image of Him Who created him*

So Beautiful In Your Sight

Lord may it be that we seek Your blessing
Lord may it be that we seek Your grace
Lord may it be that we cry for Your mercy
Lord may it be that we cry out Your holy name

Lord You tell me that we are special
That we are so beautiful in Your sight
When the world says that we are nothing
That nothing we do will ever be right
That we'll never be good enough
That we will never measure up
Lord You tell me that we are
So beautiful in Your sight

Lord may it be that we seek Your blessing
Lord may it be that we seek Your grace
Lord may it be that we cry for Your mercy
Lord may it be that we cry out Your holy name

Lord we want our love to come alive, come alive!

Lord You tell me that we are special
That we are so beautiful in Your sight
When the world says that we are nothing
That nothing we do will ever be right
That we'll never be good enough
That we will never measure up
Lord You tell me that we are
So beautiful in Your sight

1 Peter 3:3-4

Do not let your adornment be merely outward arranging the hair,
wearing gold, or putting on fine apparel, rather let it be the hidden
person of the heart, with the incorruptible beauty of a gentle
and quiet spirit, which is very precious in the sight of God.

Lord I'm Praying For Just This Moment

Lord I'm praying for just this moment
Not what was, or what will come after
Lord I'm praying for just this moment
Not yesterday, or what will come tomorrow

Lord I'm praying for just this moment
Just for Your will, only for Your truth
Lord I'm praying for just this moment, all to You

For Your perfect will, is what I'm praying for
For Your perfect will is all that I need
For Your perfect truth, is what I'm hoping for
For Your perfect will is all that I seek

From You, for me, for my eyes to see
From You, for me, for my heart to believe
To need Your will, to seek Your truth
And to feel Your love, surrounding me
And to feel Your strength, all around me

Lord I'm praying for just this moment
With all my faith, with all of my soul
Lord I'm praying for just this moment
With all my hope, with all that I know

Lord I'm praying for just this moment
Just for Your will, only for Your truth
Lord I'm praying, for just this moment, all to You
Lord I am praying, for just this moment
Lord all to You

Psalm 138:8

The Lord will perfect that which concerns me, Your mercy, O'
Lord, endures forever, do not forsake the works of Your hands.

That's When God Begins

I wish I had some other words that I might now say
I wish I had another prayer that I could now pray
I don't know what God's plan, what it is for you
All I know is that our God
He's going to help you see it through!

**So don't you give up, don't you give in
When you're at your end, that's when God begins
So don't you lose hope, don't you ever lose faith
For when you've lost your place, God will show you the way
When you're at your end, that's when God begins**

I wish I had some other news that I could now bring
I wish I had another point of view for your eyes to see
I don't know why so many things happen the way they do
All I know is that our God's holy word, it is forever true!

**Know that the sunny days
They will one day come again
And know that these tough days
They will one day come to an end**

**But it's gonna take love
It's gonna take His grace
It's gonna take some time
Take all of your faith, all of your faith**

I wish I had some other words that I might now say
I wish I had another prayer that I could now pray
I don't know what God's plan, what it is for you
All I know is that our God
He's going to help you see it through!

Psalm 27:13-14

*I would have lost heart, unless I had believed that I would
see the goodness of the Lord In the land of the living.
Wait on the Lord, be of good courage and He shall
strenghten your heart, wait, I say, on the Lord!*

Because Love Always Knows

When I am praying, You are here praying with me
When I am kneeling, You are here kneeling next to me

For when I am falling, You are here lifting me up
For when I am hurting, You are here healing me with Your love

When I am crying, You are here crying with me
When I am running, You are here catching up to me

For when I am shaking, You are here holding me close
For when I am doubting
You are here believing, because Love always knows

There has not been one minute
That You're not by my side
There has not been one moment
That You left me alone here to hide

For when I am falling, You are here lifting me up
For when I am hurting, You are here healing me with Your love

For when I am shaking, You are here holding me close
For when I am doubting, You are here believing
Because Love always knows

So when I am searching, You are here leading me home
When I am trusting, You are here making me Your very own

Colossians 3:14

But above all these things put on love,
which is the bond of perfection.

Jesus Christ!

Maybe you've taken for granted, maybe your whole life
Maybe it's your job, your home, or maybe your own wife
Maybe I'm here to tell you, that it's not too late
Maybe I'm here to show you His way

That it's the Lord, Jesus Christ!
He is the Way, the Truth, the Hope, He is the Life
And it's the Lord, Jesus Christ!

Maybe you've awakened to, maybe no one's there
Maybe on your own alone, maybe life's not fair
Maybe I'm here to find you, hold out a hand to hold
Maybe this hand to hold, it's just in time

And it's the Lord, Jesus Christ!
He is the Rock, the Prayer, the Path, He is the Light
And it is the Lord, Jesus Christ!

Maybe it has taken you, maybe now all your time
Maybe you've remained too long, standing there in line
Maybe I'm here to invite you, to open up your eyes
Maybe to wipe the tears, just as you cry

And to find the Lord, Jesus Christ!
He is the Way, the Truth, the Hope, He is the Life
And it's the Lord, Jesus Christ!
He is the Rock, the Prayer, the Path, He is the Light
And it is the Lord, Jesus Christ!

Maybe you've taken for granted, maybe your whole life

John 14:6-7

Jesus said to him, "I am the way, the truth and the life.
No one comes to the Father except through Me. If you
had known Me, you would have known My Father also
and from now on you know Him and have seen Him."

September 25TH

Even In The Moments That It Hurts

I do not know why, I do not know how
These things happen just the way that they do
I cannot explain, I can't figure out
After all of this time I'm still so confused

**All that I do know is what the Lord has told me
That all things work together for good
All that I do know is what the Lord has shown me
That all things work together just the way that they should
Even in the moments that it hurts**

I don't have all the answers, I don't have all the words
But there is something else here at play
But I can share with you, I can give to you hope
As why our hearts must get broken this way

*For it's in every sunrise and in every sunset
In every life and every death
For it's in every step we walk
Every breath we have left*

*So look upon the horizon, keep your hope hoping
So stand now in the sun, into the first light of the morning
Know that with this new day, there's great expectation
Now await the dawn, with great anticipation
So open your eyes, see the blue skies
So open your heart, today is your brand new start*

**For all that I do know is what the Lord has told me
That all things work together for good
All that I do know is what the Lord has shown me
That all things work together just the way that they should
Even in the moments that it hurts**

Psalm 34:18

*The Lord is near to those who have a broken heart,
and saves such as have a contrite spirit.*

— 278 —

When You Call Out My Name

When you're on your knees, with your eyes lifted high
Call out My name I will hear your cry

When you lift up your heart, high up to the sky
Call out My name I will hear your cry

I will hear you cry from Heaven
When you call out My name
I will hear you cry from Heaven
When you call out My name

When you lay down your soul, when you say you are Mine
Call out My name I will hear your cry

When you give me your sin, when you want a new life
Call out My name I will hear your cry

For nothing you could ever do
Could keep Me away from you
For nothing you could ever say
Could ever keep Me away from you

I will hear you cry from Heaven
When you call out My name
I will hear you cry from Heaven
When you call out My name

Psalm 18:3

I will call upon the Lord, Who is worthy to be
praised, so shall I be saved from my enemies.

The Greatness Of Our Lord

God is faithful, God is love
God is merciful, God is enough
God is hopeful, God is grace
God is beautiful, God is in this place!

**For nothing ever said in any spoken word
For nothing ever sung in any song ever heard
Could ever reach the heights of His glory
Could ever touch the greatness
The greatness of our Lord**

God is mindful, God is trust
God is wonderful, God is alive in us!

God is truthful, God is strength
God is powerful, God is His great name!

***No angel in Heaven, no man, here upon the earth
Can ever truly know all of His great love
Or may truly know all the splendor of
The greatness of our Lord, the greatness of our Lord***

**For nothing ever said in any spoken word
For nothing ever sung in any song ever heard
Could ever reach the heights of His glory
Could ever touch the greatness
The greatness of our Lord**

Nehemiah 1:5

*And I said, "I pray, Lord God of Heaven, O' great and
awesome God, You Who keep Your covenant and mercy
with those who love You and observe Your commandments.*

Come To My Altar

Come to My altar all who are broken
And I will heal your heart
Come to My altar all who are crying
And I will dry your tears
Yes I will dry your tears

**Come to My altar all who are silent
And I will sing you a new song
Come to My altar all who are hurting
And I will ease your pain
Yes I will ease your pain**

Come to My altar all who are weary
And I will be your strength
Come to My altar all who are searching
And I will find your way home
Yes I will find your way home

*And to all who have ever fallen
I will lift you up
And to all who have been afraid
I will give you hope
And to all who've been so blind
I will help you see
And to all who have ever doubted
I will give to you faith
Yes I will give to you faith*

Come to My altar all who are broken
And I will heal your heart

Matthew 5:23-24

*Therefore if you bring your gift to the altar and there
remember that your brother has something against you,
leave your gift there before the altar and go your way.
First, be reconciled to your brother and
then come and offer your gift.*

What I Believe

At the end of the day, when I close my eyes
When it is just You, Lord it's just You
Just You and I

Where I will stand on my faith
I will rest in Your grace, when at last we'll stare
Yes we will stare, eye to eye
Now face to face

**When not what I've done
Not my battles won
When all that will matter
Is what I believe**

***When this room is dark
With just the beat of one heart
And all that will matter
Is what I believe***

At the end of the day, when I close my eyes
When it is just You, Lord it's just You
Just You and I

John 20:24-29

Now Thomas, called the Twin, one of the twelve, was not with them when Jesus came. The other disciples therefore said to him, "We have seen the Lord." So he said to them, "Unless I see in His hands the print of the nails and put my finger into the print of the nails and put my hand into His side, I will not believe."

And after eight days His disciples were again inside and Thomas with them. Jesus came, the doors being shut and stood in the midst and said, "Peace to you!" Then He said to Thomas, "Reach your finger here and look at My hands and reach your hand here and put it into My side. Do not be unbelieving, but believing."

And Thomas answered and said to Him, "My Lord and my God!" Jesus said to him, "Thomas because you have seen Me, you have believed. Blessed are those who have not seen and yet have believed."

Like No Other

Lord Your strength, for it is stronger
It holds me closer when I feel alone

Lord Your grace, for it is greater
It draws me nearer when I'm far from home

**Lord my soul, it needs Your love Like no other,
Lord like no other**

Lord Your faith, for it is forever
It will keep us together for eternity to come

Lord Your love, for it is higher
And it shines brighter, brighter than the sun

**Lord my soul, it needs Your love
Like no other, Lord like no other**

*Lord Your word it is my breath of life
Lord Your truth it is my guiding light
Lord Your cross it is the only way
That I will see Your face someday*

Lord Your strength, for it is stronger
It holds me closer when I feel alone

Lord Your grace, for it is greater
It draws me nearer when I'm far from home

**Lord my soul, it needs Your love
Like no other, Lord like no other**

Isaiah 44:6

*Thus says the Lord, the King of Israel and his
Redeemer, the Lord of Hosts, "I am the First
and I am the Last, besides Me there is no God."*

October

Heaven Awaits

Heaven Awaits

Not too far off, somewhere there in the distance
Not too far away, there's a light beyond the darkness

Not too far ahead, just there out of reach
Not too far behind, a little faith is what you'll need

Heaven awaits, where the angel's sing
Preparing you a place, in the presence of the King

Heaven awaits, where His glory reigns
And where eternity is just beginning, Heaven awaits

Not too far from view, just there before the dawn
Not too far to see, cast your eyes and now look upon

Not too far out there, just beyond the morning star
Not too far in front of you, now from right where you are

Heaven awaits, where the angel's sing
Preparing you a place, in the presence of the King

Heaven awaits, where His glory reigns
And where eternity is just beginning, Heaven awaits

Not too far off, somewhere there in the distance
Not too far away, there's a light beyond the darkness

Matthew 7:13-14

Enter through the narrow gate. For wide is the gate and
broad is the road that leads to destruction and many
enter through it. But small is the gate and narrow the
road that leads to life and only a few find it.

How Can I Lift Them Up?

Lord if there's a word that may bring hope to their heart
Lord let me say it, Lord may I say it
Lord if there's a prayer that may bring peace for their soul
Lord let me pray it, Lord may I pray it

**Oh Lord I'm hoping now, Lord I'm searching how
How can I lift them up?
Lord I'm crying out, Lord I'm singing loud
How can I lift them up?
Oh Lord how can I lift them up?**

*Lord if there's a song that I may sing
Oh Lord may I sing it now
Lord if there's a gift that I can give
Oh Lord may I give it now*

**Oh Lord I'm hoping now, Lord I'm searching how
How can I lift them up?
Lord I'm crying out, Lord I'm singing loud
How can I lift them up?
Oh Lord how can I lift them up?**

Lord if there's a word that may bring hope to their heart
Lord let me say it, Lord may I say it

Isaiah 46:4

*Even to your old age, I am He and even to gray
hairs I will carry you! I have made and I will bear,
even I will carry and will deliver you.*

More Than Anything

What does it mean to be forgiven?
What does it mean to find forgiveness?

What does it mean to know salvation?
What does it mean to know saving grace?

Well it means more, more than anything
Well it means more, more than everything
More than anything

More than the wealth, all the wealth of this world
More than the power, all the power you may hold
More than anything

What does it mean to feel redemption?
What does it mean to feel His loving embrace?

What does it mean to be forgiven?
What does it mean to find forgiveness?

Well it means more, more than anything
Well it means more, more than everything
More than anything

Luke 5:19-21

And when they could not find how they might bring him in, because of the crowd, they went up on the housetop and let him down with his bed through the tiling into the midst before Jesus. When He saw their faith, He said to him, "Man, your sins are forgiven you." And the scribes and the Pharisees began to reason, saying, "Who is this Who speaks blasphemies? Who can forgive sins but God alone?"

The Lord Has Shown Me

Not long ago when I was alone
I was so lost with no way home
I was alone, I am alone no more
Not long ago when I was afraid
I was in fear seemed of everything
I was alone, I am afraid no more

For the Lord has shown me, all the strength that I need
For the Lord has shown me, all the faith to believe
For the Lord has shown me, all the grace for my soul
Enough to wash away my sin, enough for me to forgive
For a greater love, the Lord has shown me

I have stood in the shadows of my shame
For too long, for far too long
I have hoped for the healing of my heart
For so long, for so very long

Not long ago when I was ashamed
I was hiding from the mistakes I've made
I was alone, I am ashamed no more

For the Lord has shown me, all the strength that I need
For the Lord has shown me, all the faith to believe
For the Lord has shown me, all the grace for my soul
Enough to wash away my sin, enough for me to forgive
For a greater love, the Lord has shown me

Not long ago when we were apart
I was in search of just Who You are
But we were apart, we are apart no more

Psalm 31:1-5

In You O' Lord, I put my trust, let me never be ashamed, deliver
me in Your righteousness. Bow down Your ear to me, deliver me
speedily, be my rock of refuge, a fortress of defense to save me. For
You are my rock and my fortress, therefore, for Your name's sake,
lead me and guide me. Pull me out of the net which they have
secretly laid for me, for You are my strength. Into Your hand I
commit my spirit, You have redeemed me, O' Lord God of truth.

Still You Love Me

You have given me forgiveness and grace
All I've shown You is my doubt instead of faith
Yet still You love me, still You love me

You have given me salvation and love
All I've shown You is my fear instead of love
And still You love me, still You love me

You could have walked away, never turned around
Could have passed me by, never looked back and found
This lost soul searching, this soul searching

You could have kept on going, never took the time
Could have kept walking by, never knelt by my side
This broken heart hurting, this heart hurting
And still You love me, still You love me

You have given me redemption and peace
All I've shown You are my lies not the truth You seek
And yet You love me, still You love me

You could have walked away, never turned around
Could have passed me by, never looked back and found
This lost soul searching, this soul searching

You could have kept on going, never took the time
Could have kept walking by, never knelt by my side
This broken heart hurting, this heart hurting
And still You love me, still You love me

John 14:1-3

Let not your heart be troubled, you believe in God, believe also in Me. In My Father's house are many mansions, if it were not so, I would have told you. I go to prepare a place for you. And if I go and prepare a place for you, I will come again and receive you to Myself, that where I am, there you may be also.

October 6TH

Give All The Glory To God

From your very first breath
To every day you have left
Give to Him your everything

Until your very last cry
Until the day that you die
Give to Him your everything

**Give all the glory to God, all of your heart
All of your heart**

**Give all the glory to God, all that you are
All that you are**

From your first step of life
Until you see Heaven's light
Give to Him your everything

From your very first prayer
To your last dream of the night
Until you say goodnight
Give to Him your everything

**Give all the glory to God, all of your heart
All of your heart**

**Give all the glory to God, all that you are
All that you are**

Jude 24-25

*Now to Him Who is able to keep you from stumbling and to
present you faultless before the presence of His glory with
exceeding joy, to God our Savior, Who alone is wise, be
glory and majesty, dominion and power, both now and
forever. Amen!*

Always

I pray the grace of our Lord Jesus
To be with you now

And I pray the love of our Lord Jesus
To surround you now

**To forever hold you in His keep
Always hold you in His arms
To never, ever let you go
To always keep you safe from harm, always**

I pray the strength of our Lord Jesus
To lift you up, when you're down

And I pray the faith of our Lord Jesus
To have you believe, when you doubt

*You feel like your heart it has been broken
And your tears now they fall, now they fall
So lift your eyes now to Heaven
And give the Lord your very all
All you have and all you are
All your life and all of your heart
All you've been and all you'll be
All you own and all the secrets that you keep*

I pray the grace of our Lord Jesus
To be with you now

And I pray the love of our Lord Jesus
To surround you now

To always keep you safe from harm, always

John 14:27

*Peace I leave with you, My peace I give unto you, not as
the world giveth, give I unto you. Let not your heart be
troubled, neither let it be afraid.*

October 8TH

No Matter How Far

Your love won't stop loving me
Your grace won't stop forgiving me
Your light won't stop shining on me
Your faith it won't stop believing in me

Your hope won't stop healing me
Your song won't stop singing to me
Your life won't stop living in me
Your heart it won't stop searching for me

So I can try to hide, so I can try to lie
I can try to keep everything inside
So I will try to pray, so I will try to stay
So I will try to keep all of my fears
All of my tears, all of my doubts so far away

Your truth won't stop teaching me
Your word won't stop preaching to me
Your tears won't stop crying for me
Your strength it won't stop carrying me

Your hands won't stop holding me
Your voice won't stop whispering to me
Your joy won't stop lifting me
Your blood it won't stop bleeding for me

For You are always here beside me
For You are always here to guide me
Right to where You are, no matter how far

Matthew 28:19-20

Go therefore and make disciples of all the nations,
baptizing them in the name of the Father and of the Son
and of the Holy Spirit, teaching them to observe all things
that I have commanded you and lo, I am with you always,
even to the end of the age." Amen!

Goodbye

Goodbye to all that I was
Goodbye to all my life has been
Goodbye to all that I have done
Goodbye to all I have said

**For I am a new creation
Born in sin, now born again
For I am now forgiven
By His grace, by His love without end
By His grace, by His love without end**

Goodbye to all that I've done without
Goodbye to all whom I've hurt
Goodbye to all my days of doubt
Goodbye to all I thought I'd learned

*Once changed, I cannot remain the same
For my heart, my soul, my life has been remade
It has been remade*

**For I am a new creation
Born in sin, now born again
For I am now forgiven
By His grace, by His love without end
By His grace, by His love without end**

So goodbye to all to all I have ever known
Goodbye to all that this world has ever shown

1 Peter 1:23

*Having been born again, not of corruptible seed but
incorruptible, through the word of God which lives
and abides forever.*

Lord I'm Here Praying

I know You've been waiting, patiently waiting
For me to hear Your voice
I know You've been praying, constantly praying
For me to make my choice
For me to see, for me to believe

**Dear Lord I'm here, drawing ever closer to You side
With my soul open wide wanting to no longer hide
Dear Lord I'm here, kneeling down at Your cross
With my soul no longer lost
All my gain I now count as my loss
Dear Lord I am here, Lord I'm here praying**

I know You've been pleading, perfectly pleading
For me to lay my life down
I know You've been leading, endlessly leading
For me to come around
For me to see, for me to believe

*Though I may drift away
And I never find the right words to say
Lord I am here praying
Though we may drift apart
And I never quite know where to start
Lord I am here praying*

**Dear Lord I'm here, drawing ever closer to You side
With my soul open wide wanting to no longer hide
Dear Lord I'm here, kneeling down at Your cross
With my soul no longer lost
All my gain I now count as my loss
Dear Lord I am here, Lord I'm here praying**

Mark 11:25

*And whenever you stand praying, if you have anything against
anyone, forgive him, that your Father in Heaven may also
forgive you your trespasses.*

Stronger

Stronger, my faith needs to be a little stronger
Longer, my faith needs to last a little longer

**But Lord I give up far too easy
Lord I give in much too quickly
Lord fill me with Your grace
Fill me with Your strength
Lord make me stronger**

Harder, my faith needs to work a little harder
Farther, my faith needs to reach a little farther

***Make me stronger today
Lord somehow tomorrow's so far away
Stronger today
Lord right now tomorrow's a brand new day
Lord make me stronger***

Clearer, my faith needs to see a litt tlle ce clearer
Nearer, my faith needs to draw a little nearer

**But Lord I give up far too easy
Lord I give in much too quickly
Lord fill me with Your grace
Fill me with Your strength
Lord make me stronger**

***Make me stronger today
Lord somehow tomorrow's so far away
Stronger today
Lord right now tomorrow's a brand new day
Lord make me stronger***

Philippians 4:13

I can do all things through Christ who strengthens me.

Call Upon The Lord

Call upon the Lord, when your heart is broken
Just call upon the Lord
Call upon the Lord, when your last prayer is spoken
Just call upon the Lord

**For He will be at your side, for He will come just in time
He will come, yes He will come**

Call upon the Lord, when your soul is searching
Just call upon the Lord
Call upon the Lord, when your faith it has been shaken
Just call upon the Lord

**When you're alone, when you are afraid
He will be there, He will be there today
When you're in prayer, when you are in pain
He will be there, He will be there today**

**For He will be at your side, He will come just in time
He will be at your side, He will come just in time
He will come, yes He will come**

So call upon the Lord, when your soul is searching
Just upon the Lord
Call upon the Lord, when your faith it has been shaken
Just call upon the Lord

Isaiah 55:6

*Seek the Lord while He may be found, call
upon Him while He is near.*

I Am Stronger Than My Sin

We all have moments that we'd like to take back
The times in our life when it was the faith we lacked
But deep within every soul we all have the hope to know
That we can be closer to our God
That we are always close to our Lord

**For I am stronger than my sin
I will not let the devil win
I am better than my shame
I will not have the pain win again
I cannot give up and I won't give in
For I am stronger than my sin**

We all have minutes that we'd like to rewind
The days in our life when we didn't take the time
But deep within every heart we all have the hope to start
That we can be nearer to our God
That we are always near to our Lord

*It may seem like we're just too far apart
Like the distance is just too far to find our way home
It may seem that in everything we've done wrong
That we will end up here alone nd never find our way home*

**But we are stronger than our sin
We will not let the devil win
We are better than our shame
We will not have the pain win again
We cannot give up and we won't give in
For we are stronger than our sin**

Luke 6:45

*A good man out of the good treasure of his heart brings forth
good and an evil man out of the evil treasure of his heart brings
forth evil. For out of the abundance of the heart his mouth speaks.*

A New Heart It Beats Within

I believe in Jesus, in His birth and in His death
For in His resurrection, in His life I am blessed
I believe in Jesus, with every prayer and every breath
For in His salvation, my soul it finds its rest

**My every sin forgiven
And a new life now to begin
My every wrong forgotten
And a new heart it beats within
A new heart it beats within**

I believe in Jesus, in His hope and in His peace
For in His loving arms, my heart it finds His keep
I believe in Jesus, when I am strong and when I'm weak
For in His forgiveness, His cross is all I seek

**My every sin forgiven
And a new life now to begin
My every wrong forgotten
And a new heart it beats within
A new heart it beats within**

I believe in Jesus, in His birth and in His death
For in His resurrection, in His life I am blessed

Luke 5:37-39

And no one puts new wine into old wineskins, or else the new wine will burst the wineskins and be spilled and the wineskins will be ruined. But new wine must be put into new wineskins and both are preserved. And no one, having drunk old wine, immediately desires new for he says, 'The old is better.'

Only One Prayer Away

There are no tears, like the tears of a hurting heart
Yes there are no tears, like the tears of a searching soul

But know that your joy it comes in the morning
But know that your hope it is never too far away

So don't you lose your hope, do not lose your faith
Know that your hope, it's only one prayer away
So don't you lose your hope, do not lose your faith
Know that your hope, it's only one prayer away
It's only one prayer away

For there are no tears, like the tears of a fearful faith
No there are no tears, like the tears of a shaking strength

But know that your joy, it comes in the morning
But know that your hope, it's never too far away

So open up your heart and let His healing start
So let all of His love in and let His great love begin
To help your heart to see, to help your soul to believe

So don't you lose your hope, do not lose your faith
Know that your hope, it's only one prayer away
So don't you lose your hope, do not lose your faith
Know that your hope, it's only one prayer away
It's only one prayer away

There are no tears, like the tears of a hurting heart

Acts 1:14

These all continued with one accord in prayer and
supplication, with the women and Mary the mother
of Jesus and with His brothers.

Your Love

I may never climb the highest mountain
I may never swim the deepest sea
I may never cross the swiftest of rivers

**But I've been so blessed
To know your love
I've been so very blessed
To know your love**

I may never run the greatest distance
And I may never gain all the riches of this world
I may never learn all the lessons of this life

**But I've been so blessed
To know your love
I've been so very blessed
To know your love**

*For every moment's been a gift from the Lord
Every moment's been the answer to a prayer
From above, from above*

For I may never answer the hardest of questions
I may never lay all my burdens down
I just may never heal all the wounds of this heart

**But I've been so blessed
To know your love
I've been so very blessed
To know your love**

Psalm 115:1

*Not unto us, O' Lord, not unto us, but to Your name give
glory, because of Your mercy, because of Your truth.*

Even When

The love of Christ
It is always blessing me
The grace of Christ
It is always forgiving me

Even when I am alone
Even when I'm far from home

The strength of Christ
It is always holding me
The love of Christ
It is always embracing me

Even when I am afraid
Even when I'm far away

The will of Christ
It is always showing me
The truth of Christ
It is always surrounding me

Even when I am ashamed
Even when I'm so full of blame

The voice of Christ
It is always whispering to me

1 John 5:5

Who is He Who overcomes the world, but he
who believes that Jesus is the Son of God?

All By Your Hands

I trust in You my Lord, with all that I am
With all that I am
I trust in You my God, with all of my soul
With all of my soul

**For everything I hold, everything I've let go
You have made so perfect, all by Your hands
Everything I've been given, everything I have taken
You have made so perfect, all by Your hands
All by Your hands**

I trust in You my King, with all of my life
With all of my life
I trust in You my Friend, with all of my heart
With all of my heart

***I want to follow You Lord, wherever You go
Wherever You go
I want to worship You Lord, wherever I am
Wherever I am***

**For everything I hold, everything I've let go
You have made so perfect, all by Your hands
Everything I've been given, everything I have taken
You have made so perfect, all by Your hands
All by Your hands**

I trust in You my Lord, with all that I am
With all that I am
I trust in You my God, with all of my soul
With all of my soul

Psalm 91:1-2

*He Who dwells in the secret place of the Most High shall abide
under the shadow of the Almighty. I will say of the Lord, "He
is my Refuge and my Fortress my God, in Him I will trust."*

That's When You Begin

I have prayed a thousand prayers
In the hopes that You are there
I have cried a thousand times
"My God please draw me near!"

I have stayed down on my knees
Lifting up my every plea
I have known deep in my heart
That You were always there for me

**And yet I doubt when I should be sure
I fall apart when I doubt that I'm Yours
I fear when I should be strong
I just give up before too long
And just when I give in just when I give in
That's when You begin**

I have walked a thousand miles
In the hopes of finding my home
I have fallen so many times
Feeling as though I'm on my own

I've lifted up my eyes
In tears to Heaven above
I have prayed a thousand prayers
In the hope of knowing Your love

**And yet I doubt when I should be sure
I fall apart when I doubt that I'm Yours
I fear when I should be strong
I just give up before too long
And just when I give in just when I give in
That's when You begin**

Mark 11:24

*Therefore I say to you, whatever things you ask
when you pray, believe that you receive them,
and you will have them.*

October 20TH

It's Only Then

There's a truth if you take the time to find it
There's a light if you take the time to shine it
In the dark, in the dark
There's a faith if you take the time to believe it
There's a grace if you take the time to receive it
All for your sin, for your sin

It's only then when you find
His love meant for your heart
It's only then when you hear
His song meant for your soul
It's only then, it's only then

There's a life if you take the time to make it
There's a free gift if you take the time to take it
All for your heart, for your heart

Only if you open up your eyes to see
Will you ever see
Only if you open up your ears to hear
Will you ever hear
Only if you open up your heart and now let be
All He wants you now to be

It's only then when you find
His love meant for your heart
It's only then when you hear
His song meant for your soul
It's only then, it's only then

There's a love if you take the time to share it
There's a cross and He took the time to bare it
All for your soul, for your soul

Matthew 20:34

So Jesus had compassion and touched their eyes. And
immediately their eyes received sight and they followed Him.

Revive Us

Revive us Father, revive us oh Lord
Revive us Jesus, now by Your holy word
Revive us Spirit, live now within our lives
Revive us Savior, now by Your perfect truth

**Awaken our heart, awaken our soul
Awaken our life, dear Lord make it now**

**Awaken our hope, awaken our love
Awaken our faith, dear Lord have it be now**

*Restore our first love, restore our lost faith
Restore our broken hearts*

*Restore our weakened strength
Lord restore our first love, restore our lost faith*

Revive us Father, revive us oh Lord
Revive us Jesus, now by Your holy word
Revive us Spirit, live now within our lives
Revive us Savior, now by Your perfect truth

**Awaken our heart, awaken our soul
Awaken our life, dear Lord make it now**

**Awaken our hope, awaken our love
Awaken our faith, dear Lord have it be now**

*Restore our first love, restore our lost faith
Restore our broken hearts*

*Restore our weakened strength
Lord restore our first love, restore our lost faith*

So revive us Father, revive us oh Lord
Revive us Jesus, now by Your holy word

Revelation 2:4

*Nevertheless, I have somewhat against thee,
because thou hast left thy first love.*

October 22ND

All By Your Love

Lord Your Spirit is alive in me, it's always calling
And it's whispering
Always leading me through Your truth
Just where You want me to be

Lord Your Spirit is alive in me, it's always moving
And it's strengthening
Always guiding me through Your faith
Just where You want me to be

May my doubt be Your faith, my weakness be Your strength
May my heart be healed by Your love
May my wrong be Your right, my darkness be Your light
May my soul be saved by Your love, all by Your love

Lord Your Spirit is alive in me, it's always holding
And it's comforting
Always working in me through Your truth
Just where You want me to be

Lord Your Spirit is alive in me, it's always searching and forgiving Always
speaking to me through Your truth
Just where You want me to be

Your surrender, Your sacrifice
Your salvation Lord it is mine
Your forgiveness, Your kindness
Your fullness Lord it is mine

May my doubt be Your faith, my weakness be Your strength
May my heart be healed by Your love
May my wrong be Your right, my darkness be Your light
May my soul be saved by Your love, all by Your love

Isaiah 53:5

But He was wounded for our transgressions, He was bruised
for our iniquities, the chastisement for our peace was
upon Him and by His stripes we are healed.

So Very Far Away

When words they hurt my heart
I give it all up to my God
And when sin it stings my soul
I give it all up to my Lord

All of my tears and all of my pain
All of my fears, all to never know again

For I've kept inside
All of the hurt I've tried to hide
In the hopes it would never see the light of day
I've buried them so far down, deep down inside
So far away, so very far away

All of my tears and all of my pain
All of my fears, all to never know again

All of my tears and all of my pain
All of my fears, all to never know again
To never know again

So when words they hurt my heart
I give it all up to my God, all to my God
And when sin it stings my soul
I give it all up to my Lord, all to my Lord

1 Peter 3:10-11

For "He Who would love life and see good days, let him refrain
his tongue from evil and his lips from speaking deceit. Let him turn
away from evil and do good, let him seek peace and pursue it."

October 24TH

A King On A Cross

God is in control, Jesus is the King
And the Holy Spirit He is here surrounding us
His word is alive, His truth's being revealed
And His perfect grace it is here all around us

**For no matter how tough it is
Even in all of this
There's a King on a cross
Who shed His blood for all of us
And this King on a cross
Yes this King on a cross, is our Lord Jesus**

His love is our victory, His death is now our life
And His holy word it is here within us
His faith it is strong, His hope is our light
And His perfect love, it is here believing in us

*Though these times they may be tough
And sometimes we've all had enough
They make us all want to give up
They may make us all want to give in
But don't you ever give in
Just let the healing begin*

**For no matter how tough it is
Even in all of this
There's a King on a cross
Who shed His blood for all of us
And this King on a cross
Yes this King on a cross, is our Lord Jesus**

John 3:35-36

*The Father loves the Son and has given all things into His
hand. He Who believes in the Son has everlasting life and he
who does not believe the Son shall not see life, but the wrath
of God abides on him.*

Your Sacrifice Is All Of Our Blame

Your victory is our victory, Your hurt our own
Your salvation is our salvation
Your cross our hope
Your forgiveness is our forgiveness, Your blood our price
Your resurrection is our resurrection
Your death our life

**Your brokenness, it is our healing
Your suffering is all of our shame
Your faithfulness, it is our believing
And Your sacrifice is all of our blame**

Your foundation is our foundation
Your strength our rock
Your righteousness is our righteousness
Your path our walk, Your path is our walk

*You gave to us Your all
So that we would have Your all
You gave to us Your everything
So that we would have Your everything*

**Your brokenness, it is our healing
Your suffering is all of our shame
Your faithfulness, it is our believing
And Your sacrifice is all of our blame**

Your sacrifice is all of our blame

Hebrews 9:24-27

For Christ has not entered the Holy places made with hands, which are copies of the true, but into Heaven itself, now to appear in the presence of God for us, not that He should offer Himself often, as the high priest enters the Most Holy place every year with blood of another, He then would have had to suffer often since the foundation of the world but now, once at the end of the ages, He has appeared to put away sin by the sacrifice of Himself. And as it is appointed for men to die once, but after this the judgment.

October 26TH

For In Everything

I will sing of Your glory, Lord that You are holy
For Lord You are my Redeemer and in You Lord I trust
I will shout of Your beauty, Lord that You are worthy
For Lord You are my Deliverer and in You Lord I trust

**For in everything I say, for in everything I do
I want to give to You my everything, all I have to You
For in everything I am, in everything I go through
I want to give to You my everything, all I am to You**

Lord I will speak of Your mercy, Lord that You are mighty
For Lord You are my Forgiver and in You Lord I trust

I will tell of Your story, Lord that You are
For Lord You are my Forever and in You Lord I trust

*Oh Lord now sings my soul
For Lord You are my only Hope
Oh Lord now sings my soul
For Lord You are my only Home*

**For in everything I say, for in everything I do
I want to give to You my everything, all I have to You
For in everything I am, in everything I go through
I want to give to You my everything, all I am to You**

I will sing of Your glory, Lord that You are holy
For Lord You are my Redeemer and in You Lord I trust
In You Lord I trust, in You Lord I trust

Hebrews 13:8

Jesus Christ the same yesterday and today and forever.

Through The Eyes Of God

If we could see, through the eyes of God
We would see the beauty, in all of our hearts
If we could see, through the eyes of God
We would see the beauty, in all that we are

**For in the sight of Heaven, from His throne of glory
We are all so beautiful, we are all so beautiful
For in the sight of Heaven, from His seat of mercy
We are all so beautiful, we are all so beautiful**

If we could see, through the eyes of the Lord
We would see the wonder, in all of our souls
If we could see, through the eyes of the Lord
We would see the wonder, in all that we hope

*And we would see all of our mistakes
And we would see each and every second that we waste
And we would see all of our darkness
And we would see all of our soul's brokenness
All through the eyes of God*

**For in the sight of Heaven, from His throne of glory
We are all so beautiful, we are all so beautiful
For in the sight of Heaven, from His seat of mercy
We are all so beautiful, we are all so beautiful**

If we could see, through the eyes of God
We would see the beauty, in all that we are

Proverbs 15:3

*The eyes of the Lord are in every place,
keeping watch on the evil and the good.*

That's What This World Needs

What this world needs is a little bit more of Your love
A little bit more of Heaven above
That's what that this world needs

What this world needs is a little bit more of Your grace
A little bit more of Your great strength
That's what that this world needs

We've got enough greed, we've got enough pain
We've got enough need, we've got enough hate
We need more hope, we need more of Your grace
Before it's too late

What this world needs is a little bit more of Your forgiveness
A little bit more of Your loving kindness
That's what that this world needs

What this world needs is a little bit more of Your truth
A little bit more of Your hope breaking through
That's what that this world needs

We've got enough greed, we've got enough pain
We've got enough need, we've got enough hate
We need more hope, we need more of Your grace
Before it's too late!

For You are our faithful God, Your word is forever true
For You are our faithful King and what this world needs
And what this world needs, is only You, it's only You

That's what this world needs, that's what this world needs

John 15:19

If you were of the world, the world would love its own.
Yet because you are not of the world, but I chose you
out of the world, therefore the world hates you.

Shout Your Love

If you see with your eyes
And you hear with your ears
And you believe with all of your heart
You shall be saved

If you confess with your mouth
And you speak the name of Christ
And you believe with all of your heart
You shall be saved

**So stand up and tell all the nations
Stand up, atop the highest mountains
And shout your love!
So rise up with your hands held high
Rise up and try to touch the sky
And shout Your love! Yes shout Your love!
Shout Your love!**

*Oh my God of wonder, how great You are!
I will shout out my hallelujah
Oh my God of glory, how great Thou Art!
I will shout out my hallelujah
Hallelujah!*

**So stand up and tell all the nations
Stand up atop the highest mountains
And shout your love!
So rise up, with your hands held high
Rise up and try to touch the sky
And shout Your love! Yes shout Your love!
Shout Your love!**

Isaiah 42:10

*Sing to the Lord a new song and His praise from the ends
of the earth, You who go down to the sea and all that is
in it, You coastlands and you inhabitants of them!*

October 30TH

To Be Forgiven?

God is asking you to open your heart
He no longer wants you to spend time apart
So will you open your heart?

God is pleading for you to come home
He no longer wants you to walk this world alone
So will you come home?

What are you praying when you kneel down and you pray?
What are you saying to the Lord this day?
What are you thinking when you lay down your sin?
What are you hoping will come true in the end?
To be forgiven?

God is trying to sing to your soul
He no longer wants you to no longer know
So will you hear His song?

For so long He's waited, just outside of your door
Standing in the rain, the snow, or the midday sun
He's knocking upon the door of your heart
Waiting for you to let Him in
So have you let Him in?
Is today the day that you begin?

What are you praying when you kneel down and you pray?
What are you saying to the Lord this day?
What are you thinking when you lay down your sin?
What are you hoping will come true in the end?
To be forgiven?

God is asking you to open your heart

Daniel 9:9

To the Lord our God belong mercy and forgiveness,
though we have rebelled against Him.

— 314 —

For Only You Know

In Your hands is my whole life
All my plans are in Your sight
In Your arms is my whole heart
Safe from harm is where You are

For only You know where I am and where I'll go
For only You see where I've been and where I'll be
My every breath and my every prayer
My every day left and my every care
My Lord is Yours, for only You know

In Your name is my whole hope
All my praise is to You alone
In Your word is my whole faith
All my hurt is healed by Your grace

All I have I lay now down at Your feet
My every victory and my every defeat
All I believe I bring here to Your cross
My every gain and my every loss
My Lord is Yours, for only You know

For only You know where I am and where I'll go
For only You see where I've been and where I'll be
My every breath and my every prayer
My every day left and my every care

My Lord is Yours, for only You know

1 Samuel 16:7

But the Lord said to Samuel, "Do not look at his appearance
or at his physical stature, because I have refused Him. For
the Lord does not see as man sees, for man looks at the
outward appearance, but the Lord looks at the heart.

November

All Thanks Now Be To God

May All Thanks Now Be To God

Lord Your mercy is what we pray for
Lord Your wisdom is what we all need
Lord Your glory it shines all around us
Lord Your Spirit is what we all seek

**May all thanks, now be to God
May all praise, be to His holy name
May all thanks, now be to our Lord
May all thanks, now be to God**

Lord Your story is what we will tell
Lord Your blessing is from You on high
Lord Your beauty is what we all see
Lord for Your Hope is what we all cry

*May our every word give You all the glory
May our every prayer be laid at Your feet
May our every song be a symphony
May our every praise honor Your victory*

**May all thanks, now be to God
May all praise, be to His holy name
May all thanks, now be to our Lord
May all thanks, now be to God**

Lord Your mercy is what we pray for
Lord Your wisdom is what we all need

Philippians 1:3-6

*I thank my God upon every remembrance of you, always
in every prayer of mine making request for you all with joy,
for your fellowship in the gospel from the first day until now,
being confident of this very thing, that He Who has begun a
good work in you will complete it until the day of Jesus Christ.*

Make Your Way

Make your way to His cross
There you'll find you're no longer lost

Make your way to His throne
There you'll find you are finally home

**And let your soul sing, let your heart heal
Let your life live, let your faith feel
Oh make your way, oh make your way**

Make your way to His feet
There you'll know sweet victory

Make your way to His side
There you'll know His love as your guide

**And let your soul sing, let your heart heal
Let your life live, let your faith feel
Oh make your way, oh make your way**

***You kept your distance, which kept us apart
Now you are drawing near, now you are reaching out***

**So let your soul sing, let your heart heal
Let your life live, let your faith feel
Oh make your way, oh make your way
Make Your way, to His cross**

Luke 9:23

*Then He said to them all, "If anyone desires to come after Me,
let him deny himself and take up his cross daily and follow Me.*

Lord Thank You For Your Son

Beautiful Jesus, wonderful Lord
Our merciful Savior, a faithful Friend

Amazing Jesus, everlasting Lord
Our forgiving Savior, a loving Friend

**Lord thank You for Your Son
My Living Hope, my Holy One
Lord thank You for Your Son
My Gift of Grace, my Kingdom Come
Lord thank You for Your Son**

*For His life and for His death
For His birth and for His every breath
All He has done, for all He will do
All for me and all for you, all for you*

Victorious Jesus, gracious Lord
Our wondrous Savior, a precious Friend

**Lord thank You for Your Son
My Living Hope, my Holy One
Lord thank You for Your Son
My Gift of Grace, my Kingdom Come
Lord thank You for Your Son
Lord thank You for Your Son**

Genesis 31:44

*Now therefore come thou, let us make a covenant, you
and I and let it be a witness between you and Me.*

There's A Power

There's a power that will heal your broken heart
That will save your wounded soul, there's a power
There's a power that will open up your eyes to see
That will have your doubt believe, there's a power

**For the very same power that is working in your life
That raised Jesus up from the grave
For the very same power that is your guiding light
For He is so mighty to save
He is so worthy of our praise**

There's a power that will forgive your every sin
That will have your life now begin, there's a power

There's a power that now leads you by the hand
That will lift you up where you stand, there's a power

***And He is leading us on, He is leading us home
For He is so mighty to save
And He is leading us on, He is leading us home
For He is so worthy of our praise
He is so worthy of our praise***

**For the very same power that is working in your life
That raised Jesus up from the grave
For the very same power that is your guiding light
For He is so mighty to save
He is so worthy of our praise**

Colossians 1:16

*For by Him were all things created, that are in Heaven
and that are in earth, visible and invisible, whether they
be thrones, or dominions, or principalities, or powers, all
things were created by Him and for Him.*

Here With Me

There's a peace waiting on the other side
There's a river flowing strong and wide

For there's no need for you to weep
For her heart is in My keep

For there's a peace waiting on the other side
Yes there's a peace waiting on the other side

If it were not so I would have let you know
For where I go, there you will also be
Here I wait for you, My love's forever true
For where I am, there you will also be
Here with Me

There's a love waiting on that further shore
And there's a joy everlasting and forevermore

Here My arms are open wide
All to welcome her inside

For there's a love waiting on that further shore
Yes there's a love waiting on that further shore

If it were not so I would have let you know
For where I go, there you will also be
Here I wait for you, My love's forever true
For where I am, there you will also be
Here with Me

There's a peace waiting on the other side

1 Corinthians 2:9

But as it is written, eye hath not seen, nor ear heard,
neither have entered into the heart of man, the things
which God hath prepared or them that love Him.

—321—

In Less Than A Heartbeat

In less than a heartbeat, I would not do the things I do
I would with all my strength
Lord I would rise up and follow You

In less than a heartbeat, I would not say the things I say
I would with all my faith
Lord I would kneel down, love and pray

**For in less than a heartbeat
I would change who I am
In less than a heartbeat
I would change all I've done
In less than a heartbeat
I would stop running away
For in less than a heartbeat
I would change my broken life today**

*Lord I am who You say I am
A broken but I'm a healing man
Lord I am who You say I'll be
A sinful but I'm a forgiven soul set free*

**For in less than a heartbeat
I would change who I am
In less than a heartbeat
I would change all I've done
In less than a heartbeat
I would stop running away
For in less than a heartbeat
I would change my broken life today**

In less than a heartbeat

In less than a heartbeat, I would not do the things I do

Jeremiah 17:10

*I, the Lord, search the heart, I test the mind, even
to give every man according to his ways,
according to the fruit of his doings.*

Now Be Forgiven

Lord do You understand, everything I'm going through?
Lord do You understand?
Lord will You forgive me, for everything I've put You through?
For everything I put You through, will You forgive me?

**My child it's true that you have sinned
My child open up your heart
Let your life begin and be born again
Now be forgiven in Me, now be forgiven and be free**

Lord can You see me here, everything I'm gonna do?
Lord can You see me here?
Lord can you believe me, everything I'll say to You?
Everything I say to You, can You believe me?

**My child it's true that you have sinned
My child open up your heart
Let your life begin and be born again
Now be forgiven in Me
Now be forgiven and be free**

*So that when you fall
Know that I'll lift your heart, I'll lift your heart
So that when you call
I'll hear you right where you are, right where you are*

Lord do You understand, everything I'm going through?
Lord do You understand?

Acts 8:22

*Repent therefore of this your wickedness and pray God if
perhaps the thought of your heart may be forgiven you.*

November 8TH

There's A Place

For the sinners and for the believers
There's a grace, oh there's a grace
For the wanderers and seekers

For the fallen and for the survivors
There's a grace, oh there's a grace
For the victors and for the vanquished
There's a place, oh there's a place

For there's a home for your heart
There's a song for your soul
There's a place for you to rest
Where your life it will be blessed
There's a place, oh there's a place

For the promised and for the redeemed
There's a grace, oh there's a grace
For the weary and for the traveler

There's a place, oh there's a place
For the chosen and the set free
There's a grace, oh there's a place
For the forgiven and the abandoned
There's a place, oh there's a place
Home, where you'll never again be alone
Home, where you'll always be His very own

For there's a home for your heart
There's a song for your soul
There's a place for you to rest
Where your life it will be blessed
There's a place, oh there's a place

Psalm 119:10-11

With my whole heart I have sought You, oh, let me not wander
from Your commandments! Your word I have hidden in my heart,
that I might not sin against You.

I Thank You Lord

I thank You Lord for the life of Your Son
For all that You have done

I thank You Lord for the price that You paid
For Your sacrifice made

I thank You Lord for the light of Your love
For all of Heaven above

For Your blood that was shed
For Your love that rain red
For Your death on the cross
For all Your pain and Your loss
I thank You Lord, hallelujah!
I thank You Lord, amen

I thank You Lord for the power of prayer
For You are always there

I thank You Lord for Your gift of Your grace
For Your salvation and strength

I am here to thank You Lord, for Your battle won
I am here to thank You Lord, Father, Spirit, Son
Thank You for Your mercy for me, for the glory I see
Thank You for Your mercy for me
For Your glory of what my heart now seeks

From what was my death, now will be my life
From what was my depth, now will be my height
From what was my loss, now will be my gain
From what was my past
Now I will be in Your Heavenly reign!

Lord I thank You, I thank You Lord!

Colossians 3:17

And whatever you do in word or deed, do all in the name of
the Lord Jesus, giving thanks to God the Father through Him.

Lord I Need You Near

Lord I need to keep on praying
On my knees to keep on staying
My eyes need to keep on lifting all to Your cross

Lord I need to keep on hoping
In Your word to keep on trusting
My soul needs to keep on singing all to Your cross

**Lord I need You near, now more than ever Lord
I need You here, now and forever Lord
I need You near, to be always together
Lord I need You here**

Lord I need to keep on believing
By Your side to keep on walking
My heart needs to for on loving, all for Your cross

Lord I need to keep on searching
My arms to keep on holding
My life needs to keep on living, all for Your cross

*Lord I don't want to be separated any longer
Lord I want to be in Your love to be made stronger
Lord I don't want to be separated any longer*

**Lord I need You near, now more than ever Lord
I need You here, now and forever Lord
I need You near, to be always together
Lord I need You here**

Psalm 63:1-4

*O' God, You are my God, early will I seek You, my soul thirsts
for You, my flesh longs for You in dry and thirsty land where
there is no water. So I have looked for You in the sanctuary, to
see Your power and Your glory. Because Your lovingkindness is
better than life, my lips shall praise You. Thus I will bless You
while I live, I will lift up my hands in Your name.*

What Do You Hope?

Have you come here to be forgiven?
Have you come here to find salvation?
Oh tell me what do you expect to find

Have you come here in anticipation?
Have you come here for redemption?
Oh tell me what is now on your mind

What do you hope awaits you here?
The Lord He only wants to draw you near
What do you hope is now made clear?
The Lord He only wants to draw you near
To draw you near

Have you come here in a situation?
Have you come here for absolution?
Oh tell me what are you trying to hide?

Have you come here for negotiation?
Have you come here for conversation?
Oh tell me what can you say this time

For there is beauty in your brokenness
And there is healing in your hurting heart
For there is salvation in your suffering
And there is mercy in the moments
That we spend apart
So just open up your heart

So have you come here for resolution?
Have you come here for restoration?
Oh tell me what do you need to decide
What do you need to decide?

Ephesians 1:18

The eyes of your understanding being enlightened,
that you may know what is the hope of His calling, what
are the riches of the glory of His inheritance in the saints.

To You All Of The Glory

You want my life, want all my lies
You want my everything I will try to hide
You want my hurt, want all my love
You want my every breath I will ever breathe

You want all of me, all that I will ever be
All to give to You, all the of glory
You want all I have, all that I have ever had
All to give to You, to You all of the glory

You want my fear, want all my faith
You want my every prayer I will ever pray
You want my sin, want all my strength
You want my every dream I will ever dream

You want my very soul, everything I believe in
You want my very heart, everything to be forgiven
All to be forgiven

You want all of me, all that I will ever be
All to give to You, all the of glory
You want all I have, all that I have ever had
All to give to You, to You all of the glory

You want my doubt, want all of my days
You want my every tear I will ever cry
You want my time, want all my truth
You want my every chain
That has ever held me down

1 Timothy 1:17

Now to the King eternal, immortal, invisible, to God who alone is wise, be honor and glory forever and ever. Amen!

I Never Walked Alone

I never walked alone
Through the valley, or through the storm
You were there all along
In every step, as I traveled on
I never walked alone

No I never walked alone
Climbing my mountains, or finding my home
Yes You were there all along
In every mile, as I wandered around
I never walked alone

Whether You were holding my hand
When my hands they were shaking
Whether You were holding my heart
When my hopes they were fading
I never walked alone

I never walk alone
Whether through my hurt, or my victory's won
Yes You are here all along
In every step, as I travel on
I never walk alone

Matthew 5:1-10

And seeing the multitudes, He went up on a mountain and when He was seated His disciples came to Him. Then He opened His mouth and taught them, saying, "Blessed are the poor in spirit, for theirs is the Kingdom of Heaven. Blessed are those who mourn, for they shall be comforted. Blessed are the meek, for they shall inherit the earth. Blessed are those who hunger and thirst for righteousness, for they shall be filled. Blessed are the merciful, for they shall obtain mercy.

Blessed are the pure in heart, for they shall see God. Blessed are the peacemakers, for they shall be called sons of God. Blessed are those who are persecuted for righteousness sake, for theirs is the Kingdom of Heaven.

We Will All Be Made New

One day there'll be no more tears
Nothing more to cry about
One day there'll be no more fears
Nothing more to be afraid of

For all things will pass away
For all things will be made new
For all things will be forever changed
And on that glorious day, we will all be made new

One day there'll be no more pain
Nothing more will hurt again
One day there'll be no more blame
Nothing more will ever end

For in the blink of an eye, with a trumpet sound
For in the beat of a heart, bursting through the clouds
Jesus will come, Jesus will come
Oh my Lord let it be done

One day there'll be no more death
Nothing more but life will be left
One day there'll be no more doubt
Nothing more but faith will you ever shout

For all things will pass away
For all things will be made new
For all things will be forever changed
And on that glorious day, we will all be made new

One day there'll be no more lies
Nothing more but the truth will ever be heard

Revelation 21:5

Then He Who sat on the throne said, "Behold, I make all things new." And He said to me, "Write, for these words are true and faithful."

Now That I Am Here

When the darkness, seems the darkest
Lord it's then You shine Your light

When my weakness, seems the weakest
Lord it's then You show Your might

**And You pick me up, off of the ground
And You hold me close to Your side
And You whisper so softly to me at first
Then You tell me that it's all right
You tell me that it's all right
Now that I am here, now that I am here**

*I've never known such love
Such love as You have shown
I've never known such forgiveness
I've never felt such grace
Such grace as You have shown*

When the darkness, seems the darkest
Lord it's then You shine Your light

**And You pick me up, off of the ground
And You hold me close to Your side
And You whisper so softly to me at first
Then You tell me that it's all right
You tell me that it's all right
Now that I am here, now that I am here**

Ephesians 2:4-5

*But God, Who is rich in mercy, because of His great love with
which He loved us, even when we were dead in trespasses,
made us alive together with Christ (by grace you
have been saved.)*

So How Can I Ever Thank You

Only by Your sacrifice
Do I live, do I breathe
Only by Your surrender
I'm alive, Lord I'm alive!

So how can I ever thank You
For all You've done for me
How You've set me free
So how can I ever show You
The way my soul believes
How You've opened my eyes to see
My eyes to see

Only by Your suffering
Can I now sing, can I now praise
Only by Your salvation
I'm alive, yes I'm alive!

So how can I ever thank You
For all You've done for me
How You've set me free
So how can I ever show You
The way my soul believes
How You've opened my eyes to see
My eyes to see

Only by Your sacrifice
Do I live, do I breathe

Colossians 4:2

Continue earnestly in prayer, being vigilant
in it with thanksgiving.

The First Step

There is a Savior, reaching out His arms
There is a Savior, Who's calling you home

There is a Savior, hoping that you come
There is a Savior, Jesus our Holy One

**Just take the first step and believe
And look into the eyes of Love
Open up your heart and you will see
All the glory Jesus is speaking of
So take that first step**

There is a Savior, so ready to forgive
There is a Savior, whispering your name

There is a Savior, Who's inviting you in
There is a Savior, Who bore all your blame

**Just take the first step and believe
And look into the eyes of Love
Open up your heart and you will see
All the glory Jesus is speaking of
So take that first step**

There is a Savior, reaching out His arms
There is a Savior, Who's calling you home

Psalm 37:23

*The steps of a good man are ordered by
the Lord and He delights in his way.*

God Be Merciful

God be merciful, God be merciful to me
For my soul it trusts in You
Under the shadow of Your wings
God be merciful, God be merciful to me

**And I will cry out to God most high
Yes I will cry out to God most high
I will cry out to God most high
Oh God be merciful, oh God be merciful
Be merciful to me**

God be merciful, God be merciful to me
For my soul it rests in You
Until You set this soul free
God be merciful, God be merciful to me

**And I will cry out to God most high
Yes I will cry out to God most high
I will cry out to God most high
Oh God be merciful, oh God be merciful
Be merciful to me**

God be merciful, God be merciful to me
For my soul it waits for You
Until Your hands calm the sea
God be merciful, God be merciful to me

**Oh God be merciful, oh God be merciful
Be merciful to me**

Deuteronomy 4:31

*(For the Lord your God is a merciful God), He will
not forsake you nor destroy you, nor forget the
covenant of your fathers which He swore to them*

Lord I Pray That We Pray

Lord I pray that we pray, in every moment we're alive
In every moment we survive

Lord I pray that we pray, in every moment of the ride
In every moment of our lives

**For it is only in prayer that you will get through
For it is only in prayer that you will hear all His truth**

Lord I pray that we pray, in every moment we're around
In every moment we're feeling down

Lord I pray that we pray, in every moment we're in pain
In every moment we remain

**For only upon your knees is only when you'll see
His love, His hope, His grace, His forgiveness and strength**

So I pray that we pray, for the ones that we love
All to Heaven above

I pray that we pray, for the strength that we need
For the faith that we seek

*When we are searching, when we are hurting
When we are joyful, when we are sorrowful
Lord I pray that we pray*

I pray that we pray, for the truth that we need
For all our hurt to heal

*If you want answers to all the questions that you have,
and if you want to know all of what God has planned
for your life, then lift up everything in prayer!
You need to lay down all that you are!*

Matthew 26:41

*Watch and pray, lest you enter into temptation.
the spirit indeed is willing, but the flesh is weak.*

Lord I Lay Down

Lord I lay down all I was
Lord I lay down all that I'll be
Lord I lay down all I've been
Lord I lay down all that You see

**For only You know just who I am
Here so deep inside
For only You know the depths of my soul
And all the sin I try to hide**

Lord I lay down all I own
Lord I lay down all of my heart
Lord I lay down all I love
Lord I lay down to all You are

Lord I lay down all my hurt
Lord I lay down all of my life
Lord I lay down all my tears
Lord I lay down all of my lies

***Oh Lord this is my offering
For only You Lord
Gave to me Your everything
Oh Lord this is my offering
Lord I thank You for all Your suffering
Oh Lord this is my offering***

**For only You know just who I am
Here so deep inside
For only You know the depths of my soul
And all the sin I try to hide**

Ephesians 6:18

*Praying always with all prayer and supplication
in the Spirit, being watchful to this end with all
perseverance and supplication for all the saints.*

There's A Still Small Voice

In the quiet of a moment
In the silence of a prayer
In the light of the dawn
In the falling of one tear

There's a still small voice
And it's whispering

In the cry of a child
In the faith of one last plea
In the first breath of the wind
In the hope of you and me

There's a still small voice
And it's whispering

It's in all of the thoughts
That now lie in between
In that falling of just one tear
In all of the hurt that remains unseen
In every moment
That we try to hold so dear

In the quiet of a moment
In the silence of a prayer
In the light of the dawn
In the falling of one tear

There's a still small voice
And it's whispering

1 Kings 19:12

And after the earthquake a fire, but the Lord was
not in the fire and after the fire a still small voice.

The Love Of The Lord

There's enough in this world, that makes you cry
There's enough in this world, that makes you sad
To make you feel a little overwhelmed
To make you feel a little under pressure and mad

There's enough in this world, that breaks your heart
There's enough in this world, that tears you apart
To make you feel a little upset
To make you feel a little downhearted so far

For every step you've gone, He has led you here
For every battle won, He has made it so clear
That the love of the Lord draws you near

But don't let it get you down
Don't let it keep you pinned to the ground
Take this chance to stand tall
Take this chance to rise above it all, it all
And to know His hope within your heart
To sing His song within your soul
This is all He wants you to do
That in Your trials He leads you through
So let the love of the Lord lead you through

For there's enough in this world, that makes you cry

Psalm 91:2

I will say of the Lord, "He is my Refuge and
my Fortress, my God, in Him I will trust."

All Jesus Did For Me

He died, so my life may know life
He cried, so my heart may feel joy
He came, so my soul may have a home
He prayed, so my prayers may be His own

All Jesus did for me, He can do for you
All Jesus did for me, He will do for you
So lay down all of your doubt
And lift up your very life
All Jesus did for me, He will do for you

He fell, so in death I would rise again
He knelt, so I'd see a world without end
He bled, so my wounds would one day heal
He led, so my feet may follow His lead

With every step that He walked
With every tear that He shed
Washed away your every sin
As far from the east is to the west
And He will forgive, He will forget
He will forgive, He will forget

All Jesus did for me, He can do for you
All Jesus did for me, He will do for you
So lay down all of your doubt
And lift up your very life
All Jesus did for me, He will do for you

John 3:17

For God did not send His Son into the world to condemn
the world, but that the world through Him might be saved.

Heaven

Each and every move we make
We're a little bit closer here along the way, to Heaven

Each and every day we spend
We're a little bit closer to the end, to Heaven
We're just a prayer away

**And on that glorious day, when I close my eyes I pray
When my eyes are opened wide, I'll see You and I'll cry
And on that glorious day, I just want to hear You say
"Well done My little child and welcome, to Heaven!"**

Each and every tear we cry
Will be wiped away, all will be dried in Heaven

Each and every sin we sin
Will all be forgotten, all will be forgiven in Heaven
We're just a prayer away

*And all of the angels, they will gather around His throne
And a choir of all the angels, they will welcome us home*

**And on that glorious day, when I close my eyes I pray
When my eyes are opened wide, I'll see You and I'll cry
And on that glorious day, I just want to hear You say
"Well done My little child and welcome to, Heaven!"**

Each and every move we make
We're a little bit closer here along the way, to Heaven
We're just a prayer away

1 John 3:2-3

*Beloved, now we are children of God and it has not yet been
revealed what we shall be, but we know that when He is revealed,
we shall be like Him, for we shall see Him as He is. And everyone
who has this hope in Him purifies himself, just as He is pure.*

Only Your Perfect Love

Save me my Lord, save me by Your grace
Hear my prayers, 'O my God, save me my Lord
Save me my Lord

Teach me my Lord, teach me in Your truth
Hear my lies, 'O my God, teach me my Lord
Teach me my Lord

For only Your perfect love, can ever save my soul
For only Your perfect love, can ever heal my heart
Can be my light in my darkness
My strength in my weakness
Only Your perfect love

Heal me my Lord, heal me with Your love
Hear my cry, 'O my God, heal me my Lord
Heal me my Lord

For no longer do I cry, without any hope
For no longer am I lost, without a home
For no longer do I pray, without any faith
For no longer do I just believe, I am no longer afraid

Guide me my Lord, guide me by Your hand
Hear my plea, 'O my God, guide me my Lord
Guide me my Lord

For only Your perfect love, can ever save my soul
For only Your perfect love, can ever heal my heart
Can be my light in my darkness
My strength in my weakness
Only Your perfect love

1 John 4:18

There is no fear in love, but perfect love casts out
fear, because fear involves torment. But he who
fears has not been made perfect in love.

My Beloved Child

My beloved child
Let Me hold you in My arms
Take you here beneath My wings
And keep you safe from all harm

My beloved child
Let Me take you far from here
May My love surround you now
And always draw you near
My beloved child

Let Me heal your hurting heart
Let Me sing to your lost soul
Let Me lead your broken life
So that you may always know
Let Me hold your trembling hands
Let Me guide you as you go
Let Me find your wandering faith
So that you may always know

That I love you more
That I listen to your every breath
That I will always keep you close
In every day that you have left
Oh My beloved child
My beloved child

My beloved child
Let Me hold you in My arms
Take you here beneath My wings
And keep you safe from all harm
My beloved child
Let Me hold you in My arms

1 John 3:1

Behold what manner of love the Father has bestowed on us, that we should be called children of God! Therefore the world does not know us, because it did not know Him.

My Thanksgiving

For my Savior and for Your love
For the peace that's in my soul
My Lord You alone are my Thanksgiving

For my prayers and for Your light
For the love that's in my life
My Lord You alone are my Thanksgiving

For the faith that's in my heart
For the truth that You are
Oh my Lord, my Lord
You're my Thanksgiving

For my mercy and for Your grace
For the joy that's in my praise
My Lord You alone are my Thanksgiving

For my faith and for Your strength
For the power that's in Your name
My Lord You alone are my Thanksgiving

For the faith that's in my heart
For the truth that You are
Oh my Lord, my Lord
You're my Thanksgiving
Oh my Lord, my Lord
You're my Thanksgiving

Colossians 3:15

And let the peace of God rule in your hearts, to which
also you were called in one body and be thankful.

For No One Else

For I am rescued, by my Rescuer
For I am healed by my Healer
For I am redeemed by my Redeemer
For I am saved by my Savior

**For no one else, no other name
Holds my heart, Who loves me the same
For no one else, no one I know
Sings to my soul, so let the blessings flow**

For I am restored by my Restorer
For I am delivered by my Deliverer
For I am forgiven by my Forgiver
For I am comforted by my Comforter

*For I will be forever lifted up
I will be forever made free
For I will be forever set apart
I will be forever made whole
By Your mercy, by Your mercy*

**For no one else, no other name
Holds my heart, Who loves me the same
For no one else, no one I know
Sings to my soul, so let the blessings flow**

For I am rescued by my Rescuer
For I am healed by my Healer
For I am redeemed by my Redeemer
For I am saved by my Savior

Isaiah 43:1

*But now, thus says the Lord, Who created you, O' Jacob,
and He Who formed you, O' Israel, "Fear not, for
I have redeemed you, I have called you
by your name, you are Mine.*

Lord I Need To Pray More

Lord I need to pray more, to be found upon my knees
Lord I need to come before
Your cross and fall down at Your feet

I need to have the words to say
Change my life in every way
Lord I need, Lord I need, to pray more

Lord I need to pray more, to pour out all of my heart
Lord I need to make sure
That my prayers are just the start

For there is no mountain that I cannot climb
Without Your strength aiding me from behind
For there is no ocean that I cannot cross
For without Your strength
I would be so lost, so very lost

Lord I need to pray more, to be found upon my knees
Lord I need to come before
Your cross and fall down at Your feet

I need to have the words to say
Change my life in every way
Lord I need, Lord I need, to pray more

Prayer is an overflowing fountain of praise, adoration and
thanksgiving to God. This kind of prayer erupts without
hesitation from the soul. One does not have to make
oneself do it, for it comes .as naturally as breathing
By Gilbert W. Stafford

Romans 1:9

For God is my witness, Whom I serve with my spirit in
the Gospel of His Son, that without ceasing I make
mention of You always in my prayers.

November 30TH

I Pray So

If I could have just one more word to say to You
What would it be? What would it be?

If I could pray just one more prayer and kneel with You
What would it be? What would it be?

Would I fall down to my knees?
Would I lift up all of my hopes on high?
Would I stand in praise and lift up my teary eyes?
I pray so, I pray so

I will know one day in glory, all that God has planned
I will know what His story was for you, what it was for me
For both you and I, for only then will we understand
I pray so, I pray so

If I had just one song I could sing with You
What would it be? What would it be?

If I could have just one more word to say to You
What would it be? What would it be?

Would I fall down to my knees?
Would I lift up all of my loves on high?
Would I stand in praise and lift up my teary eyes?
I pray so, I pray so

I John 5:14-15

Now this is the confidence that we have in Him, that if
we ask anything according to His will, He hears us. And
if we know that He hears us, whatever we ask, we know
that we have the petitions that we have asked of Him.

December

LOVE CAME DOWN

Love Came Down

Love came down, from Heaven above
Love came down, as a gift of His love
Love came down, to the earth below
Love came down, so all the world it may know

**Know Christ the Lord, Christ the King
The Lord of all and our Everything**

Love came down, to Bethlehem
Love came down, as the Savior to all men
Love came down, in a manger to lay
Love came down, born to light the way

**It was Christ the Lord, Christ the King
The Lord of all and our Everything**

Love came down, to change your heart
Love came down, just to where you are
Love came down, to save your soul
Love came down, so that you may know

**Know Christ the Lord, Christ the King
The Lord of all and our Everything
Love came down**

Psalm 96:11-13

*Let the Heavens rejoice and let the earth be glad, let the sea
roar and all its fullness, let the field be joyful and all that is in it.
Then all the trees of the woods will rejoice before the Lord. For
He is coming, for He is coming to judge the earth. He shall judge
the world with righteousness and the peoples with His truth.*

The Bells Of Heaven

Hear the bells of Heaven ring
Hear the choir of the angels sing
All glory to the Newborn King
Glory to the Lord

See the Child in a manger lay
See Love born this very day
All glory now to come His way
Glory to the Lord

**Lord I will praise and worship You
Lord I will praise and worship You, my Lord**

Angels sing as the shepherds draw near
Angels sing as the wise men gather there
All glory now as angels appear
Glory to the Lord

**Lord I will praise and worship You
Lord I will praise and worship You, my Lord**

A world awakens as our Savior is born
A world awakens, as a new day it dawns
All glory now for our King He has come
Glory to the Lord

Luke 2:12

*And this will be the sign to you will find a Babe
wrapped in swaddling cloths, lying in a manger.*

A Son Is Given

For He will be called Wonderful, Counselor, Mighty God
Our Everlasting Father, our Prince of Peace
For He will be called Faithful, Majesty, Mighty God
Our Emmanuel, our King of kings

For He will be called Beautiful, Deliverer, Mighty God
Our Amazing Grace, our Hosts of Hosts
For He will be called Merciful, Glorious, Mighty God
Our Everything, our All in All

**For unto us a Child is born, for unto us a Son is given
To every nation under God
To every nation under Heaven, a Son is given**

For He will be called Messiah, Redeemer, Mighty God
Our Beginning, our Lord of lords
For He will be called Beloved, Savior, Mighty God
Our Morning Star, our Gift of God

**For unto us a Child is born, for unto us a Son is given
To every nation under God
To every nation under Heaven, a Son is given**

For He will be called Wonderful, Counselor, Mighty God
Our Everlasting Father, our Prince of Peace

Isaiah 9:6-7

*For unto us a Child is born, unto us a Son is given and the
government will be upon His shoulder. And His name will be
called Wonderful, Counselor, Mighty God, Everlasting Father,
Prince of Peace. Of the increase of His government and
peace there will be no end, upon the throne of David and
over His Kingdom, to order it and establish it with judgment
and justice from that time forward, even forever. The zeal of
the Lord of hosts will perform this.*

Angels Gathered

It was a night, a night of glory
The night the Christ Child was born
It was a night, a night so holy
The night our Savior had come

**And when the angels gathered
To declare the birth of the Lord
They all sang hallelujah
They all sang "Glory to the Lord"**

It was a night, a night of worship
The night shepherds they came
It was a night, a night of rejoicing
The night in a manger He lay

**And when the angels gathered
To declare the birth of the Lord
They all sang hallelujah
They all sang "Glory to the Lord"**

*And all of creation
They all sang in perfect harmony
And all of the nations
They all sang a perfect melody*

It was a night, a night of celebration
The night the King of kings appeared
It was a night, a night of wonder
The night our God drew us near

Luke 2:13-14

*And suddenly there was with the angel a multitude
of the Heavenly host praising God and saying,
"Glory to God in the highest and on earth peace,
goodwill toward men!"*

December 5TH

It's Christmas All Around

Well it looks like another white Christmas
And the manger scene just opened downtown

And the church bells they are ringing
And the church choirs they are singing
And it looks like it's Christmas all around

Well the first snow of the season has now fallen
And all the joy lost all the year's been found

And the children they are wishing
And our loved ones we are missing
And it looks like it's Christmas all around

All for this little Child born in Bethlehem
For He was sent to be the Savior to all men
For this little Child was given from Heaven above
He was born to be the Gift of the Fathers love

Well it looks like another Christmas morning
And all the presents lie so scattered up and down

And everyone is reminiscing
For this day is such a blessing
And it looks like it's Christmas all around
Yes it looks like it's Christmas all around

It's so true that Christmas time can be so busy, but know that this is not the reason for the season, Jesus is the reason for the season. So, this year how about we all find that reason, let's find that meaning in all we do. Make this the year, more than ever, let's find it before the season is gone. Let us all find the meaning of it all, Jesus!

*So no matter where we are, no matter what we do, let's tell loved ones, lost friends or maybe even a stranger on the street that **JESUS REALLY LOVES THEM!** Why? Because He really does! Let us all make sure that they know this, it just may be the very first time that they've **EVER** heard these words. Imagine that! It may be the perfect words to warm their heart and possibly save their soul!*

— 352 —

Mercy And Peace

Some may say Merry Christmas
And they pray now to the Savior
Some may hope now for a miracle
Some may know His love like no other

Some they speak of the joy of the season
Some they sing from so deep in their soul
Some they seek to now find the reason
Some they bring gifts before His throne

So come find your hope, come find your grace
Come find forgiveness, mercy and peace
Come find your love, come find your joy
Come find salvation, mercy and peace
Mercy and peace

For He's lying in a manger low
A Heavenly light shines to the earth below
For He is crying for all the world to see
So that the world might too believe

So come find your hope, come find your grace
Come find forgiveness, mercy and peace
Come find your love, come find your joy
Come find salvation, mercy and peace
Mercy and peace

Some may say Merry Christmas
And they pray now to the Savior
Some may love now for a miracle

Some may know His love like no other

Matthew 1:20-21

But while he thought about these things, behold, an angel of the Lord appeared to him in a dream, saying, "Joseph, son of David, do not be afraid to take to you Mary your wife, for that which is conceived in her is of the Holy Spirit. And she will bring forth a Son and you shall call His name Jesus, for He will save His people from their sins.

December 7TH

Christmas 'Morn

Lord may all of Your people, may all of Your children now sing
May they sing of their worship
And their praise for this Newborn King

Lord may all of creation, may all of Heaven now sing
May they sing of Your glory
And the hope that this small Child brings

So praise the Lord, so praise His holy name
So praise the night, the night which He came
So praise the Child and the manger where He was laid
So praise the Lord, so praise the Lord
On this Christmas 'Morn!

Lord may all of the Nations, may all Your faithful now sing
May they sing "Lord You are worthy!"
And of every gift that we now bring

So praise the Lord, so praise His holy name
So praise the night, the night which He came
So praise the Child and the manger where He was laid
So praise the Lord, so praise the Lord
On this Christmas 'Morn!

The morning's sun it has now risen
As a sleeping world now awakes
For Love has come to all the earth
For Love has come to all the world
Love He has come, Grace He is here

Love has arrived, now draw now to His side

On this Christmas 'Morn

Luke 1:30-31

Then the angel said to her, "Do not be afraid, Mary, for you have found favor with God. And behold, you will conceive in your womb and bring forth a Son and shall call His name Jesus

So Happy Christmas

Lord we pray for peace on earth
We give thanks for our Saviors birth, our Saviors birth
Lord we pray for all mankind
That Your grace that each may find, that each may find

So happy Christmas everyone
So happy Christmas one and all, one and all

Lord we pray for the life to come
We lift our praise to the Promised One, to the Promised One
Lord we pray for every soul
That Your love that each may know, that each may know

So happy Christmas everyone
So happy Christmas one and all, one and all

So may the light of our God, surround you now
So may His love, His love now fill your soul
So may the light of our Lord, find you where you are
May His love, His grace now hold your heart

So happy Christmas everyone
So happy Christmas one and all, one and all

Lord we pray for peace on earth
We give thanks for our Saviors birth, for our Saviors birth

2 Corinthians 9:14-15

And by their prayer for you, who long for you because
of the exceeding grace of God in you. Thanks be to
God for His indescribable gift!

December 9TH

All Because Of Christmas

You have peace, you have love
You have angels, singing from above
You have hope, you have a star
You have wise men, traveling from afar

You have grace, you have a promise kept
You have shepherds
Watching from where they slept
You have a light, now shining down

You have a Father's love
And it's here all around, it's here all around

All because of Christmas
All because of this small Child
All because of Jesus Christ
All because of His new life
Born this very night
All because of Christmas
On a night like no other night
A holy light like no other light
A star its shines, yes a star it shines
A Child born like no other child
A Love like no other love
And a star it shines, yes a star shines

You have peace, you have love
You have angels, singing from above

All because of Christmas

Colossians 1:15-18

He is the image of the invisible God, the Firstborn over all creation
For by Him all things were created that are in Heaven and that are
on earth, visible and invisible, whether thrones or dominions or
principalities or powers. All things were created through Him and
for Him. And He is before all things and in Him all things consist.
And He is the head of the body, the church, Who is the beginning,
the Firstborn from the dead, that in all things He may
have the preeminence.

Oh My Little Child

Oh my little child, I'll dry your every tear
I'll calm your every fear, whenever you're afraid

Oh my little child, I'll hold your trembling hand
I'll help you to understand, whenever you feel betrayed

**Know that I am here
When you close your eyes to pray
When you lift up love this day
With you I'll always stay**

Oh my little child, I'll hear your every prayer
I'll always draw you near, whenever you leave My side

Oh my little child, I'll show you the way home
I'll never leave you alone, though you want to run and hide

**Know that I am here
When you close your eyes to pray
When you lift up love this day
With you I'll always stay
Know that I am here
When you reach out your arms to hold
When you lay down your very soul
You will hear My Heavenly song**

*And I will sing, I'll sing just for you
Yes I will sing, so you will always know the truth
Yes I will sing, come rain or shine
Know I'm forever yours, know your forever Mine*

Oh my little child, I'll dry your every tear
I'll calm your every fear, whenever you're afraid

Matthew 18:4-5

Therefore whoever humbles himself as this little child is the greatest in the Kingdom of Heaven. Whoever receives one little child like this in My name receives Me.

Christmas Is Here

The snow is now falling
And loved ones are now calling
For Christmas is here, at this time of the year
The choir is now singing
And our gifts we are now bringing
For Christmas is here, at this time of the year

The wreath we've placed on our front door
The tree is standing like all the years before
The holly is hung upon our fireplace
So many smiles on everyone's face

The church is now filling
And the candles are now glowing
For Christmas is here, at this time of the year

The wreath we've placed on our front door
The tree is standing like all the years before
The holly is hung upon our fireplace
So many smiles on everyone's face

For the faithful are praying
And such faithful words they're all saying
For Christmas is here, for Christmas is here
At this time of the year
For Christmas is here, at this time of the year

Luke 2:20

And the shepherds returned, glorifying and
praising God for all the things that they had heard
and seen, as it was told unto them.

The Blessing That Is Christmas

The love of Christmas
It will heal your heart
The hope of Christmas
It will find you where you are

The grace of Christmas
It will have you follow a star
The light of Christmas
It will shine throughout the dark

**Such is the blessing that is Christmas
Such is the birth of our Lord Jesus Christ
Such is the blessing that is Christmas
Such is the gift of this Holy Child
Such is the blessing
The blessing that is Christmas**

*If you are alone
It will comfort your soul
If you are afraid
It will help you find, your way home
Your way back home*

**Such is the blessing that is Christmas
Such is the birth of our Lord Jesus Christ
Such is the blessing that is Christmas
Such is the gift of this Holy Child
Such is the blessing
The blessing that is Christmas**

1 John 5:11

*And this is the testimony, God has given
us eternal life and this life is in His Son.*

Upon This Holy Night

Upon this holy night, a Child for He is born
Born in Bethlehem, the Savior to all men

Upon this holy night, a King for He has come
Light to all the world and Hope to everyone

For God has given to us
The perfect gift of His precious Son
For God has shown to us
The depths of His love
The depths of His love

Upon this holy night, a world now sleeps in peace
Unaware of the love this sleeping Child now brings

Upon this holy night, a Star in the sky now shines
Leading every soul to Salvation's great design

For God He has given to us
The gift of His precious Son
For God He has shown to us
The depths of His love
The depths of His love

Upon this holy night, a Child for He is born
Born in Bethlehem, the Savior to all men

Luke 2:15-19

*So it was, when the angels had gone away from them into
Heaven, that the shepherds said to one another, "Let us now go
to Bethlehem and see this thing that has come to pass, which
the Lord has made known to us." And they came with haste and
found Mary and Joseph and the Babe lying in a manger. Now
when they had seen Him, they made widely known the saying
which was told them concerning this Child. And all those who
heard it marveled at those things which were told them by the
shepherds. But Mary kept all these things and pondered them
in her heart.*

Maybe It's Christmas Out There

Maybe it's the new-fallen snow lying upon the ground
Or maybe it's the gifts placed under the tree that I've found
Or maybe it's the bells ringing in the little church downtown
Maybe it's that time of year, maybe it's Christmas out there

Maybe it's Santa there waving at the Old Wilson's Store
Or maybe it's the brand new wreath hanging on my front door
Or maybe it's that everyone now seems to care just a little more
Maybe it's that time of year, maybe it's Christmas out there

There's just no other feeling
Than when the Spirit comes alive
There's just no better feeling
Than when you feel His love inside
Maybe it's that time of year
Maybe it's Christmas out there

Maybe it's the manger scene placed under main streets lights
Or maybe it's the church choir singing all their praise tonight
Or maybe it's the Salvation Army Band playing "Silent Night"
Maybe it's that time of year, maybe it's Christmas out there

There's just no other feeling
Than when the Spirit comes alive
There's just no better feeling
Than when you feel His love inside
Maybe it's that time of year
Maybe it's Christmas out there

Maybe it's that time of year, maybe it's Christmas out there

Philippians 4:4

Rejoice in the Lord always, again I will say, rejoice.

All Because of Christmas

You have peace, you have love
You have angels, singing from above
You have hope, you have a star
You have wise men, traveling from afar
All because of Christmas
You have grace, you have a promise kept
You have shepherds
Watching from where they slept

You have a light, now shining down
You have a Father's love
And it's here all around, it's here all around
All because of Christmas

All because of this small Child
All because of Jesus Christ
All because of His new life
Born this very night

All because ofcchristmas
On a night like no other night
A holy light like no other light
A star it shines, yes a star it shines

A Child born like no other child
A Love like no other Love
And a star it shines, yes a star shines
You have peace, you have love

You have angels, singing from above

Psalm 148:1-4

Praise the Lord! Praise the Lord from the Heavens, praise Him in the heights! Praise Him, all His angels, Praise Him, all His hosts! Praise Him, sun and moon, Praise Him, all you stars of light! Praise Him you Heavens of Heavens and you waters above the Heavens!

This Christmas Day

On this Christmas may we once again find the meaning
On this Christmas may we once again embrace the Reason
Of this Child born in Bethlehem
And why our God He chose to make a way
On this Christmas day

On this Christmas may we once again remember
On this Christmas may we once again worship our Savior
And share in the love of His Son
And why our God He chose His Gift of Grace
On this Christmas day

For this very Child, is the Man, Who will die for our sins
For this very Child, is the Man, Who will wear the scars
Of our forgiveness, of our forgiveness

So on this Christmas may we once again find the meaning
On this Christmas may we once again embrace the Reason
Of this Child born this day
And why our God He chose to make a way
On this, on this, Christmas day

Matthew 2:9-11

When they heard the king, they departed and behold, the star which they had seen in the East went before them, till it came and stood over where the young Child was. When they saw the star, they rejoiced with exceedingly great joy. And when they had come into the house, they saw the young Child with Mary His mother and fell down and worshiped Him. And when they had opened their treasures, they presented gifts to Him, gold, frankincense and myrrh.

Our Savior He Is Born

There's a Child lying in a manger
There is hope in every beat of His heart
There's a star shining in the darkness
There's a light streaming down from afar

There's a song being sung by angels
There is love in every breath that He breathes
There's a cry coming now from the faithful
There's a prayer rising from every soul from their knees

Glory, glory, glory hallelujah
For upon this night, our King He has come
Glory, glory, glory hallelujah
For tonight Jesus Christ, our Savior He is born

And all of the earth, all of the world now awakens
Without ever knowing, of the grace this Child will give
And all of the earth, all of the world has now awoken
Without ever knowing, of the life, this Child will live

Glory, glory, glory hallelujah
For upon this night, our King He has come
Glory, glory, glory hallelujah
For tonight Jesus Christ, for tonight Jesus Christ
Our Savior He is born

Luke 2:4-7

Joseph also went up from Galilee, out of the city of Nazareth,
into Judea, to the city of David, which is called Bethlehem, because
he was of the house and lineage of David, to be registered with Mary,
his betrothed wife, who was with Child.

So it was, that while they were there, the days were completed for her
to be delivered. And she brought forth her Firstborn Son and wrapped
Him in swaddling cloths and laid Him in a manger, because there was
no room for them in the inn.

Tonight

Tonight angels and shepherds, will all worship together
Tonight kings and paupers, will all bow down at His throne
Tonight saints and sinners, will all rejoice forever
Tonight the lost and the found, will all find their way home

**For He's the Light of the world
There'll be no more darkness
For He's the Hope to the earth
There'll be no more sadness**

*For He will sing with those who sing
He will pray with those who pray
For He will cry with those who cry
And kneel with those who kneel
And speak truth to those who seek truth
And pray prayers with those who will draw near
So come, so come*

**For He's the Light of the world
There'll be no more darkness
For He's the Hope to the earth
There'll be no more sadness**

**For He will sing with those who sing
He will pray with those who pray
For He will cry with those who cry
And kneel with those who kneel**

For He's the Light of the world!

Tonight angels and shepherds will, all worship together
Tonight kings and paupers, will all bow down at His throne
Tonight saints and sinners, will all rejoice forever

Luke 2:8-10

*Now there were in the same country shepherds living out in the
fields, keeping watch over their flock by night. And behold, an angel
of the Lord stood before them and the glory of the Lord shone around
them, and they were greatly afraid. Then the angel said to them,
"Do not be afraid, for behold, I bring you good tidings of great
joy, which will be to all people.*

December 19TH

The Love Of Christmas

Everyone needs to feel the love of Jesus
Everyone needs to feel that love inside
We all need to feel the love of Christmas
We all need the love of this beautiful Child

Why is it only at this time of year
That we hold this precious Child so dear?
Why isn't the answer now any more clear?
When all He longs for is to hold each of us near

Everyone wants to know the love of Jesus
Everyone wants to know that love inside
We all want to feel the love of Christmas
We all want the love of this wonderful Child

Why is it only at this time of year
That we hold this precious Child so dear?
Why isn't the answer now any more clear?
When all He longs for is to hold each of us near

His only desire is to be with us forever
His only prayer is to bring us all together
His only reason is to keep us all closer
His only purpose is to have us all be kinder to one another
Here in the love, here in the love of Christmas

Everyone seeks to find the love of Jesus
Everyone seeks to find that love inside
We all seek to find the love of Christmas
We all seek the love of this beautiful Child

2 Corinthians 5:14-15

For the love of Christ compels us, because we judge thus, that
if One died for all, then all died and He died for all, that those
who live should live no longer for themselves, but for Him Who
died for them and rose again.

On This Christmas Day

Lord if I had one wish, just one prayer
On this Christmas day
My Lord it would be for the world to join with me
All in one voice and to pray

And Lord to have Your love
Be the gift that we give
And to be our hope this day
Lord to have Your love
Be the life that we live
And to be our hope this day
This prayer Lord I pray
On this Christmas day

Lord now if the world
Could all just sing along
All in one choir, all now in one song
If we could all stand together
We could all now praise forever
We could walk hand in hand
All across this land
On this Christmas day

So Lord if I had one wish, yes just one prayer
On this Christmas day
My Lord it would be for the world to join with me
All in one voice and pray
On this Christmas day

Luke 1:14

And you will have joy and gladness
and many will rejoice at His birth.

I Will Pray A Prayer This Christmas

I will pray a prayer this Christmas
That love is what you may find
That once again you will place Jesus
Somewhere near the front of the line

Not to be just a thought
That you have once in a while
Not to be just a hope
That you use to make you smile
So I will pray, I will pray a prayer this Christmas

**For You simply cannot draw a line
And divide what divides one's heart
You simply cannot, not take the time
And not try to heal what has been broken apart
So I will pray, I will pray a prayer this Christmas**

*For every good and perfect thing
It comes from God's love
It comes from Heaven above*

*For every good and perfect thing
It comes from God's grace
It comes from God's perfect grace*

So I will pray a prayer this Christmas
That peace is the gift you may give
That once again you will keep Jesus
As the most important part of life that you live
So I will pray, I will pray a prayer this Christmas

Matthew 1:22-23

*So all this was done that it might be fulfilled which was
spoken by the Lord through the Prophet, saying, "Behold, the
virgin shall be with Child and bear a Son and they shall call
His name Immanuel," which is translated "God with us."*

The Promised One

A Gift of grace, a Gift of Love
Born for us the Lord Jesus

A Gift of hope, a Gift of Peace
Given to us the Lord Jesus

**Do not be afraid, for your Savior He is here
Now on a midnight clear
Heaven has now drawn near
So do not be afraid, for your Savior He has come
For this world to save
Our Father's only Son, the Promised One**

*The shepherds heard the voice of all the angels sing
"All glory be to God and to this Newborn King!
Peace be to all the earth and peace be to all men
For on this day a Child is born to be a Gift from Heaven"*

**Do not be afraid, for your Savior He is here
Now on a midnight clear
Heaven has now drawn near
So do not be afraid, for your Savior He has come
For this world to save
Our Father God's only Son, the Promised One**

A Gift of grace, a Gift of Love
Born for us the Lord Jesus

Acts 13:23

*From this man's seed, according to the promise,
God raised up for Israel a Savior, Jesus.*

A Child Is Born

A Child is born in Bethlehem, the Savior to the world
A Child is born, this holy night, a Light to all the earth
A Light to all the earth

Our Lord has come, our Holy One
Let all the nations rise, our Lord is here
May all who seek, draw near
Let all the nations rise, let all the nations rise

A Child is born the Son of God, the Hope of every man
A Child is born, is Christ the King, a Gift of the Father's love
A Gift of the Father's love

Our Lord has come, our Holy One
Let all the nations rise, our Lord is here
May all who seek, draw near
Let all the nations rise, let all the nations rise

Lord Jesus, the Son of God, the Savior to the world
Lord Jesus, the Son of God, the Light to all the earth
The Light to all the earth

Lord may You shine, Lord may You shine!

A Child is born in Bethlehem, the Savior to the world
A Child is born, this holy night, a Light to all the earth
A Light to all the earth

Lord may You shine!

John 1:14

And the Word became flesh and dwelt among us
and we beheld His glory, the glory as of the only
Begotten of the Father, full of grace and truth.

Awaken Bethlehem

Don't ever be afraid
There's no need to ever tremble at the sight
For the Lord thy God has come to all the earth
Don't ever close your eyes
There's no need to ever turn away and hide
For the Lord thy God has come to all the world

**So awaken, awaken Bethlehem
Your Savior is here, your Deliverer is near
Born in a manger low, so all the world it may know
So awaken, awaken Bethlehem**

*All glory now to God in the highest
Peace to His people on the earth
All glory now to God in the highest
Peace to His people on the earth
Peace to His people here upon the earth*

**For your Messiah is born, your Redeemer has come
Your Father on high has heard your cry
For your Messiah is born, your Redeemer has come**

**Your Father on high has heard your cry
So awaken, awaken Bethlehem**

Don't ever be afraid

Romans 13:11

*And do this, knowing the time, that now it is
high time to awake out of sleep, for now our
Salvation is nearer than when we first believed.*

Christmas Day

For it is now Christmas day
All across the earth
And we sing to You our praise
Now at our Saviors birth

Glory, glory to our Newborn King
Holy is the Lord
Hear the choir of the angels sing
"Holy is the Lord, holy is the Lord!"

For it is now Christmas day
All around the world
And we bring to You our praise
Every boy and girl

Glory, glory to our Newborn King
Holy is the Lord
Hear the choir of the angels sing
"Holy is the Lord, holy is the Lord!"

Glory, glory to our Newborn King
Holy, is the Lord
Hear the choir of the angels sing
"Holy is the Lord, holy is the Lord!"

For it is now Christmas day
All across the earth
And we sing to You our praise
And we sing to You our praise
Now at our Saviors birth

Luke 2:11

For there is born to you this day in the city
of David a Savior, Who is Christ the Lord.

The Greatest Gift Of Christmas

The Greatest gift of Christmas
Was never left under a tree
For you or for me
The Greatest gift of Christmas
Was never wrapped up with a bow
Just so that you know

**He was born in a manger
Under Heaven's light
Oh such a beautiful sight
He was a gift of Father
To make every wrong right
On such a perfect night
Under Heaven's light**

The Greatest gift of Christmas
Was never for sale in a store
For it is so much more
The Greatest gift of Christmas
Was never written down in a book
So come on and take a look

**He was born in a manger
Under Heaven's light
Oh such a beautiful sight
He was a gift of the Father
To make every wrong right
On such a perfect night
Under Heaven's light**

*Oh this little Boy, this sweet small Child
Born to be our Savior, to be our Mercy Mild
For He has come to save, to take our sins away*

The Greatest gift of Christmas
Was born on Christmas Day
He is so mighty to save

Psalm 62:1-2

*Truly my soul silently waits for God, from Him comes
my salvation. He only is my Rock and my Salvation,
He is my Defense, I shall not be greatly moved.*

For Only Then

Lay down your life, give up your shame
Call upon the Lord cry out His name

Lift up your heart, pray for His grace
Call upon the Lord, cry out His name

**For only then will your sin ever be forgiven
Only then will your soul ever be made new
Only then will your heart ever be forever changed
For only then will your sin ever be forgiven**

*For salvation it can be yours
With His open arms, He now awaits
Reach out now, with all your strength
Please don't wait, please don't you hesitate!*

**For only then will your sin ever be forgiven
Only then will your soul ever be made new
Only then will your heart ever be forever changed
For only then will your sin ever be forgiven**

Lift up your heart, pray for His grace
Call upon the Lord, cry out His name

1 Corinthians 6:9-10

*Do you not know that the unrighteous will not inherit the
Kingdom of God? Do not be deceived.*

1 John 1:9

*If we confess our sins, He is faithful and just and will
forgive us our sins and purify us from all unrighteousness.*

1 John 1:6-7

*If we say that we have fellowship with Him and walk in darkness,
we lie and do not practice the truth. But if we walk in the light as
He is in the light, we have fellowship with one another and the
blood of Jesus Christ His Son cleanses us from all sin.*

Lord Only You Know

Lord my heart is healing now
For only You have healed me by Your love
Lord my life is changing now
For only You have changed me by Your love

So Lord here in this place, fill our hearts with Your grace
Lord here in this church, Lord take away our hurt

For only You know my heart, even the deepest part
Only You know my soul and every secret that it holds
Lord only You know, Lord only You know

For only You know my life, the dark and the light
Only You know my heart, just who I am, who I'm not
Lord only You know, Lord only You know

Lord my soul is searching now
For only You have searched me by Your love
Lord my sin is forgiven now
For only You've forgiven me by Your love

So Lord here in this place, fill our hearts with Your grace
Lord here in this church, Lord take away our hurt

For only You know my heart, even the deepest part
Only You know my soul and every secret that it holds
Lord only You know, Lord only You know

For only You know my life, the dark and the light
Only You know my heart, just who I am, who I'm not
Lord only You know, Lord only You know

Hebrews 4:12

For the Word of God is living and powerful and sharper
than any two-edged sword, piercing even to the division
of soul and spirit and of joints and marrow and is a
discerner of the thoughts and intents of the heart.

You Are Blessed

You are loved, by God above
You are held safe within His arms
You are known, by God alone
You are kept safe from all harm

**All your sins He has forgiven
As far as the east is from the west
All your wrongs He has forgotten
You are perfect, you are loved, you are blessed**

*And high up in the Heavens
Your Heavenly Father is sending blessings
Blessings to you*

*And high up in the Heavens
Your Heavenly Father is always praying for you
Praying for you
He's praying just for you*

**All your sins He has forgiven
As far as the east is from the west
All your wrongs He has forgotten
You are perfect, you are loved, You are perfect
You are loved, you are blessed**

You are loved by God above
You are held safe within His arms
You are known by God alone
You are kept safe from all harm
You are kept safe from all harm

Matthew 5:12

*Rejoice and be exceedingly glad, for great is your reward in
Heaven, for so they persecuted the prophets who were before you.*

My Soul Will Forever Sing Your Praise

I find my hope in Jesus Christ
In the cross that claimed His life
I find my grace in Jesus's blood
In the depths of His love, His forgiving flood

I find my faith in Jesus's scars
In the wounds that for me He wore
I find my strength in Jesus's heart
In the heights of His love, in the Great Thou Art

My soul will forever sing Your praise
My soul will forever cry Your name
My soul will forever sing Your praise
For all of my days

Oh what a love, oh what a love
Oh what a love, the love of Christ

My soul will forever sing Your praise
My soul will forever cry Your name
My soul will forever sing Your praise
For all of my days

I find my hope in Jesus Christ
In the cross that claimed His life
I find my grace in Jesus's blood
In the depths of His love, His forgiving flood

Psalm 30:12

To the end that my glory may sing praise to You and not be
silent. O' Lord my God, I will give thanks to You forever!

It's A Great Day In Heavens

There is a stirring in Heaven, as your name it is called
A crowd begins to gather, in Heaven's great hall
The faithful stand together, holding hands, singing songs
Surrounded by every angel, one by one they sing along

It's a great day in Heaven, when the lost they come home
Yes it's a great day in Heaven, when your soul it knows
You'll never again be alone

Your loved ones are there to greet you
For it's been such a long, long time
With open arms they reach to hold you
To be forever by your side

And then Jesus He stands before you
His eyes they meet your eyes
In a whisper He says to you
"Welcome home, well done My child!"

It's a great day in Heaven, when the lost they come home
Yes it's a great day in Heaven, when your soul it knows
You'll never again be alone

And then with a trumpet sound
The Lord appears in the clouds, with a shout!
Just then eternity begins, all your sins He forgives
Oh the Lord He forgives!

It's a great day in Heaven, when the lost they come home
It's a great day in Heaven, when your soul it knows
It's a great day in Heaven, when the lost they come home
It's a great day in Heaven, when your soul it knows
When your soul it knows, you'll never again be alone

1 Thessalonians 4:16-17

For the Lord Himself will descend from Heaven with a shout,
with the voice of an archangel, and with the trumpet of God. And
the dead in Christ will rise first. Then we who are live and remain shall
be caught up together with them in the clouds to meet the Lord
in the air. And thus we shall always be with the Lord.

My Dedication Page

Your Beautiful Light

You make my life worth the living
My every dream it has come true in you
My every prayer it has been answered
I'm so beyond blessed all because of you

**Know that your every breath fills my lungs with life
Know that your every smile fills my heart with
Your beautiful light, your beautiful light**

You make this fight worth the fighting
My every hope is now alive in you
My every wish it has been granted
I'm so beyond blessed all because of you

**Know that your every breath fills my lungs with life
Know that your every smile fills my heart with
Your beautiful light, your beautiful light**

You make my life worth the living
My every dream it has come true in you
My every prayer, it has been answered
I'm so beyond blessed all because of you

~ * ~

*"Your Beautiful Light" is dedicated
To all the beautiful lights in my life*

Kohen - September 26th / Madison - January 25th
Owen - January 30th / Michael - December 10th
Cody Bear- November 26th / Gabriel - June 16th
Quinn - February 8th / Dylan - July 14th
Chloe - September 15th / Kim - July 19th
Jessica & Nichole - July 23rd / Teresa - September 14th
Ava - December 30th / Charlotte - July 2021

*May God's light always shine upon you
May His beautiful light always show you the way!*

All my love - Joe, DAD & your Pepe

May God Bless Your Journey Home

May God bless your journey home
For your battle it is done
For your victory it is won

Into His arms may you now fly
Into His keep may you now stay
Into His love may you now find
All of your dreams to come true
There along the way

May God bless your journey home
For your soul it is born
For your heart it is home

Into His arms may you now fly
Into His keep may you now stay
Into His love may you now find
All of your dreams to come true
There along the way

So may God bless your journey home
For your rest may you now find
For your peace may you now know

May your eyes now forever see the glory of the King
May your ears now forever hear the bells of Heaven ring
May your soul now forever be at home
May your heart now forever
Be as one with the Lord, with the King

This is a dedication to everyone we have
lost and miss each and every day!

May God bless our journey home!

I Pray Father To Be Worthy

I pray Father to be worthy
Of the prayers that I now pray
I pray Father to be worthy
Right up to my dying day

**How can it be any other way?
How can it be that I not choose to stay?
Down on my knees, down on my knees**

I pray Father to be worthy
Of the words that I now speak
I pray Father to be worthy
For Your will is all I seek

**How can it be any other way?
How can it be that I not choose to stay?
Down on my knees, down on my knees**

I pray Father to be worthy
Of the prayers that I now pray

*This song absolutely changed my prayer life,
I pray with all of my heart that it may do the very
same for you, as you travel along your very
own Soul Road!*

God Bless!

J.R. Canuel